The Capra Touch

The Capra Touch

*A Study of the Director's
Hollywood Classics and
War Documentaries, 1934–1945*

MATTHEW C. GUNTER

McFarland & Company, Inc., Publishers
Jefferson, North Carolina, and London

LIBRARY OF CONGRESS CATALOGUING-IN-PUBLICATION DATA

Gunter, Matthew C., 1974–
　　The Capra touch : a study of the director's Hollywood classics and war documentaries, 1934–1945 / Matthew C. Gunter.
　　　　p.　　cm.
　　Includes bibliographical references and index.

　　ISBN 978-0-7864-6402-9
　　softcover : acid free paper ∞

　　1. Capra, Frank, 1897–1991 — Criticism and interpretation.
2. World War, 1939–1945 — Motion pictures and the war.
3. Motion pictures in propaganda.　I. Title.
PN1998.3.C3G86　2012
791.4302'33092 — dc23　　　　　　　　　　　　2011042541

BRITISH LIBRARY CATALOGUING DATA ARE AVAILABLE

© 2012 Matthew C. Gunter. All rights reserved

No part of this book may be reproduced or transmitted in any form or by any means, electronic or mechanical, including photocopying or recording, or by any information storage and retrieval system, without permission in writing from the publisher.

On the cover: Frank Capra, mid–1940s (Photofest)

Manufactured in the United States of America

McFarland & Company, Inc., Publishers
　Box 611, Jefferson, North Carolina 28640
　　www.mcfarlandpub.com

To my wife and family, who continually support
my ambitions and academic endeavors

Table of Contents

Preface — 1

1. Pre-War Capra — 11
2. The Capra Formula — 59
3. The Roots of *Why We Fight* — 101
4. Mr. Capra Goes to War — 117
5. The Capra Formula in His War Documentaries — 138
6. *It's a Wonderful Life* and Beyond — 172
7. Capra's Legacy — 207

Chapter Notes — 221
Bibliography — 233
Index — 237

Preface

On December 8, 1941, the day after the Japanese bombed Pearl Harbor, two Army officers arrived on the Warner Bros. soundstage of *Arsenic and Old Lace*, starring Cary Grant and Priscilla Lane. They were not there for a sightseeing visit or to collect autographs. They were there to swear the film's Academy Award-winning director, Frank Capra, into the armed services. The ceremony did not come as a surprise to the 44-year-old, as earlier that year on a trip to Washington Capra had accepted a position as a major in the U.S. Army Signal Corps. According to Capra's autobiography, *The Name Above the Title*, he took the oath on the soundstage that very day.[1] Accounts in Capra's autobiography, however, should be treated with a degree of skepticism. As in many Hollywood memoirs, reality and truth tend to take a backseat to drama and showmanship.

According to Joseph McBride, a biographer of Capra who debunked much of the "history" described in *The Name Above the Title*, it was on December 12 that Capra agreed to join the Signal Corps and announced his decision to the press. When he did take the oath, on January 29, 1942, it was not on a soundstage but at the Southern California Military District Headquarters in Los Angeles.[2] So, which is true? While researching this book, I found that anyone writing about Frank Capra and his work must first reconcile the differences between Capra's autobiography and McBride's well-researched biography, *Frank Capra: The Catastrophe of Success*. The question becomes, what tells us more about Frank Capra — a book written by the man himself, whose flawed versions of events perhaps allow us to understand him all the more, or an objective version, which seeks truths the autobiographer cleverly tries to hide? While it is true that Capra had a penchant for exchanging truth for metaphors and imagery, it is also true that McBride, throughout his book, repeatedly points out the flaws in Capra's version of history, either caused by Capra's faulty memory, his ego, or his desire to make events more dramatic. Although McBride can claim that his version of events is "truer" because it incorporates more research and accounts, Capra's book is much more entertaining and engrossing.

Director Frank Capra (far right) takes time out on the set of *Arsenic and Old Lace*, with stars Priscilla Lane and Cary Grant. *Arsenic and Old Lace* would be the last film Frank Capra would direct before joining the army during World War II (Warner Bros./Photofest).

Throughout our history, Americans have continually shown a preference for metaphors and symbols over reality — this is especially true of moviegoers, who flock to theaters to escape from cold reality and experience well-told lies. Capra simply wrote his book the same way he made his movies — for an audience, who prefer to be entertained rather than informed, who have frequently chosen myth over reality. The real question, then, is whether or not the mythical, subjective version of events should replace the objective, "actual" version. It was this very question that Capra was forced to answer when he took on the *Why We Fight* series. It is a delicate balance, fusing research with subjectivity, especially when one is trying to be entertaining. In this book, therefore, when facts are needed in order to inform the reader or give a more complete picture, McBride's version will most definitely win out. *The Name Above the Title* will be quoted and referenced when Capra's point of view is necessary. When discussing Capra's films after *It's a Wonderful Life*, I will also much more readily lean on Capra's book, as Chapter 6 deals more with the techniques used in the films themselves than the events leading up to them.

This discussion brings us back to the aforementioned example, whether or not Capra was actually sworn into service on a studio backlot on December 8. While I prefer the symbolism of Capra's version, the merging of one career into another, McBride's version is backed by the facts. Despite which account is actually true, the most essential piece of information needed from the story is not only incorporated in both stories, but is frankly, the most fascinating — that Frank Capra, the Italian American director of the popular Depression-era films *It Happened One Night, Mr. Deeds Goes to Town, You Can't Take It with You, Mr. Smith Goes to Washington,* and *Meet John Doe* surrendered his lucrative position as one of America's most sought-after directors to work for the United States Army during the war. John Ford, another major filmmaker at the time, did the same, giving up his Hollywood career to produce films like *Battle for Midway* and *December 7th.* Such an occurrence, where two Academy Award-winning directors of popular films became willing participants in the creation of propaganda for the United States government, has rarely taken place in American history.[3] Such an event merits study for both its impact on history and on the filmmaking process. How, for instance, does a director of popular films adapt his style to produce films for the purpose of indoctrinating troops? How are the messages of the earlier narrative films altered under the watchful and censoring eye of the federal government? How much authorship does a director retain when switching from fiction filmmaking, where one can choose the angles from which to shoot a scene, to documentary filmmaking, where one primarily uses found footage and editing to recreate reality? These are the questions that seized my imagination and led to the composing of this book. I believe such questions need and should be answered in order to better appreciate the entirety of Capra's work.

As such, this book will focus primarily on the major works of Frank Capra from *It Happened One Night* to *It's a Wonderful Life* — including his war documentaries, most especially the *Why We Fight* series. Unlike Ford, who always remained aloof when asked by reporters about his film career, Capra was usually uninhibited when he discussed his films, even if he did sometimes sacrifice truth for dramatic flair. This wealth of information provided directly by Capra (as well as other notable biographers) can be combined with a study of *all* of his films during his most successful period (1934–1946) to more accurately define Capra's unique style.

As of yet, no major work has been written about the important connection between Capra's fictional Hollywood films and his *Why We Fight* series. Scholarly texts which analyze the films of Capra, such as Ray Carney's *American Vision,* hardly mention Capra's war documentaries at all. In his book *Another Frank Capra,* Leland Poague writes lengthy chapters on *Mr. Deeds Goes to Town, Mr. Smith Goes to Washington, Meet John Doe,* and *It's a Won-*

derful Life, but completely neglects Capra's war career which appeared at the same time period. Charles Maland lauds Capra's *It's a Wonderful Life* as the filmmaker's masterpiece, but spends less than ten pages in his book on Capra's three-year stint in the army which directly preceded the film. Other texts, like Thomas Bohn's detailed *Historical and Descriptive Analysis of the Why We Fight Films* or LTC Barry Cardwell's "Film and Motivation: The 'Why We Fight' Series," focus entirely on the documentaries themselves without delving into Capra's previous career as a Hollywood film director. Most analysis, whether in the form of individual articles or full text, takes an either/or approach to Capra's filmmaking — either one discusses the ideology and techniques presented in films like *Mr. Deeds Goes to Town, Mr. Smith Goes to Washington, Meet John Doe,* and *It's a Wonderful Life,* or one thoroughly analyzes the techniques and effects of the films Capra produced during the war. Capra's *The Name Above the Title* and Joseph McBride's *Frank Capra: The Catastrophe of Success* both provide meaningful details about the production of both of these film genres, but offer no significant analysis of the films themselves. Peter Rollins's brief article "Frank Capra's *Why We Fight* Film Series and Our American Dream," first published in the *Journal of American Culture,* suggests the possibility of a connection between Capra's fiction and propaganda films, asserting that Capra's films of the thirties provide a "good basic training" for his war documentaries, but is too narrowly focused, mainly remarking on the connection between the patriotic montage sequence in *Mr. Smith Goes to Washington* and the main ideas of *Why We Fight*.

Why no thorough analysis has been written about the similarities and differences between the two types of films Capra made during his career is indeed perplexing. Such analysis will not only generate greater insight into the nature of Capra's ideology, themes, and filmmaking techniques, but would also lead to a greater understanding of how Capra's Army films fit into Capra's filmography as a whole. Noting the similarities and differences between these two genres leads to important conclusions about the relationship between fiction and propaganda films, including the techniques used in both genres when they have similar agendas — in this case, providing clarity, comfort, and solutions to Americans during times of national crisis.

Perhaps this lack of scholarship derives from the fact that documentaries are viewed as substantially different from narrative films in that they deal with real events and real people. In both genres, however, images are either chosen or "left on the cutting-room floor," structure and themes are imposed through the writing of dialogue and/or narration, editing is employed to affect the pace and generate relationships between images, and music is specifically composed to heighten the drama or generate an emotional response in the audience. Capra had a hand in each of these aspects of production in both his thirties films and his wartime career. As historian Arthur Schlesinger, Jr., once wrote:

> The line between the documentary and the fiction film is tenuous indeed. Both are artifacts; both are contrivances. Both are created by editing and selection. Both, wittingly or not, embody a viewpoint. The fact that one eschews and the other employs professional actors becomes in the end an economic detail.[4]

Not to disagree in any way with an opinion that so clearly supports the premise of this book, but the fact that these films did not use professional actors (save for narration) did hurt Capra's authorship a great deal. Capra was terrific with actors, and his clever use of spontaneity on the set adds a flavor to his narrative films that is definitely missed in his documentary films. James Stewart, Gary Cooper, Jean Arthur, and Barbara Stanwyck are more than just economic details; they added an emotional weight and realism to Capra's narrative films that gave increased resonance to Capra's messages and ideas. Capra would have to rely on narration and realistic images to make up for the emotional reality created by these famous stars. As discussed in later chapters, however, one of Capra's greatest talents as a director is often neglected by critics. As Capra tended to shoot a great amount of footage on the set, many of his films were shaped in the editing process, during which Capra took an active part. In an interview for the American Film Institute, Capra stated that he'd be in the cutting room with the editor the whole time he edited his pictures, adding "they couldn't get rid of me no matter what."[5] As will be shown, Frank Capra's skill as an editor is well documented by a variety of sources, both during his narrative and wartime careers.

Capra scholars may also concur with Charles Maland's assessment that if one discovered traces of the director's social vision from his narrative films in his *Why We Fight* series, it was because his worldview already coincided with and followed American policy and not vice versa.[6] Much of Maland's argument, however, is based on his assumption that the U.S. government strictly censored Capra's work at this time, thereby limiting his authorship. Additionally, this argument suggests that Capra's ideology was not entirely distinctive, that he did not make deliberate creative choices during the production of these films, and that his documentaries were no different than any other documentaries produced by the government at the time. This simply goes against much of what we know about Capra's personality and work habits. In Hollywood, Capra's success in the mid to late 1930s awarded him a great degree of creative control over his pictures while at Columbia, even under the dictatorial power of studio head Harry Cohn. And control he most certainly took — Capra was known for being actively involved in every one of his productions, from the time the first word was put on paper to the film's premiere. In a later interview, Capra himself described his work ethic during a production, saying, "I never left the set. I stayed right there.... I liked to be a part of everything that went on."[7] It was no different, it seems, when Capra worked on the war films. When interviewed about the production of the films in 1957, Capra claimed that he took a "personal hand in all the operations—conceiving, the writing, the editing, the cutting to the final completion of the films."[8] Later in life, Capra mused that this ability to work independently, without the need for upper level involvement, may have been the primary reason General Marshall elected him to make the *Why We Fight* series in the first place.[9] General Marshall, in fact, had so much confidence in Capra's abilities that he not only allowed Capra to form his own division, but also permitted him to move his entire production from Washington (where it was originally housed) to Los Angeles. Capra himself later claimed that he was given "full power over the selection and editing on the *Why We Fight* films because there was no precedent for what they were doing."[10] Furthermore, as this book will prove, there are too many distinct similarities between Capra's fictional films and his documentaries for Maland's argument to be true. Capra employed many of the same filmmaking techniques in both types of films, and the study of these techniques leads to greater insight into how Capra was able to manipulate his audiences into agreeing with his own personal ideology. Truth be told, Capra made propaganda films long before he joined the Army. It is, therefore, the intention of this book to prove that these influential war documentaries were not produced in a vacuum. There can be no doubt that Capra's previous history and the work of several other documentary filmmakers certainly had an effect on how Capra's war documentaries were constructed. Such roots will be explained further in chapters dealing with Capra's war documentaries. As Capra was the guiding creative force behind the films of the 834th Photographic Detachment, however, the films made for his unit share the most in common with the narrative films he directed before the war. As such, this book will devote most of its pages to establishing the connection between Capra's popular Depression-era films and the films he made during World War II. It is my assertion that Capra did not cease to become a filmmaker simply because he was making a different type of film.

Over the course of several films in the 1930s, Frank Capra established an extremely popular formula that resonated with the American people during the Great Depression. This formula, first established in films like *It Happened One Night* and *Mr. Deeds Goes to Town*, would, in turn, make him extremely successful and extremely rich. It would be illogical, therefore, to assume that he would abandon such effective methods simply because the genre had changed. While it is true that Capra did not actually *shoot* much footage for these films, he did play a major part in their construction, their writing, their choice of shots, and their editing. Capra's idealistic vision of America found new expression in government propaganda, allowing a single Hollywood director to profoundly shape the way American soldiers viewed their country and their role in the greatest war in human history.

And so, this book intends to more clearly define the film techniques Capra used in his most successful period, starting with *It Happened One Night* and ending with *It's a Wonderful Life*—including his war propaganda. It is believed that including these films will yield greater insight into this productive part of Capra's career, as well as bridge the gap between *Meet John Doe* and *It's a Wonderful Life*. Such analysis will also more completely define Capra's worldview and ideology — an ideology that was extremely influential throughout the Great Depression and World War II. During this period, the United States was attempting to redefine itself, and Capra came to be one of the primary voices of this transformation.

According to film historian Thomas Schatz, the popularity of Capra's films, like that of John Ford, was part of a larger trend at the time. Like the comedy of Will Rogers and the films of Shirley Temple, the films of these two directors fulfilled the wish of audiences for simpler times and simpler folk. According to Schatz, both Capra and Ford made films that "evoked a way of life that was fading or already vanished for most Americans."[11] While the country was dealing with its position as a modern superpower in a chaotic world, Capra wanted to ensure that its people would not lose the traditional values of the past. Whether Capra was ultimately successful in this goal is a matter of opinion; however, it remains a subject worth examining to students of film and history. It is indeed rare that a successful Hollywood filmmaker would give up a lucrative career in the motion picture industry and devote three years to the service of his country. Whatever the underlying motives were for this decision (which will be explored in a later chapter), the act itself should be commended, for in his own way, Capra's service helped to bring about the destruction of the Third Reich.

In order to complete this book, I have had to watch many Capra films over and over again. As a professor of film history, I have shown *It Happened One Night* numerous times in my classes. As a result, even before deciding to write this book, I had seen the film enough times to know every scene in detail. In addition, *It's a Wonderful Life* had been mandatory viewing in my house every holiday season. When I was tasked to write a thesis for my master of liberal studies degree at Rollins College, these repeated viewings came to mind and I chose Capra's war films as my topic. I consciously chose from the beginning of the writing of this thesis (which would eventually become the foundation of this book), that I would study the *Why We Fight* films first, before thoroughly analyzing any of Capra's narrative films that came before and after. This decision assisted me in becoming more attuned to the connection between the two types of films; when I rewatched the Capra narrative films, I was more aware of the films' similarities than their differences. I saved the viewing of *It's a Wonderful Life* for last, as it was the most familiar to me, and because (along with many critics) I see the film as a culmination of Capra's work. These repeated viewings of Capra's films have accorded me a newfound respect for the consistency and depth of his vision.

The premise of this book also allied me more with Capra scholars Leland Poague and Ray Carney, who are more willing to accept the "one man, one film" stance of Capra, than with Joseph McBride, who tends to give greater credit to Capra's collaborators than to the man himself. Although Capra's authorship of some of the war documentaries produced by the 834th detachment is questionable (most especially *The Negro Soldier* and the later *Why We Fight* films), there is little doubt of Capra's authority over the unit. Moreover, Capra's signature stylistic touches and themes are prevalent in many of the documentary films over which he had direct control, namely *Prelude to War, The Nazis Strike, Divide and Conquer,* and *Tunisian Victory*. In all of Capra's films, the dedication to the craft is felt in every frame. The consistency in Capra's technique, most especially in the films he made from 1934 to 1945, yields great rewards both in the viewing experience and in the subsequent analysis. It is hoped that after reading this book, and perhaps after watching many of the Capra films mentioned in this book, the reader will feel the same.

In many ways, Capra's films are more accessible than ever before. *It's a Wonderful Life* has recently been released on Blu-Ray, and a few years ago, Columbia (now Sony) released a DVD box set of five Capra films and an additional documentary on Capra's life. As Capra's war documentaries and *Meet John Doe* are in the public domain, one can find them in numerous places, including several sites online, although the quality is not always stellar. Either way, it is hoped that this book will increase interest in Capra's career, both at Columbia Pictures and in the U.S. Army. In the opening chapter of his book, *Regarding Frank Capra*, Eric Smoodin wrote that Capra "participated in more kinds of filmmaking than perhaps any other major director from the period" as he made independent films, studio films, educational films, and propaganda films.[12] This author could not agree more, as Capra's diversity is one of the most intriguing aspects of his long career. As such, it is time Capra's non-fiction work takes its rightful place in the Capra scholarship.

As mentioned previously, this book will primarily deal with the most celebrated time in Capra's career, between *It Happened One Night*, his first blockbuster success, and *It's a Wonderful Life*, his most celebrated and most enduring film. Chapter 1 will chronicle Capra's early career and will provide summaries of his major pre-war films, starting with *The Bitter Tea of General*

Yen and ending with *Arsenic and Old Lace*. This chapter will also provide the reader with the historical context necessary for the analysis of these films, which will be related in great detail in Chapter 2. That chapter will discuss the techniques and ideologies of these early films in an attempt to provide a foundation for similarities between these films and Capra's war films. Chapter 3 will provide insight into why Capra joined the Army in 1941, as well as trace the historical roots of Capra's war films. Chapter 4 details the production process of Capra's war films and provides a short summary and the historical context for each. Chapter 5 attempts to connect the techniques and ideas of Capra's successful pre-war films to his war documentaries. Chapter 6 will provide analysis of Capra's films after the war, most especially his masterpiece *It's a Wonderful Life*, in relationship to the insights discovered in the previous chapters. Finally, Chapter 7 will discuss the legacy of Capra and the continued influence of Capra's work on modern filmmakers.

It is hoped that, after reading this book, one will not only come away with a new perspective of Capra's work, but also a renewed appreciation of the medium itself. Because motion pictures were *the* art form of the 20th century, it is imperative that they continually be studied and analyzed. Too often we watch films without understanding how they influence our behavior and change our worldview. Only after watching Capra's films over and over again did I become aware of Capra's subtle (and sometimes not so subtle) influence. Most especially, I became aware that all of Capra's pre-war films after *Bitter Tea of General Yen* in some way dealt with the concept of freedom. In many of the films, the central characters struggle to be themselves and find their voice under oppressive and powerful regimes. In some of the situations, these same characters must either conform to the higher authority and lose a piece of themselves, or fight against them and risk losing everything they hold dear. By researching the historical context behind these films, as well as by discovering recurring patterns and themes, I was also able to come away with a better understanding of the power of the medium itself. Motion pictures are by their very nature manipulative, and their power to evoke emotion is unequalled by any other medium. This is why (as early as 1929) Edward Bernays, the "Father of Propaganda," called the American motion picture the "greatest unconscious carrier of propaganda in the world today."[13] It is imperative, then, that all viewers be aware of this manipulation, in order to remain free-thinking, autonomous adults. Frank Capra was well aware of the power of his films. Throughout his career, he remained consistent but subtle in his agenda, hoping the people watching would decipher his clues. In that way, all of Capra's films could be considered propaganda.

1
Pre-War Capra

There is no documentation detailing why Frank Capra was chosen to make the *Why We Fight* films. In an interview in 1984, Capra claimed that John Ford had mentioned his name to General George Marshall, but there is no existing paperwork to back up this claim.[1] There is little doubt that Marshall knew about the three-time Academy Award-winner, who had appeared on the cover of *Time* magazine in 1938. Perhaps General George Marshall realized that Capra possessed all three of the major qualities Edward Bernays listed in 1929 as important for creators of propaganda — natural leadership or charisma, the ability to read what people want, and a key position in the social structure.[2] Perhaps he simply understood, like Joseph McBride, that two of Capra's most successful films, *Mr. Deeds Goes to Town* and *Mr. Smith Goes to Washington*, were actually orientation films themselves, using the power of story to assist common Americans in their transition from insular, small-town life to the growing industrial society without losing their souls.[3] Perhaps he just trusted "that fellow Capra"[4] knew what he was doing, showing little worry about Capra's lack of experience with the documentary format. In fact, when Capra protested that he had never made a documentary before, Marshall responded: "Capra, I've never been Chief of Staff before. Thousands of young Americans have never had their legs shot off before. Boys are commanding ships today who a year ago had never seen the ocean before."[5] Immediately understanding Marshall's response, Capra quickly apologized and took the job. Marshall had finally gotten his man.

Unlike Capra scholars Ray Carney and Leland Poague, who devote very little time to analyzing the connection between Capra's fictional films and Army films, General Marshall seemed to understand the connection quite well. He was, in fact, counting on it. He understood that in order to accomplish his goal, he did not need a filmmaker experienced in documentary techniques, but a person with the unique ability to communicate ideas to an audience without coming across as condescending or heavy-handed. Capra's successful filmmaking career before the war proved that he was the perfect candidate, a director who could employ a variety of filmmaking techniques

Frank Capra (far left) poses in a publicity shot with Clark Gable and Claudette Colbert for the Academy Award–winning *It Happened One Night* (Columbia, Pictures/Photofest).

to connect with an audience of ordinary American citizens. Strangely enough, the Capra formula fits extremely well into the subject matter of the documentary series because it deals intimately with topics like patriotism, fascism, liberty, groupthink, and individualism. Thus, by carefully analyzing the themes and techniques of Capra's most famous films as well as his wartime documentaries, one can see remarkable similarities between these films. Discovering these similarities in turn leads to greater insight and understanding of Capra's life and work, which had enormous influence on how Americans defined themselves before and during World War II.

A brief outline of Frank Capra's career is necessary to provide the proper context for his films. Unfortunately, tracing Capra's history can be troublesome because, as mentioned in the introduction, he often showed a penchant for rewriting history in order to promote the myth of himself as a self made man guided by fate. Capra, for instance, reimagined the story of his entry into the film business in his autobiography, claiming that he blindly stumbled into the industry after the Great War, directing his first film, *Fulta Fisher's Boarding House*, without any previous experience. Such storytelling on Capra's part made it appear that he possessed some kind of God-given talent for directing, eliminating some important details that directly relate to his production of the war documentaries two decades later. In truth, he was interested in films while attending Throop Polytechnic Institute. For his Junior English class, in December of 1917, he wrote "A Treatise on Moving Pictures," wherein he put down some of his thoughts about the new art form. In the essay, he stated that films were better than the stage in terms of presenting spectacle and *thematic* material. He concluded this essay by listing the benefits of film as a medium for *persuasion, education*, and *information*, which would edify the average citizen.[6] While still in college, he helped newsreel cameraman Roy Wiggins photograph the Mount Wilson observatory and may have even been employed as a film editor for Mack Sennett.[7] In addition, Capra's study of engineering and his scientific training at Throop could have led to his success at Columbia years later. In an interview with Arthur Friedman in 1957, Capra stated that his technical training in college gave him an "organized mind," which, in turn, allowed him to face problems on his sets in a cool, objective manner.[8] This scientific background also helped him study and objectively analyze audience reactions to his films, which he did during preview screenings, often implementing minor changes to the films at the last minute to maximize their effectiveness. This background also made him a perfect choice for making the *Why We Fight* series. Edward Bernays, strangely enough, mentioned in his groundbreaking book *Propaganda*, that in order to be effective, modern propagandists should systematically and objectively study "the material with which he is working in the spirit of the laboratory."[9]

After college and a brief teaching career in the army during the First World War, Capra had a difficult time finding a job in engineering. He traveled throughout the West for three years, moving from job to job, sometimes working as a traveling salesman. These sales jobs helped to develop the "huckster" aspect of his personality as well as his imagination. In one instance, in an attempt to get people to buy a set of books, he fabricated a story about being an orphan who was taught the sales trade by a bookbinder who took pity on him.[10] These instances became the first moments in Capra's life in which he could gage the immediate effectiveness of his emotional stories to an audience of ordinary people. In addition, this period in Capra's life put him in close contact for the first time with small-town America, as most of his life up to that time was spent in the bustling city of Los Angeles. Capra described these years in a later interview: "I met the American people, day to day- farmer, gambler, saloon keeper, doctor, dentist. And I got to know them very well, got to like them."[11]

Capra's hunting for work eventually landed him in San Francisco at the Ball Film Laboratory, where he processed feature film dailies and newsreels, and edited and shot various small projects. Such experience is key to our understanding of Capra's talent for editing, an ability he would use a great deal in his World War II films. After working for the lab, Capra was then approached to direct a series of short films based on famous poems for Fireside Productions—his first film being *Fultah Fisher's Boarding House*. From then on, he only worked in film. He explains his passion for the medium in his autobiography as follows:

> Film is a disease. When it infects your bloodstream, it takes over as the Number One hormone; it bosses the enzymes; directs your pineal gland; plays Iago to your psyche. As with Heroin, the antidote for film is more film. Withdrawal from junk tortures a mainliner's body. But kicking the film habit wracks a filmmaker's soul—his essential nature.[12]

Having been bitten by the "film bug," Capra moved back to Los Angeles, where he worked as a writer for Hal Roach and Mack Sennett. After a few years, he was assigned to write for Harry Langdon, who, like all silent comedians, was desperately looking for a niche that would differentiate himself in the crowded and competitive Hollywood market. Capra's idea was to make Langdon an innocent, whose inherent goodness would always win out over his enemies. According to Capra, the success of the material he wrote for Langdon worked because it "had a theme behind it."[13] This theme, the power of decency over the powers of evil and hypocrisy, would be rediscovered by Capra in his most influential films of the 1930s, and to some extent, his war documentaries. After working successfully as a writer for Langdon, Capra was promoted to director of *The Strong Man*, which was to be his first feature for Sennett in 1926. After a falling-out with Langdon, Capra found himself unemployed once again.

After a short time, Capra ended up at Columbia Pictures through sheer luck (studio head Harry Cohn apparently hired Capra because his name appeared on top of a list of unemployed directors). He would make 25 pictures for Cohn, from 1927 to 1939, including *It Happened One Night, Mr. Deeds*

Goes to Town, Lost Horizon, You Can't Take It with You, and *Mr. Smith Goes to Washington.* The quantity of Capra's output was greatest in his first years at Columbia. In 1928 alone, he made seven films. Unfortunately, the prints of many of these early films including *The Younger Generation, That Certain Thing,* and *The Power of the Press* have been lost. Overall, the partnership between Cohn and Capra, although contentious at times, would be regarded as one of the most successful in film history. According to film historian Neal Gabler, Capra got along with Cohn not only because they had similar personalities, but also because they had similar goals. Their relationship was basically an "alliance between outsiders," as they both had a driving need to be acknowledged by the Hollywood establishment. While Cohn desired power, Capra desired recognition.[14] In the 1930s, this desire would drive Capra to serve as president of the Academy of Motion Picture Arts and Sciences (AMPAS) for four years (1935–1939), and president of the Screen Director's Guild for two (1939–1941). After *Mr. Smith Goes to Washington,* Capra left Columbia to form Frank Capra Productions. In 1941, he released *Meet John Doe,* a joint venture with Warner Brothers, a fascinating but troubled work that did not make enough of a profit to keep the independent venture operational. Capra would make one more film for Warner Brothers before enlisting in the Army—*Arsenic and Old Lace,* which was based on a stage play and shot in only four weeks.

As stated earlier, this book will primarily concentrate on the Capra films most relevant in subject matter to the *Why We Fight* series, dealing primarily with the American people and their relationships with idealized heroes and ruthless, powerful men: *Mr. Deeds Goes to Town, Mr. Smith Goes to Washington,* and *Meet John Doe.* These films, two of which were written by Robert Riskin, are epitomes of the label "Capracorn," which is often used to describe the bulk of Capra's work of this time. In these films, personable, boyish men take on corrupt authoritarian powers and ultimately win the day through the sheer power of their decency. Nowadays, the term "Capracorn" is usually used in a derogatory way, criticizing Capra for his penchant for sentimentalism, ideology, and happy endings. Three other films, *It Happened One Night, Lost Horizon,* and *You Can't Take It with You,* will also be studied as they helped to establish Capra's trademark visual and dramatic techniques, as well as contributed to his phenomenal success in the '30s. Lesser-known Capra films— such as *Lady for a Day, Bitter Tea for General Yen, American Madness, Broadway Bill,* and *Arsenic and Old Lace*—will be discussed as well, as these films helped develop and solidify the Capra style, even though they do not have as much directly in common with his wartime films.

In order for the reader to best understand the context of each film, the background and synopsis of each is necessary.

Capra's Early Talkies

Capra's early talkies for Columbia can be separated into three primary categories—adventure films, comedy films, and Barbara Stanwyck films. The three adventure films—*Submarine*, *Flight*, and *Dirigible*, all starring Jack Holt and Ralph Graves, are basically Columbia's attempt to capitalize on the enormous success of Paramount's *Wings* (1927). In these films, action scenes are interplayed with dramatic scenes involving a love triangle, and in the end, the friendship of the two male characters overcomes both the triangle and the perilous situations in which they are placed. The three films in this category are only worth mentioning because they move at a much quicker pace than most talkies of the time, and because of the timeliness of the topics (*Submarine* was based on two actual submarine disasters in the 1920s; the story of *Flight* involves the U.S. military's Nicaraguan involvement in 1928; and *Dirigible*'s story echoes Admiral Byrd's expedition to the South Pole.) While *Flight* is notable because it marks the first time Capra worked with the U.S. military as a film director, according to Maland, *Dirigible* is the best of the three mainly because it was written by Jo Swerling. Swerling helped Capra develop a moral center to his film and would write the bulk of the director's films in the early thirties, including *Ladies of Leisure*, *Rain or Shine*, *The Miracle Woman*, and *Forbidden*. Myles Connolly, another friend of Capra at the time, was also pushing Capra to make more personal, moral films instead of just popular ones.[15]

Of the two comedies directed by Capra in the early sound era, *Rain or Shine* and *Platinum Blonde*, only the latter is important in the discussion in the evolution of Capra's thematic style. Although the talented Jo Swerling receives credit for the writing of *Rain or Shine*, the film was actually based on a Broadway musical, with all the songs removed. *Rain or Shine* is basically a derivative circus film ending with a climactic fire.

Platinum Blonde, on the other hand, has survived obscurity as it stars the doomed Hollywood icon Jean Harlow and her trend setting titular hairdo, and because it is the first Capra film on which Robert Riskin worked (although Swerling was credited with the adaptation, Riskin wrote much of the dialogue). The future Capra collaborator would go on to write many of Capra's most famous films, including *It Happened One Night* and *Mr. Deeds Goes to Town*. His touches add spice to the dialogue and a sense of playfulness to the characters, which makes the whole film more enjoyable than it otherwise would be. *Platinum Blonde* also hits on a subject which Capra would revisit in later films—the difficulties of mixing the vibrant, worldly middle class with the snobbish leisure class. The plot of the film involves a marriage between a middle class reporter and an upper crust girl (Harlow). The marriage falls apart as the groom ultimately tells off his wife and mother-in-law and returns to the world where he realizes he ultimately belongs. The film is the first of Capra's to recognize the powerful tensions between the classes underlying the Great Depression. The story admits to the temptations of money and power, but ultimately rejects the values of that world for the values of the working class. According to Maland, the film not only says that the two worlds are irreconcilable, but it also holds up the middle class world as superior to the other.[16]

Of the three different categories, the Barbara Stanwyck films—*The Miracle Woman, Forbidden, Ladies of Leisure,* and *The Bitter Tea of General Yen*— are the most interesting not only because they star one of cinema's most enduring leading ladies at the start of her career, but also because they include the strong thematic content which would become the hallmark of Capra's greatest films. In *Ladies of Leisure* (1930), Ralph Graves plays idealist artist Jerry Strong, the son of a wealthy businessman, who is struck by the beauty of working girl Kay Arnold (Stanwyck, in her first film with Capra) and longs to paint her. Over time, the male hero's idealism wins over the cynical worldview of the female lead (shades of *Mr. Deeds* and *Mr. Smith*), while his upper-crust family attempts to tear them apart. The melodramatic film ends with Kay's attempted suicide and Jerry rushing to her bedside, dedicated as ever to preserving their relationship. Capra was sure the film, which premiered in March of 1930 to generally positive reviews, would be recognized by the Academy of Motion Pictures Arts and Sciences. When neither he nor his star was nominated, Capra was sure it was due to the minor status of Columbia in the established Hollywood system. His repeated complaints about the Academy's neglect of the smaller studios, eventually led to his invitation to join the organization the following year. *Ladies of Leisure* gave Capra the taste of Oscar, and his appetite would not be satiated until he won the award.

The Miracle Woman (1931) was the second Capra film to star Stanwyck and ended up a failure at the box office, a rarity for Capra in his most productive and successful decade. Based on a play by Robert Riskin and John Meehan, and adapted by Jo Swerling, *The Miracle Woman* stars Stanwyck as Florence Fallon, a minister's daughter who becomes a faith healer in order to seek revenge on the hypocritical followers of the faith who unfairly ousted her father from the church. Led by the capitalist villain Hornsby (Sam Hardy), Florence becomes a sensation, but in a twist similar to *Meet John Doe*, what was supposed to be a hoax ends up actually helping people. In one particular instance, John (David Manners), a blind songwriter, hears her voice on the radio and decides not to kill himself. A romance between this blind songwriter and Florence eventually blossoms, and Florence (like Kay in *Ladies of Leisure*) becomes softened by the idealism of her love interest. Her outlook on life suddenly changes: she decides to tell the truth about herself to her audience in her final sermon and end the charade. Before she can do this, Hornsby cuts off her microphone and a fire is accidentally started. John miraculously, if not improbably, saves Florence from the fire. The film's final scene shows Florence working at the Salvation Army, where she receives a telegram from John informing her that his eyesight may be restored and that he is asking her to marry him.

As mentioned earlier, the film was not a success for Capra, who felt the film's failure was due to his inability to take it where it needed to go. Instead of committing to the idea that Florence was the villain, Capra claimed to have chickened out by adding a villain who was not only unnecessary, but made the audience unsure of Florence's sincerity. As Capra stated in his autobiography, "I dove into the pool of powerful ideas—and came up with a can of claptrap and corn."[17] Although the film ultimately doesn't work, *The Miracle Woman* contains many ideas which would work in Capra's later films. Florence's ability to become successful by using the mass media as a tool of persuasion is not only explored in *Meet John Doe* (with which the film shares many similarities) but also in his war documentaries. The relative ease by which the masses can be manipulated by hypocritical drivel in the film not only forecasts the mindless mobs of *American Madness*, *Broadway Bill*, and *Meet John Doe*, but could also be seen as an indictment against the Hollywood establishment, which Capra often criticized for trading sincerity and values for profits and popularity.

Forbidden (1932) was based on a story by Frank Capra himself, who described the film decades later as "two hours of soggy, 99.44% pure soap opera."[18] He devoted only a single page to the film in his autobiography and claimed that the only aspect of the film that saved it from being a total disaster was the performances. The film centers around Lulu (Stanwyck) and her relationship with a married politician named Robert Conover (Adolphe Menjou, who would, strangely enough, play another politician with the same last name in Capra's *State of the Union*.) The film plays out the standard fallen-woman melodrama. Lulu ends up pregnant by Conover but gives the child up for adoption to Conover's wife, who raises the child as her own. She then marries a news editor (Ralph Bellamy), who confronts Lulu about the truth of the Conovers' "adopted" child. Lulu kills her husband, but is pardoned by Conover, who, on his death bed, gives her a paper recognizing Lulu as the mother of his child and granting her half of his estate. Immediately after Conover dies, Lulu rips up the paper and exits out into a crowded street. Although Maland mentions several similarities between *Forbidden* and Orson Welles's masterpiece *Citizen Kane*,[19] the film is nearly humorless, and all but drowns in its own melodrama. It contains none of the complexities of Capra's best early talkie with Barbara Stanwyck, the vastly underrated and underappreciated *The Bitter Tea of General Yen.*

American Madness
(released August 1932)

Although it would make sense at this point to delve directly into *The Bitter Tea of General Yen*, I believe it is important to break from continuity and take a more chronological approach to Capra's films. By doing so, one can better trace the evolution of the director's thematic style, which starts with *American Madness* and does not really end until *It's a Wonderful Life* 14 years later.

American Madness, the first Capra film written entirely by Robert Riskin, has much to recommend it. So much so, that Columbia (now Sony) included the film with other Capra classics in its Frank Capra DVD box set in 2006.

The story of *American Madness* revolves around two men of principle and the decisions they make to preserve a bank's future. The first man introduced is Matt (Pat O'Brien), a responsible cashier in love with the bank president's secretary. The bank president, Tom Dickson (Walter Huston), is the other hero of the story; Dickson is a workaholic who believes that money should be loaned out on the basis of character. This philosophy has put him at odds with the bank's board of directors, who visit Dickson at the beginning of the film to discuss his risky lending policies. A third man in the picture, the Bank Manager, Cluett (Gavin Gordon), lacks the scruples of our heroes, and ends up jeopardizing the entire bank with his selfish schemes. It seems Cluett owes gangsters $50,000 in gambling debts and cannot pay them. The gangsters propose an alternate plan to recoup their money, asking Cluett to turn the vault alarm off when the bank closes so they can rob it. Cluett, realizing he needs an alibi, attempts to charm his way into the favors of Dickson's neglected wife, Phyllis (Kay Johnson). Matt accidentally interrupts Cluett and Phyllis in Cluett's office and interprets their embrace as an act of infidelity. At first, everything goes according to Cluett's design. Angry because her husband has to go out of town on the night of their anniversary, Phyllis agrees to go out with the smooth-talking manager, providing him with a perfect alibi. In addition, Cluett is able to successfully turn the alarm off by distracting Matt at the end of the day. While the bank is being robbed at midnight, Cluett, still on his date with Phyllis, asks the married woman up to his apartment. Upon entering, he is surprised to find Matt there waiting for them. Matt urges Phyllis to remain faithful to Tom, and Phyllis guiltily consents, leaving with him. The next day, the police accuse Matt of intentionally turning off the alarm. Feeling that he must protect Tom from the knowledge of his wife's indiscretion, Matt will not explain where he was on the night of the robbery, which makes him appear guilty. Eventually, Cluett is found to be the guilty party, exonerating the honest Matt, but not without revealing Matt's secret. Meanwhile, news of the robbery has spread like wildfire, and mobs of people, feeling their money is unsafe, rush the bank to withdraw their funds. Tom, devastated by news of his wife's unfaithfulness, gives up trying to halt the run and decides to resign his position as president. Matt, however, desperately attempts to stop the run on the bank by encouraging customers who are loyal to Tom to deposit more of their money. The plan works, bringing an end to the bank run, and inspiring Tom to tear up his resignation. He then forces the board members to start depositing their money into the bank as well. The film ends with the bank returning to its normal routine, and Tom booking a honeymoon trip for himself and his wife.

For Capra *American Madness* represents a welcome return to timely topics, a trend that would continue through most of his famous films of the thirties. It also marks the beginning of a new style for Capra, who intentionally "kicked up the pace" of the film by speeding up the delivery of the actors while filming, overlapping speeches, and avoiding dissolves and long walks. Although technically closer to *Forbidden* and *Bitter Tea of General Yen* with its ornate sets and camera moves, the theme of *American Madness*—a man's moral character determines his success—is closer to that used in his later films. Both heroes in *American Madness* become martyrs for their idealistic causes and are effectively silenced by their enemies, only to be rejuvenated by the acts of the ordinary people whose lives they touched. As such, Matt and Tom become prototypes for Capra's most famous film heroes—Longfellow Deeds, Jefferson Smith, and George Bailey. In this author's opinion, as entertaining as the characters of Matt and Tom are, the two-hero split in the narrative hurts the overall power of the film. As we shall see with *Mr. Deeds Goes to Town* and Capra's later films, this director wisely combined the innocent, sincere qualities of Matt with the active, idealistic aspects of Tom into a single hero on whom the audience's attention could be appropriately and effectively focused.

While *American Madness* was a success for Capra, it did not receive any recognition by the Academy that year. Capra, believing that only "arty" films were nominated, subsequently decided to go for Oscar gold by proving that he could direct artistic films as well as anyone. Although *The Bitter Tea of General Yen* would prove to be a critical and box-office disappointment, it remains one of Capra's most interesting and complex works.

1. Pre-War Capra 21

The Bitter Tea of General Yen
(released January 1933)

The Bitter Tea of General Yen is basically a tragic love story about two worlds which cannot coexist. In his quest for a Best Picture nod, Capra stepped out of his comfort zone to make a film which not only took place outside America (a rarity for Capra), but also dealt with the controversial subject of miscegenation. Based on a novel of the same name, *Bitter Tea* is also one of the few films directed by Capra in his "golden age" that was not written by Robert Riskin. Although it is neglected by many Capra scholars who tend to start Capra's greatest period with the Oscar nominated *Lady for a Day*, I believe *The Bitter Tea of General Yen* deserves recognition not only because it is a poetic, interesting film, but because it deals with the clash of traditional American/Christian values and the values of fascist dictators — the main focus of Capra's war films.

The film begins with the arrival of Megan Davis (Barbara Stanwyck) to Shanghai the night of her marriage to American missionary Dr. Robert Strike (Gavin Gordon). The wedding is postponed however, when she and her fiancé resolve to save a group of orphans in a nearby town plagued by violent riots. In order to travel out of Shanghai, Bob requests a pass from the local warlord, General Yen (Nils Asther, a Swedish actor made up to look Chinese). General Yen agrees to the good doctor's request in person, but sneakily writes him a false pass instead. Megan and Bob travel to the town and save the orphans, but the false pass issued by Yen forces them all to escape quickly to the rail station to avoid any further entanglements with the law. At the station, Megan and Bob are separated and Megan is knocked out. When she awakes, she finds herself in the charge of General Yen and his servant girl, Mah-Li (Toshia Mori). After being transferred to Yen's castle, where she is told she cannot leave for her own safety, Megan meets Mr. Jones (Walter Connolly), a shrewd American in charge of Yen's finances and business dealings. From here on, the story plays out like a doomed version of *Beauty and the Beast*. As Megan learns to look beyond her own prejudices to see the complexity and cold passion of Yen (illustrated by a remarkably filmed dream sequence), Yen learns to appreciate Megan's capability for compassion and love. Their relationship is tested when the general decides to put Mah-Li to death for passing notes to the enemy. Megan's Christian ethics cannot stand for this pagan brutality, and she offers to be responsible for Mah-Li from that point on. General Yen, deciding to push Megan's compassion to the ultimate limit, agrees to her demand, but only if she puts herself up as collateral. Megan agrees, but is betrayed by Mah-Li, who once again gives essential information to the enemy, bringing about the collapse of Yen's small empire. Megan appears before Yen, prepared to give up her life to atone for Mah-Li's betrayal, but Yen intimates that the bargain was not for her life but for her body. This sudden change of tactics startles Megan, but in the end, Yen decides he cannot take what is not freely given. Megan, still reeling from General Yen's words, returns to her room and dresses herself in Chinese robes, seemingly prepared to give herself over to the general. She does not know, however, that the general has decided to commit suicide in his own room by stoically drinking a tea of bitter poison. He dies with the sobbing Megan at his feet, the only major Capra character to successfully die by his own hand. The film ends with Megan and Jones on a boat headed to Shanghai, saddened by the death of Yen, but hopeful that they both will see him again in the afterlife.

Although the film was not a success (it did not receive any Oscar nominations and was banned in Great Britain and the British commonwealth countries), *The Bitter Tea of General Yen* deserves to be more than a footnote in the Capra filmography. Not only is the film historically important (it was the first film to play in Radio City Music Hall), but it is also thematically significant because it is the first of Capra's films to deal with the thorny subject of fascism. Although visually it bears no resemblance to any of the Capra films that followed (save *Lost Horizon*), *The Bitter Tea of General Yen*, like the best of his films, treats its subject honestly and seriously. And while the film does not condone fascism, it does not condemn it either. The film, therefore, accurately reflects Capra's own mixed feelings at the time about fascism. Although Capra was an avowed lover of liberty, he was also—like Harry Cohn—a professed admirer of Benito Mussolini (who at this time had not yet invaded Ethiopia.) As will be discussed later, Capra was also distrustful of large crowds of people, and felt safe by making it clear that *he* was the ultimate authority on the set. *Bitter Tea* is also notable for its association of American capitalism with fascism, illustrated by the morally relative and perpetually cynical Jones. In a few short years, the basic characteristics of this clever and devious character would provide the foundation for memorable villains like John Cedar, D.B. Norton, and Mr. Potter. In the end, *Bitter Tea for General Yen* forces us to question not only our own prejudices and beliefs, but our very notions of compassion and sacrifice, even though it does not provide the viewer with any real answers. In many ways, it is Capra's most intellectual film. Its failure, however, marked a turning point for the director. According to Philip Scheuer, who interviewed Capra for the *Los Angeles Times*, the fate of *Bitter Tea* "bore out Capra's declaration that the great mass of paying patrons are not intellectually inclined."[20] And so, after *Bitter Tea*, Frank Capra forsook the ambiguity and complexity of artistic films for the straightforward, people-pleasing comedies that would become his hallmark. The first of these films, *Lady for a Day*, would also be the first of his films to be nominated for Best Picture, placing the elusive statuette Oscar closer to Capra than it had ever been.

Lady for a Day
Based on the story "Madame La Gimp" by Damon Runyon (released September 1933)

The failure of *The Bitter Tea of General Yen* left Capra confused, upset, and insecure about his future in the industry. Instead of taking the risk that another high-minded venture would fail, Capra resolved that his next film would be completely different. He explained his motives in his autobiography:

> *Bitter Tea* had a cool, blue tinge. Why not try the other end of the story spectrum — the warmer, red end — by filming one of Runyon's muggy Cinderella tales? Who knows? At least the British Commonwealth couldn't ban a fairy tale. Harry Cohn hadn't let me forget that "that arty drek" had lost him money, "and," he superstitiously nudged, "it broke up your winning streak, you louse."[21]

Even after convincing Cohn to buy the rights for the short story "Madame La Gimp" by Damon Runyon, Capra was unsure of the project until Robert Riskin talked him into it. Riskin suggested the title *Lady for a Day*, and the two escaped to Palm Springs to work on the script. It was a trip they would subsequently make at the start of every film they made together.

Lady for a Day is a makeover story, a Cinderella story filled with quirky Runyonesque characters and fast-paced dialogue. Like *American Madness*, the hero's role is split between Apple Annie (May Robson), a poor old woman who sells apples in the streets, and Dave the Dude (Warren William), a superstitious gangster who buys Annie's apples for luck. The first part of the story centers around Annie, who we find out has been sending money to her daughter overseas. The daughter, Louise (Jean Parker) is ignorant of her mother's lowly position. In fact, Annie has fooled Louise into thinking she is a woman of means by writing to her on stationery stolen from a local ritzy hotel. The ruse works until Annie receives a letter from Louise telling her that she is coming for a visit — and bringing her fiancé and his father over with her. Realizing that it would be impossible for Louise's fiancé's family to accept her as she is (they are members of Spanish royalty), Annie collapses in despair — much to the chagrin of Dave the Dude, who counts on Annie's apples to bring him good luck. In a display of unbelievable generosity, Dave decides to help Annie so he can continue his streak of good luck. With the assistance of his girlfriend and Annie's friends, Dave transforms Annie into a lady, finds her a fake husband (Guy Kibbee), and rents her a suite at the ritzy hotel. The story then focuses on Dave the Dude's trials and tribulations as he tries to balance his own business dealings with the increasingly complicated scheme to pass Annie off as a lady. Dave is forced to kidnap some reporters to keep Annie's story quiet, and gathers all his men together to rehearse for an upcoming reception for Annie's daughter. These events raise the suspicion of the police, who arrest him on the night the reception is to take place. He pleads his case to the police chief, seemingly to know avail, and requests an audience with the governor. Meanwhile, Annie, Louise, her fiancé, his father, Count Romero (Walter Connolly), and others await the arrival of Dave's ersatz guests to the party, unaware that they too have been detained, along with Dave. Just as Annie is about to reveal the truth to Louise, the *real* mayor and governor arrive to save the day. Touched by Dave's generosity towards Annie, they have decided to go along with the charade, much to Annie's amazement. The film ends with Annie waving goodbye to Louise, her fiancé, and the count from the boat docks, Louise never aware of her mother's lowly condition.

Lady for a Day is a touching but overly schmaltzy love story. It leaves one with a warm feeling (the arrival of the actual mayor and governor to the reception cannot help but generate a smile), but the film, like *American Madness*, suffers from the incorporation of two main characters. When Capra and Riskin switch from Annie's story to Dave the Dude's, we forget about Annie's existence, and when the plot returns to Annie the night of the reception, Dave the Dude is not even permitted to share the emotional moment with her. Furthermore, the motives behind Dave's generosity are basically selfish and superficial, which makes him a difficult character with whom to sympathize. Only his sincere speech at the police station really connects him with the audience.

That being said, *Lady for a Day* is notable for instituting several story techniques that Capra would later use in his most famous films. Scholar Raymond Carney, for instance, sees *Lady for a Day* as a key Capra film because it is the first to combine "visionary dreaming and pragmatic scheming."[22] Rather than simply wishing for change to happen, Dave the Dude has to work and suffer to make both his and Annie's dreams come true. Dave the Dude becomes the first in a long line of Capra heroes who make a conscious choice to change the lives of others, even at the risk of their own well-being. In addition, like Dave the Dude, Capra's most successful heroes have no real dreams or goals other than the maintenance of the status quo. When that status quo is endangered by unforeseen circumstances, the heroes are forced to engage, as Leland Poague describes it, in a series of "moment to moment improvisations."[23] Dave has no real plan for how to pull off the near-impossible task of passing Annie off as the elegant E. Worthington Manville, but jumps in with both feet to accomplish the goal. This impetuous decision not only generates numerous comedic situations, but also creates an unpredictable, improvisational reality which stimulates audience interest and piques its curiosity. One only wishes while watching *Lady for a Day* that Dave the Dude could look like he's having more fun while doing it.

With *Lady for a Day*, Capra finally received attention from the Academy. The film was nominated for Best Picture, Best Writing, Best Directing, and Best Actress. Although the film did not win in any of the categories for which it was nominated (much to Capra's great disappointment), *Lady for a Day* was a financial success for both Capra and Columbia Pictures. As such, Capra was free to choose his next picture. Wanting to film an "exterior picture," Capra persuaded Cohn to buy the rights to the short story "Night Bus."[24] The resulting film would become one of Capra's greatest successes and would make Oscar history.

It Happened One Night
(Based on the story "Night Bus"
by Samuel Hopkins Adams) (released February 1934)

Before Capra made his first Oscar winner, he was loaned out to Irving Thalberg to make a films for the biggest studio at the time, Metro-Goldwyn-Mayer. The film, titled *Soviet,* a melodrama about an American engineer hired to build a dam in Russia, would have been the director's biggest picture to date, populated with some of Hollywood's biggest stars—Wallace Beery, Marie Dressler, Joan Crawford, and Clark Gable. When Thalberg's illness forced him to travel to Europe to recover, studio head Louis B. Mayer immediately axed the project, sending Capra out of the major leagues and back to Columbia Pictures and the "Night Bus" project. MGM would, however, still have to honor its contract with Cohn, promising one of its stars to Columbia. Mayer sent over Clark Gable, wishing to exile the young star because he dared to ask for more money. Gable left MGM as persona non grata, but returned a star. Similarly, actress Claudette Colbert had no real interest in Capra's upcoming project, agreeing only if the mostly "outdoor" picture could be shot in a nearly impossible four weeks. Capra agreed. He had his two stars, and he hoped his script about heiresses and autocamps would be worthy of their great reputations.

It Happened One Night begins with the spoiled Ellie Andrews (Claudette Colbert) leaping off her family yacht to escape the imprisonment of her father (Walter Connolly) who objects to her hasty marriage to King Westley (Jameson Thomas), a playboy aviator. Her plan is to travel up the east coast to New

York, where she will meet up with Westley, and thus consummate her marriage. Once on dry land in Miami, she meets Peter Warne (Clark Gable), a recently unemployed reporter (changed from a painter in the original story), who recognizes the famous fugitive and offers to help Ellie get to Westley in exchange for the exclusive story. The couple is forced to travel by bus, then by foot, then by car, in order to reach New York in time. In one especially memorable scene, the two fugitives pose as a married couple in a motor lodge to throw off a couple of detectives. Along the way, Ellie becomes less rigid and condescending, while Peter softens, gradually opening up and becoming less class conscious. They fall in love, but after a misunderstanding on their last night together, Ellie runs away to accept her repentant father's offer to remarry Westley. On the day of the wedding, Ellie's father clears up the misunderstanding while walking the bride down the aisle. She breaks away at the last minute and escapes into the back of a car, which had been waiting the whole time to take her to Peter.

It Happened One Night brings back the love-versus-class struggle plot lines of earlier films like *Platinum Blonde* and *Ladies of Leisure*, but successfully resolves the crisis by having Ellie's father actually approve of the low class but honest Peter over the wealthy but shallow Westley. The script's brilliant pace and casual approach to storytelling also allows the characters to shine. Peter and Ellie are extremely likeable because they are allowed to *be*, and their arcs and motivations are believable. As pointed out by Charles Maland, *It Happened One Night* also hit upon a major structural center that Capra would use for *Mr. Deeds Goes to Town*, *Mr. Smith Goes to Washington*, and *Meet John Doe*—the use of a main character who acts as both a romantic and a moral figure in order to convert a heroine to his cause.[25] Like *Lady for a Day*, the main characters' decision to take on a difficult challenge without a well thought-out plan, allows them to engage in improvisatory behavior, leading to both "real" and humorous situations. The film's most entertaining moments come from these scenes: a busload of passengers start singing "Man on the Flying Trapeze"; Peter and Ellie pretend to be an arguing married couple; and—the most famous scene in the movie—the hitchhiking Ellie stops a car by showing her leg. These instances catch the viewer by surprise and prove that the two characters truly belong together. *American Madness* and *Lady for a Day* had some warm comedic touches (I particularly love how Matt and Tom are introduced in the former), but their heavy reliance on plot weighs them down, especially at the films' climaxes. The freeing "road movie" structure of *It Happened One Night* hits just the right balance, never letting its plot get in the way of its playfulness. For every obligatory and expository scene, we are treated to a scene of carefree improvisation that has very little bearing on the story, other than to increase the enjoyment of watching it.

The success of *It Happened One Night* took the whole industry by surprise, perhaps because it occurred so gradually. It opened in February to mediocre reviews and made only $80,000 in its first week.[26] By the end of the year, however, it had become a phenomenon, earning $4.4 million on a budget of $300, 000.[27] It was the first Capra film to make the prestigious *New York Times* Top Ten list and ended up winning all five major Academy Awards: Best Director, Best Picture, Best Actor, Best Actress, and Best Screenplay. In the history of the Oscars, only two other films have equaled this achievement — *One Flew Over the Cuckoo's Nest* and *Silence of the Lambs*. The success of the film shocked Capra, who had been itching to win an Oscar ever since he lost the year before for *Lady for a Day*. In his autobiography, he wrote: "Externally, I accepted the laurels with a show of grace. But inwardly, I had become a pillar of jello; haunted by fear that my next picture would fail. In short, I made the major leagues — and choked up."[28]

Capra's fear of failure and his reluctance to make another film manifested itself into an imagined sickness, which quickly developed into a real one, complete with night sweats and high fever. While recovering from this baffling illness, alternately diagnosed as "Galloping Tuberculosis" and "California pneumonia," Capra received a visit from a "faceless" little man who, without introducing himself, verbally assaulted Capra in his bed. Pointing to the radio, out of which Hitler's voice was blaring, the man called Capra a coward and castigated him for not making more of his talent. In his autobiography, Capra quoted the mysterious man's speech word for word:

> That evil man [Hitler] is desperately trying to poison the world with hate. How many can he talk to? Fifteen million — twenty million? And for how long — twenty minutes? You, sir, you can talk to *hundreds* of millions, for two hours — and in the dark. The talents you have, Mr. Capra, are not your own, *not* self acquired. God gave you those talents; they are His gifts to you, to use for His purpose. And when you don't *use* the gifts God blessed you with — you are an offense to God — and to humanity. Good day, sir.[29]

It is important to note, that Capra biographer Joseph McBride believes most of this encounter, if not all of it, is pure invention. The story first appeared in a talk between Capra and UCLA professor Arthur Friedman in the late 1950s, and at that time, Capra mistakenly placed his illness in 1936, after *Mr. Deeds*.[30] In actuality, Capra became deathly ill *before It Happened One Night* swept the Academy Awards of 1935, missing the Radio City Music Hall premiere of his next film, *Broadway Bill,* which was held on Thanksgiving Day, 1934.[31]

The reason for making up this story remains unclear, but provides us with some insight into what Capra was thinking at the time of his first major success. The sudden success made him feel like a fake, one who should be using his talent and power to better mankind rather than to simply make money. This revelation would be a key factor in his decision to join the Army. It would also start a major trend in the films Capra made thereafter. Capra would change the "gradual" conversions of his characters in earlier films like *It Happened One Night*, *Bitter Tea of General Yen*, and *Miracle Woman* to the "sudden" conversions of characters in *Mr. Deeds*, *Lost Horizon*, *You Can't Take it With You*, and *Mr. Smith Goes to Washington*. Whether it came from a pep talk from a faceless little man, or from inside his own heart, Capra's style of filmmaking clearly changed in 1935. Starting with *Mr. Deeds Goes to Town*, (the next film he made for Columbia), Capra decided his films would *say* something. "From then on," he wrote, "my scripts would take six months to a year to write and rewrite, to carefully — and subtly — integrate ideals and entertainment into a meaningful tale."[32]

"Capracorn" was born.

Broadway Bill
(Released November 1934)

Although the momentum created by the dramatic story of Capra's sickness and resulting conversion seems to require us to move directly into *Mr. Deeds Goes to Town*, doing so would not only violate my adherence to chronology but would also unfairly neglect one of Capra's most engaging films. Too often, scholars neglect *Broadway Bill* because of its unfortunate placement in the Capra timeline — between the premiere of *It Happened One Night* and the 1935 Academy Award ceremony during which the Gable/Colbert film won big. *It Happened One Night*'s blockbuster success dwarfs the modest success of *Bill*; even Capra neglects to mention the production of the film between *It Happened One Night* and *Mr. Deeds Goes to Town* in his own autobiography. *Broadway Bill* has been viewed as a speed bump on the way to Capra's second Oscar winner. Such treatment is not worthy of this thoroughly entertaining film, which not only contains winning performances by Warner Baxter and Myrna Loy, but initiates and strengthens several key Capraesque elements.

The dilemma of Dan Brooks (Warner Baxter), the hero of *Broadway Bill*, is strikingly similar to that of Stew Smith in *Platinum Blonde*. Dan has married into a wealthy family but wants none of the trappings of the leisure class. Although his father-in-law, the rich and powerful J.L. Higgins (Walter Connolly), for the most part approves of the man his daughter married, Dan himself feels unfulfilled as acting president of the Higgins Paper Box company. He would rather race horses, a passion shared by his friend Whitey (Clarence Muse) and his sister-in-law Alice (Myrna Loy), the only daughter of J.L. not married. At a ritualistic dinner with the whole upper-crust family, Dan finally quits the box company to follow his passion, running off to the racetrack with Whitey and his horse, Broadway Bill. His wife, Margaret (Helen Vinson), does not join her husband on his quest, choosing instead to wait him out while living in the lap of her father's luxury. Alice, however, does join Dan, helping him financially when she can and supporting him emotionally through every ordeal — of which there are quite a few. First, Bill and his owners are forced to room in a ramshackle stable, whose roof leaks during a violent storm, causing Bill to become deathly ill. Dan must also raise money for the several fees the track must charge. He receives help from Colonel Pettigrew (Raymond Walburn), a friendly and colorful con artist who happens to be just as broke as Dan. Eventually, he is assisted by Eddie Morgan (Douglas Dumbrille) a rich horse owner who needs Broadway Bill in the race so the odds on his own horse will be greater. Eventually, Bill recovers from his illness and becomes the favorite of the working class, an underdog everyone wants to win. Despite the crooked tricks of Eddie Morgan, Broadway Bill actually wins the race, but his heart bursts as he crosses the finish line and he dies right on the track, in full view of the audience who had cheered for him. Dan, Whitey, and Alice are devastated by Bill's sudden demise. At the emotional funeral, the racing commissioner says Bill's story is more than a story, it is a "lesson in courage and loyalty." Whitey and Dan walk off into the sunset, heads hanging down, as Alice returns home with her father. In a surprisingly upbeat coda, at another family dinner, J.L. Higgins tells his sons-in-law that he is selling all of his companies. He is interrupted by Dan, honking the horn outside the dining room. He has come for Alice, as he and Whitey have new horses to race. Alice runs outside, only to be joined by her newly "converted" father, who runs out after them.

Broadway Bill, like *It Happened One Night*, is as likeable and entertaining as its leading stars. *Broadway Bill* has its moments of spontaneity and playfulness, and Warner Baxter seems sincerely joyful at every upturn in their fortunes. The only difficulty is its ending. Bill's death is so overpowering and emotional that no tacked-on "happy ending" could possibly overcome it. Dan comes the closest of any previous Capra character to the heroes of his most famous films, but like *American Madness*, he shares the role with another character in the film — Broadway Bill. While Dan is playful, spontaneous, and idealistic, Bill is the character who inspires the working man to support him — and Bill is the one who becomes a martyr to the cause, surprisingly winning the race even though the game was rigged from the start. *Broadway Bill* also shows the powerful ability of idealists and martyrs to convert the rich and the cynical (both J.L. Higgins *and* Eddie Morgan show up at Bill's funeral, genuinely moved), a theme Capra would employ time and time again in his later, more famous films. With *Broadway Bill,* Capra also seemed to hitting his stride. The "artsy" camera movements and rich set design used in *American Madness* and *Bitter Tea* are sacrificed for more character moments and a quicker, more economical pace. Furthermore, the fast-paced, quickly cut racing scene at the film's climax may very well be one of the greatest sequences Capra ever filmed, and deserves to be ranked alongside the best of the genre.

Mr. Deeds Goes to Town
(Based on the serial "Opera Hat" by Clarence Budington Kelland) (Released April 1936)

With Capra's success assured after sweeping the Academy Awards in 1935, the Oscar-winning director returned to Columbia with renewed vigor and an increased passion to make movies that mattered. In an interview with *American Classic Screen* nearly 35 years later, Capra admitted that he was not fully committed to film as a career until the success of *It Happened One Night.* After that motion picture, he said, "I had to marry one or the other — science or film — and I married the harlot. Then I began to concentrate on using films to express ideas."[33] As described in his "conversion" story, this decision to make "idea" films, may have also been a reaction to the terrible news he and his fellow Americans were hearing about the rise of Hitler overseas. In an interview in 1957, he stated that at the time: "I began to react against these institutions, against the one man dominating individuals, shooting people in large numbers, and I suppose subconsciously I began to put up the fight for man as an individual, and the triumph of the human spirit over obstacles."[34] Capra was no longer split over his feelings towards fascism and oppression. He saw himself as a fighter for freedom, a man who could use his newfound popularity to tell stories about the importance of individualism and liberty. This theme would take a central role in Capra's most examined films as well as the films he made for the U.S. government during World War II. No longer would greedy capitalists, conformists, and fascist "bosses" help his heroes achieve success as they did in *It Happened One Night, American Madness,* and *Broadway Bill,* nor could they be reformed. With the exception of *You Can't Take It with You,* the powerful villains in Capra's films for the next 12 years would remain on the opposite side of his heroes, setting up continued showdowns between the rich and the ordinary, the cynical and the idealistic, the conformist and the rebel.

It is hard to believe that Capra found the perfect story to illustrate that theme in "Opera Hat," a detective story about the murder of a 22-year-old millionaire while attending the opera. It was the character of Mr. Deeds, however, that attracted Capra to the story, and eventually he and Robert Riskin jettisoned most of the story to focus the film on that character entirely.[35] The plot of the film is rather light as it is more of a character piece than anything else. Even Frank Nugent, a *New York Times* film critic who reviewed the film, understood that a simple outline of the film's plot could not "attempt to capture the gay, harebrained, but entirely ingratiating quality of the picture."[36] In an effort to preserve continuity, however, I will attempt such a plot summary, although like many of Capra's films, plot summaries in no way compensate for the actual viewing of the film.

In *Mr. Deeds Goes to Town*, Longfellow Deeds (Gary Cooper), tuba player and greeting card writer of Mandrake Falls, Vermont, learns that he has inherited $20 million from his rich Uncle Martin Semple, who died in an automobile accident. Even though he argues that he does not want or need the money, he is talked into moving to his uncle's mansion in New York City by his uncle's lawyer, John Cedar (Douglas Dumbrille), and his uncle's bodyguard, "Corny" Cobb (Lionel Stander). Once in New York, he runs into Babe Bennett (Jean Arthur), a wisecracking reporter who pretends to be a starving small-town girl named Mary Dawson. Babe continues this charade, going out on dates with Deeds while poking fun at his impulsive behavior in her articles behind his back, cruelly dubbing him the "Cinderella Man." The name sticks, and the honest, small-town Deeds becomes the laughingstock of the Big Apple. Longfellow eventually discovers Mary's real identity through Cobb, the morning after he proposes to her. Filled with despair over Babe's betrayal, Longfellow decides to leave New York permanently, but in a scene remarkably close to Capra's "faceless man" episode, the "common man" millionaire is confronted by a farmer who scolds him for being frivolous with his money and not helping people who really need it. Touched by the farmer's story, Deeds resolves to loan out his money to unemployed farmers, but is stopped by the lawyer Cedar, who, on behalf of Semple's nephew, declares him mentally unfit to receive the inheritance, cruelly using Babe's articles as evidence. In his sanity hearing, Deeds at first offers no resistance to Cedar's arguments, but after Babe confesses her love for him on the stand, he defends his sanity by deconstructing Cedar's attacks, one by one, with plain, honest, common sense— ending his argument by punching Cedar in the face. True to the "Capracorn" formula, the judge is won over by Deeds's inherent honesty and declares him sane. The courtroom spectators go wild and carry Deeds out of the courtroom on their shoulders. In the film's final moments, Deeds escapes from the crowd and makes his way back to the courtroom for Babe. He scoops her up in his arms and kisses her as we hear "For He's a Jolly Good Fellow."

Mr. Deeds Goes to Town was a very successful film for Capra. Not only did it win him a second Oscar for Best Director, it made $2.3 million at the box office, nearly three times its budget. According to the book *George Lucas's Blockbusting*, this is equivalent in today's box office to making $59 million on an $11 million budget.[37] It broke box-office records of all kinds and nearly bested the other hit of that year, *Modern Times*.[38] And more so than *It Happened One Night*, *Mr. Deeds* established a winning formula for Capra that would be worked into *Mr. Smith Goes to Washington* and *Meet John Doe*, as well as his war documentaries. As mentioned earlier, from the beginning, Capra saw *Mr. Deeds* as a vehicle through which he could abandon the light, screwball comedy of *It Happened One Night* for much more serious political and social themes.[39] In a somewhat related note, with *Mr. Deeds*, Capra also abandoned the "outdoorsy" feel of *Broadway Bill* and *It Happened One Night* for interior sets and soundstages. This preference would continue for the rest of Capra's films, save for *Riding High*, his 1950 musical remake of *Broadway Bill* starring Bing Crosby. For these reasons, according to Capra scholar Leland Poague, "Just about everyone agrees that *Mr. Deeds Goes to Town* marks a crucial turning point in Capra's relationship to his craft and his public."[40] Although many elements and techniques used in *Deeds* pop up in earlier Capra films like *American Madness* and *Broadway Bill*, I tend to concur.

According to Capra, it was the film's strong thematic content that caused it to be such a hit. Longfellow Deeds, Capra wrote, was a symbol of the deep resistance Americans at the time felt about being compartmentalized. Deeds asserted the rights of the individual over the "massiveness" of the 1930s—mass production, mass thought, and mass conformity.[41] Like many of Capra's films, *Mr. Deeds* seems to exist both in its own time and outside it. Although it brings up the Depression, its idealism and humanistic themes are timeless. On a personal note, less than a month ago, the head of the Criminal Justice Department at the university where I work, caught me doodling during a faculty meeting. The use of the word led him to ask me if I had seen *Mr. Deeds Goes to Town* (he was unaware I was working on this book). I nodded and he mentioned that the film was one of his favorites. Such reactions, I find are not uncommon with Capra's works, which, like the heavily thematic films of Walt Disney, continue to resonate from generation to generation.

Lost Horizon
(Based on the novel by James Hilton)
(Released March 2, 1938)

Frank Capra read the book *Lost Horizon* by James Hilton just before shooting *Mr. Deeds*. The theme of the novel, man's search for solace and understanding in a world where nations were devoted not to wisdom but to vulgar passions and the will to destroy, seemed remarkably current to Capra, so he asked Cohn to buy the rights to the book. Cohn bought the six-month option for the film, wary about spending the amount needed to bring the story to life. The success of *Mr. Deeds*, however, convinced Cohn to take the risk on his most popular director, and *Lost Horizon* became Capra's next film.

Capra understood from the beginning that turning *Lost Horizon* into a film would be especially difficult. The story was essentially a poetic saga, filled with allegory and idealized locations, which, if treated wrongly, would be resented by the audience if they knew what the director was up to before they were "conditioned."[42] To guard against this, Capra decided to photograph the early scenes of the film with a "stark, documentary reality."[43] This technique would later be employed in the *Why We Fight* series, wherein he used realistic war footage to add legitimacy to the ideology being sold.

The story of *Lost Horizon* is essentially an "imperialist fantasy."[44] The film begins in China, where diplomat Robert Conway (Ronald Colman) is tasked to rescue trapped Westerners from the rioting city of Baskul. He flies out with the last batch of evacuees, just ahead of the armed revolutionaries, but crash lands deep in the Himalayas. Conway and his fellow Westerners, including his brother, George (John Howard), are rescued by Chang (H.B. Warner) and taken to Shangri-La, a beautiful and peaceful valley sheltered from the cold, with magical properties that keep people from growing old. While there, Conway meets Sondra Bizet (Jane Wyatt), a white woman raised by a Belgian priest who civilized the valley 200 years ago. Eventually, Conway gets an audience with this spiritual leader (Sam Jaffe), called the High Lama, who tells the British diplomat his plane crash was no accident. Conway, in fact, was purposely taken to Shangri-La to replace the dying leader. Sondra, having read Conway's writings before his arrival, had advised the High Lama that Conway would be the best man to protect this utopia, as he possesses a great understanding of the ways of the modern world. Conway, however, is torn between staying in this paradise and leaving with George, who doubts the High Lama's fantastic story. Conway chooses to leave with George and his lover, Maria (Margot), but after a grueling journey, Maria collapses and dies, having been magically transformed into an old woman. George, horrified, leaps to his death, leaving Conway as the lone survivor to be picked up by a search party. The ordeal causes Conway to lose his memory, which is regained on the voyage back to England. He jumps ship and travels back to the Himalayas, returning in the final scene to the elusive paradise.

Everything about *Lost Horizon* was big. It became the most expensive picture Columbia Pictures had ever produced, costing a reported $1.6 million.[45] In addition, the initial cut of the film was nearly six hours long, cut down to 132 minutes for its premiere, which Capra did not attend. The film did not make a profit until it was reissued in 1942, and negatively affected Columbia's net profits between 1937 and 1938.[46] In a candid moment during an interview in the 1950s with Arthur Friedman, Capra confessed that he got lost in the "never-never land" of Shangri-La, making the theme of the picture more important than the human beings in it.[47] Capra seemed unsure of himself with such a large production, endlessly shooting multiple takes and multiple endings. One of Capra's favorite stories, related nearly four decades later on *The Dick Cavett Show*, involved a disastrous preview screening of the film, which resulted in Capra burning the first two reels in order to give the beginning of the film the punch it needed. The final shooting ratio of the film, however, would be an astonishing 93 to one, seven times the amount of film used for *Mr. Deeds*.[48] In addition, the shooting would last a hundred days, 34 days over schedule and 53 days longer than *Mr. Deeds*.[49] Biographer Charles Maland believed that Capra's insecurity about the film dealt with the inherent problem with the story itself, as there is no believable reason the confident, serene Robert Conway would ever leave Shangri-La. Though absence of any real conflict "may create a wonderful society," he wrote, "it's no way to construct a film."[50] Even Capra concurred that the film missed the mark. In an interview over 20 years later, he admitted that he was "disappointed" in *Lost Horizon* because the film "should have been better than it was."[51]

At the time, *Lost Horizon*'s utopian theme was judged anti-war, stirring up pundits from the far right and far left. A Nazi paper in Germany called the film "decadent drivel from a decaying democracy," as they believed the ideology of the film was opposite to Hitler's aggressive point of view.[52] To many middle- and lower-class Americans at the time, however, Capra's vision of utopia had its benefits. Not only did Shangri-La offer its citizens the freedom to pursue their own passions, Leland Pogue points out that it also proposed a world where the "ordinary life" was "protected from the extraordinary pressures of a world gone communally mad."[53]

Despite its troubles, *Lost Horizon* was still considered by many critics of the time to be a successful film. Frank Nugent of the *New York Times*, for instance, wrote that *Lost Horizon* was a "grand adventure film, magnificently staged, beautifully photographed, and capitally played."[54] In addition, the film won two Academy Awards for Best Art Direction and Best Film Editing and was placed on the *New York Times* list as one of the ten best films of 1937. More importantly, its large scope elevated Capra's status in Hollywood to a "director's director."[55] According to Capra, the film had a strong fan base, with Columbia receiving letters from thousands of fans who said they had seen the film "as many as twenty times."⁵⁶ Actor/Director Gene Kelly, for instance, once wrote "the best of all Capra's work," [was] "contained in *Lost Horizon*."⁵⁷

Like *Arsenic and Old Lace*, *Lost Horizon* remains troubling to Capra scholars because it seems so different from the other work that made the director famous. Its hero is a well-spoken intellectual, not a stammering everyman, and everything about the film is grand and epic rather than personal and intimate. Some Capra scholars have discussed the relationship between the film and *The Bitter Tea of General Yen*, especially in its Asian-influenced production design. Both of these films also revolve around characters, who, although they are captives in an unfamiliar environment, learn to adapt and even enjoy their strange surroundings. Perhaps these plots illustrate Capra's own mixed feelings about working for Columbia Pictures when his popularity and success should have allowed him to move up to more prestigious surroundings. (Changing studios, however, would have also meant giving up the substantial creative freedom he was used to having at Columbia.) In addition to its similarities to *Bitter Tea*, Leland Poague also pointed out in his book *Another Frank Capra*, that *Lost Horizon* is surprisingly similar to *Mr. Deeds*. Both films, for instance, involve a hero being transported against his will to palatial foreign surroundings, as well as dealing with the differences between competing ideas of community and service.⁵⁸

Finally, Capra's difficulty with the film's disastrous initial test screenings forced him to come to terms with the audience's importance in the filmmaking process. While a book is aimed at an audience of one, he wrote, a "motion picture is aimed at communicating with hundreds, or, hopefully, thousands of viewers at each showing.... The line between the sublime and the ridiculous is rather wide and indefinite to an audience of one; thinner and sharper to an audience of many — the larger the audience, the thinner the line."⁵⁹ Capra would carry this important lesson with him when working on his Army-orientation films, knowing they would be seen by thousands of U.S. troops during the war.

You Can't Take It with You
(Based on the play by George S. Kaufman and Moss Hart)
(Released September 2, 1938)

During the international press tour for *Lost Horizon*, Capra discovered that his boss, Harry Cohn, had put the director's name on a film he did not make. Livid, Capra decided to sue Columbia Pictures. After a long, protracted court battle (during which time Capra could not work), he finally agreed to drop the lawsuit. One of the conditions upon his return to the studio was that Cohn buy the rights to the hit play *You Can't Take It with You* by Moss Hart and George S. Kaufman. Capra saw the play's focus on individuality and loving one's neighbor to be a perfect fit for his style. With Riskin, he "amplified" the play for the screen, paying more attention to the father/son relationship between Anthony Kirby (Edward Arnold) and Tony Jr. (James Stewart) and adding scenes like the night court which were only hinted at in the play.[60] In fact, almost all the memorable scenes in the film — Tony Jr. and Alice's date, the scene between Vanderhof and Kirby Sr. in the jail, as well as the climactic boardroom scene with Anthony Kirby, Sr., were added to the content of the play. Most of these scenes either open up the play to other locations, create a sense of spontaneity and playfulness, add to the Kirby storyline, or enhance the theme of individuality. These additions, however, greatly change the tone of the play, which was meant to be satirical. In an interview with the *Christian Science Monitor* at the time, Capra defended his decision to change the play's tongue-in-cheek atmosphere to one of honest sincerity. He claimed that plays, by necessity, must be changed when adapted to film in order to play to a larger audience, adding that "you can't make sport with an audience's cherished beliefs and have a very wide audience."[61]

The film begins with ruthless banker Anthony P. Kirby detailing his plan to buy up all the land around a competitor to put him out of business. The only holdout is Martin Vanderhof (Lionel Barrymore), who refuses to sell his home (an element added to the film to bring greater complexity to the Kirby/Vanderhof relationship). Unbeknownst to Kirby Sr., Tony Kirby, Jr., has just proposed to his stenographer, Alice Sycamore (Jean Arthur), who also happens to be Vanderhof's granddaughter. That night, Tony Jr. meets the entire family, all of whom live together in the Vanderhof house and are free to pursue their own individual passions. Tony, charmed by their uniqueness, agrees to bring his parents by for dinner in order for them to meet his fiancée's family. Afraid that Alice will force her family to change in order to impress his parents, Tony purposely brings his mother and father by a day early. The plan goes disastrously awry. After a series of misunderstandings involving firework ads touting a "revolution," the police arrive and arrest everyone in the house — including the Kirbys. While in jail, Grandpa Vanderhof learns that Anthony Kirby, Sr., was the man who had been pestering him about selling his house. In a speech written specifically for the film, Vanderhof castigates Kirby Sr. about his warped priorities in front of the common rabble of the jail cell. Immediately regretting the exchange, Grandpa gives Kirby Sr. a harmonica as a peacemaking gesture. During the trial, Vanderhof lets the Kirbys off the hook by testifying that they had nothing to do with the trouble and that Kirby Sr. was only visiting to buy his house. Alice, angry that Tony is protecting his family by not announcing the real reason his parents were there, tells the court the truth and storms out. The couple splits, Alice moves out, and Vanderhof ultimately decides to sell his house. Kirby Sr. profoundly affected by the trial, his son's resignation, and the bitter words of his business competitor on the day of his huge deal, leaves work and decides to visit the Vanderhof house once again. After a harmonica duet with Grandpa Vanderhof, he sees that Tony Jr. is there as well and has made up with Alice. In the end, Kirby Sr. decides not to buy the house and joins the family for dinner, this time participating in their revelry rather than judging it.

You Can't Take It with You earned Capra his third Oscar for directing and his second for Best Picture. Most critics at the time believed Capra's film was an improvement on the play. *Variety* called the film "wholly American, wholesome, homespun, human, appealing, and touching in turn."[62] Additionally, *You Can't Take It with You* was one of the top 15 money-makers of 1938–39. Capra said little about the film's financial success, however, as its release coincided with a more significant personal event: the death of his three-and-a-half-year-old son John during a routine tonsillectomy.

When studying Capra's films chronologically, three aspects of *You Can't Take It with You* stand out. For one, the film relies more on music than perhaps any other Capra film before it, save *It Happened One Night*, which started the trend. Throughout the film, music brings people together. Alice and Tony Jr. dance in the park during their date; the men in the drunk tank sing and dance to Grandpa Vanderhof's harmonica; and Grandpa Vanderhof and Anthony Kirby, Sr., bond over a harmonica duet. Anthony Kirby, Sr.'s conversion is also an unusual aspect of the film, not only because it was specifically added to the play by Capra, but because this conversion becomes a major focus of the film. I have a sneaking suspicion that Capra added the conversion to the film in order to force it to "mean something." Whether or not I am right, the focus on the millionaire's change of heart *does* lead to the film's more "preachy" moments. Although Charles Maland believed that Anthony Kirby, Sr.'s conversion strained credibility,[63] I believe it was adequately developed throughout the film, especially in the second half, during which he nearly loses his son. The other aspect of Kirby's conversion that bears note is the sheer unlikelihood of its occurrence in any of Capra's other films. Perhaps Capra was feeling a bit more optimistic about businessmen after he won his legal battle with Harry Cohn, or perhaps he simply believed that Kirby should be a model for other businessman during the Depression. Either way, *You Can't Take It with You* marks the last time the major villain of a Capra film is converted to the hero's cause. Finally, in his book *Another Frank Capra*, Leland Poague pays a great deal of attention to the fireworks scene in the film, when the high-key comedy lighting quickly gives way to the low-key lighting and fast intercutting of a dark action film. This drastic change of tone not only proves that Capra could work in any genre of filmmaking equally well, it also gives the film a much-needed energy boost.[64] Additionally, the chaotic scene carries the audience's attention into the pivotal jail scene, during which the film's ideology is laid bare. Capra's ability to abruptly change tone not only serves him well in films like *Meet John Doe*, *Arsenic and Old Lace*, and *It's a Wonderful Life*, but also in his war documentaries, wherein he needed to balance gripping battle scenes with idealistic, patriotic content.

Mr. Smith Goes to Washington
(Based on Lewis R. Foster's short story
"The Gentleman from Montana"
and the play *Both Your Houses* by Maxwell Anderson)
(Released October 1939)

By the late 1930s, Capra well understood the type of material that would perfectly fit his style. Thus, when the novelistic treatment "The Gentleman from Montana" came across his desk, he knew immediately that he "wanted that story!"[65] In fact, the two-page treatment was so inspiring to Capra, he never sat down and actually read the finished book.[66] Capra even tried to get Gary Cooper to revise his earlier role and call it *Mr. Deeds Goes to Washington*. But when Samuel Goldwyn refused to loan Cooper to Columbia, James Stewart was tapped to be the leading man. Frequent collaborator Robert Riskin was also tied up with Samuel Goldwyn as a scriptwriter and script "doctor," so Capra turned to Sidney Buchman to help him write the script. The choice of adapting so political a book raised many eyebrows in Hollywood. Joseph Breen, head of the Production Code Administration, cautioned the studio against making the film, saying the material might be "loaded with dynamite."[67] In the end, however, Breen deferred to his boss, Will Hays, who allowed the film to be made only so long as "the studio exercise the greatest possible care in indicating that the indictment of members of the Congress is not a wholesale indictment."[68]

The controversial story revolves around Jefferson Smith (Stewart), a scout leader who is appointed to the Senate when the previous office holder, Senator Foley, dies unexpectedly. Smith, who is not introduced until 20 minutes into the film, is beloved by the kids in his state and is known as the type of man who can cite Lincoln and Jefferson by heart. On his first day in Washington, the wide-eyed Smith ditches his "handlers" to take a tour of Washington, D.C., visiting all the historical landmarks. When he finally shows up in his office, he meets his secretary, Clarissa Saunders (Jean Arthur), a jaded and opportunistic Washington insider. In a press meeting, Smith talks about his plans to open a national Boy Ranger's Camp, but the press betrays him, running false headlines about Smith and manipulating photos of him to make him appear foolish. Smith responds by going out on the warpath, seeking out each of them and punching them in the jaw. Saunders, meanwhile, is charged by Senator Joseph Paine (Claude Rains), the senior senator from Smith's state, to keep Jeff away from a Willett Creek dam bill proposed by Paine that will favor his state's political boss Jim Taylor (Edward Arnold) and other legislative insiders. Instead, Saunders helps Smith draft his Boy Ranger's Camp proposal which plans on using the same Willett Creek. When Jeff refuses to back down on his bill after Taylor turns up the heat, Paine and Taylor conspire to have Smith thrown out of the Senate on corruption charges. Jeff, feeling betrayed by Paine and disillusioned by democracy, visits the Lincoln Memorial, where Saunders finds him and encourages him to fight back. Smith decides to filibuster the dam bill on the floor of the Senate, where his endurance and emotional stand against the legislation inspires his fellow senators and provokes Paine into an attempted suicide and, finally, a full confession.

Sidney Buchman, although proud of the script, later confessed that he hated the ending, which he always avoided watching. His biggest problem was the attempted suicide, the idea of which came from Capra, who Buchman claimed was not able to "avoid falling into moments of violence." This melodramatic touch, he felt, lessened the overall political impact of the film.[69] Sam Girgus, author of *Hollywood Renaissance: The Cinema of Democracy in the Era of Ford, Capra, and Kazan*, respectfully disagrees with Buchman. To Girgus, the ending underlies the film's theme of martyrdom and the necessity of idealistic "lost causes." He adds that, by attempting suicide, Paine is attempting to relieve his guilt of not living up to the ideals of Smith's father. Paine attempts to shoot himself, therefore, as a "masochistic craving to take the place of his victim," Jefferson Smith, who has proven he can take punishment as a true martyr to his lost cause.[70] In my opinion, while Paine's attempted suicide is not only believable but also dramatically necessary, the film tries to accomplish too much in the film's final minutes, as if Capra was attempting to tie up all the loose ends without boring the audience. Either way, the rushed, chaotic ending of *Mr. Smith* proves that Capra had no problem resorting to heavy-handed melodrama to solve story problems, especially if that melodrama reinforced the film's serious themes.

Mr. Smith Goes to Washington became a hit in 1939 — the golden year of Hollywood hits — earning $3.3 million dollars on a budget of $1.9 million, a gross second only to *Gone with the Wind*. In 2005 dollars, the budget would be about $26 million and its gross would be nearly $93 million.[71] *Mr. Smith* earned 11 Academy Award nominations, the most nominations of any Capra movie, and won for Best Original Story. The small touches, more than its melodrama, attracted most of the critics to the film. The *New York Times* critic Frank Nugent, for instance, lauded the simple, human details, including Jeff's voice cracking as he reads his bill and fumbling with his hat while talking to Senator Paine's attractive daughter.[72] *Mr. Smith Goes to Washington*, however, marked the end of Capra's critical success, which started only half a decade earlier with *It Happened One Night*. It would be the last film of Capra's to make the *New York Times* Top Ten list.[73]

Mr. Smith was not so well received by the Washington elite, who interpreted the film as a criticism rather than a compliment. This criticism deeply hurt Capra, and as will be discussed in Chapter 3, may have contributed to his decision to enter the Army during World War II. Both the critics and the American people, however, enjoyed the film a great deal, and its reputation has only improved over time. It was recently ranked by the American Film Institute as the 26th best film of all time, higher on the list than *It Happened One Night*. Once the initial controversy over *Mr. Smith* died down, the film was no longer seen as a criticism of democracy, but a testament to one man's power to influence it. Presidential candidate George McGovern, for instance, once wrote that *Mr. Smith* helped "awaken [his] early interest in our national government."[74] In some ways, *Mr. Smith* illustrates how the government works from a childlike point of view, brimming with drama and exaggerations. In truth, Capra often exaggerated events in order to simplify important points to a mass audience, many of whom did not graduate from high school. The exaggerations in *Mr. Smith Goes to Washington* were offensive to congressmen because the film seemed to tell people that when senators voted it came down to a moral choice — one could either vote for one's own self-interest or for the interests of others. Although this is not always the case in reality, Sam Girgus points out that many of the exaggerations in *Mr. Smith* have actually "turned into prophecies of serious relevance to contemporary life and politics."[75] (Personally, I have found that students who watch the film rarely believe the film is unfair in its depiction of how government works.)

When studying all of Capra's films from the thirties, one aspect of *Mr. Smith* stands out from the rest, and that is the treatment of its titular hero, Jefferson Smith. Part of this certainly has to do with the heartfelt performance of Jimmy Stewart, but also because he is much more innocent than any of Capra's previous heroes. Longfellow Deeds may have been a martyr, but he was adept at smelling out rats, as could Peter Warne and Grandpa Vanderhof. Jeff never knows when he is being mocked or betrayed, which makes those scenes all the more painful to watch. Like Grandpa Vanderhof, Smith possesses a core set of beliefs. But where Vanderhof's beliefs are never substantially tested (he always seems to know what is going to happen), Smith's ideals—

a mixture of liberty and Christian love — are continually challenged by outside forces. The stakes are much higher for him than they are in *You Can't Take It with You* and *Mr. Deeds Goes to Town*. Jefferson Smith is much more alone than his fictional predecessors; his punishment is much more severe, and his task much more difficult, pushing him (literally) to the point of exhaustion. In the end, as in *It's a Wonderful Life*, all of Smith's struggles come down to one issue: faith. It is Smith's faith in the importance of his ideals (which he claims are also the ideals of the Founding Fathers) which resonates so strongly with audiences, especially audiences of the time, who saw in Smith's ideals an attempt to give America the identity it needed to fight against the rising fascist philosophy in Europe. It is no wonder that this philosophy would also provide Capra with a solid foundation on which to make the *Why We Fight* series a few years later.

Meet John Doe
(Based on the treatment "The Life and Death of John Doe"
by Robert Presnell and Richard Connell)
(Released May 3, 1941)

Meet John Doe became the culmination of the "common man" pictures Capra directed before the war. It also marked the reunion between the director and his writing partner Robert Riskin, who joined with Capra to found Frank Capra Productions, an independent film company. *John Doe* was the company's first picture, and they both knew it had to be good if they were going to keep their independent status alive. But with *Meet John Doe*, Capra was aiming for more than popular success. He wanted critical success as well. In his autobiography, he wrote:

> An ego like mine needed — nay, required — the plaudits of sophisticated criticism. Childlike, creativity thirsts for the heady wine of the connoisseur's acclaim. The "Capra-corn" barbs had pierced the outer blubber.
> And so, *Meet John Doe*, my first completely independent film venture, was *aimed* at winning critical praises.[76]

Strange as it may seem, Frank Capra — winner of three Academy Awards for Best Director, president of the Academy of Motion Picture Arts and Sciences, and the subject of a *Time* magazine cover story — still yearned for the special kind of legitimacy that only comes from approbation of the elite.[77] Furthermore, the success of *Mr. Smith* and its strong ideological content provoked Capra into pushing the issues explored in that film even further. As the situation in Europe grew steadily worse, Capra and Riskin decided to pull out all the stops on this film, putting their creative minds to the test. Years later, Capra explained the lofty intentions of *Meet John Doe* to interviewer Richard Schickel, saying:

> *John Doe* was to me an important film because it did dig pretty deeply into the tempo and the mood of our times, which was fear of military aggression, fear of losing our sense of well-being and our sense of satisfaction, and fear that we might lose everything that we ever stood for. Hitler was a real, real problem.[78]

Capra believed his first film outside the studio system would help alleviate the anxiety and uncertainty that Germany had brought into the world. Unfortunately, while making the film, Capra and Riskin would discover that the negative forces they had amassed against the heroes in *Meet John Doe* were too great for them to realistically overcome. The inability to successfully resolve this conflict would push Capra and Riskin to their creative limits, and would result in the first failure of their long partnership. This failure, at the height of Capra's popularity, however, makes *Meet John Doe* one of his most fascinating works.

Meet John Doe begins like a documentary film, showing several "stock" shots of ordinary men and women working throughout America, ending on the name plaque of the *New Bulletin*, a newspaper advertising itself as "A Streamlined Newspaper for a Streamlined Era." Writer Ann Mitchell (Barbara Stanwyck), a victim of the *New Bulletin*'s restructuring, in one last desperate attempt to keep her job, fabricates a story about a man, John Doe, who threatens to throw himself off the roof of City Hall on Christmas Eve to protest the state of the world. The story becomes a sensation, and Ann is rehired to milk the story for all it is worth. Because the story is fake, Ann and her editor, Henry Connell (James Gleason), must find the perfect person to pretend to be John Doe. As if in answer to their prayers, in walks Long John Willoughby (Gary Cooper), an out-of-work pitcher, who agrees to pretend to be John Doe if the newspaper gives him the money to fix his bad "wing" so he can pitch again. The plan is immediately seen as trouble by Willoughby's skeptical friend, the "colonel" (Walter Brennan), who decides to stay, if only to prevent John from being manipulated. With John Doe's popularity increasing, the paper's owner D.B. Norton (Edward Arnold) decides to take John's voice to the radio. Inspired by her father's diary, Ann writes a moving speech about loving one's neighbor for John to read over the airwaves. John, falling in love with Ann, resists the $5,000 offer to come clean by a competitor of *The Bulletin* and reads Ann's speech live on the air. Taken aback by the audience's strong reception, he escapes the station with the colonel, returning only when he learns his speech has inspired "John Doe Clubs" all over the country. John, seeing his popularity as a chance to do good, goes on a press tour with Ann, visiting and speaking to the clubs, which claim no political affiliation and are "unselfishly" funded by Norton. At the peak of the clubs' popularity, however, Ann learns that Norton plans to use the upcoming John Doe Convention as a platform for the John Doe political party, which will nominate Norton for president. She reluctantly agrees to go along with the plan, which the paper's editor, Connell — in a crisis of conscience — reveals to John on the night of the convention. John, furious, visits Norton and sees Ann there, along with several other political bosses who are celebrating the success of their endeavor. After a long speech berating Norton and his fascist plans, John escapes from Norton's house and arrives at the convention. Ann is arrested before she can join him and apologize. Just as John is able to expose Norton's plot to the massive crowd of "John Does," Norton's cronies distribute papers exposing him as a fraud. His microphone unplugged, John is unable to defend himself against the shouts of detractors. He barely escapes with his life and disappears from the world, disillusioned and hopeless. The John Doe movement has fallen apart. As promised in Ann's original letter, John shows up on the roof of City Hall on Christmas Eve to kill himself. Norton is there as well, telling John that his suicide would ultimately be worthless, as his people have orders to remove any evidence that he was ever there. Ann, Connell, the colonel, and several John Doe club members, however, arrive on the roof as well, pleading with him not to kill himself, telling him that he needs to live in order to continue the movement. John, especially touched by Ann's moving speech, decides not to kill himself and walks off with the people, carrying Ann in his arms.

Meet John Doe was a moderate hit, winning over some critics but ultimately failing to connect with the American public, as *Mr. Deeds* and *Mr. Smith* had. Most critics agree that the biggest problem with the film is the ending, which Capra reshot and re-edited several times. Capra understood that he could not kill off Gary Cooper at the end of *Meet John Doe*, although that ending would have shown Willoughby as a hero truly committed to his cause. In an interview in 1971, Capra confessed that he did not allow John Willoughby to commit suicide because it would be too negative, adding that "it would be like St. George slew the dragon and got slain in the act."[79] The suicide ending simply would not work because such a dark and tragic ending went against the optimistic light tone Capra had set up throughout the picture. (Although *It's a Wonderful Life* in many ways goes even darker that *Meet John Doe*, it works because the film is set up as a fantasy, where miracles and supernatural interference are possible.)

The original ending had a crowd outside City Hall waiting for him to jump, and Norton recanting, asking Connell to print Doe's real suicide letter in the paper so all "John Does could know the truth." This ending was not well received, so Capra removed Norton's conversion. Capra reshot a new ending on March 23, adding Bert and the other John Doe Club members to the rooftop asking him to live, and removed the shots of the crowd outside City Hall.[80] The ending to this day remains unsatisfying. Critic Elliot Stein, in 1980, went so far as to say that the last reel of *Meet John Doe* was "Capra's Waterloo as an artist."[81] Capra had simply made the stakes too great for his hero to realistically triumph over them. As Glenn Phelps remarked in his essay, "Frank Capra and the Political Hero: A New Reading of *Meet John Doe*," through the course of constructing the film, Capra realized that "one individual, no matter how ideologically 'true,' no matter how virtuous, cannot reverse the entrenched institutions" represented by D.B. Norton.[82] The ending suggests that the only way to beat a man like Norton is through teamwork, which, although it makes sense both realistically and ideologically, limits John Willoughby's power as an autonomous individual. Thus, the film's active hero becomes both silent and powerless in the film's final reel, which is ultimately unsatisfying for the viewer. In an interview with Richard Schickel, Capra himself confessed that he was disappointed by the film's ending, saying:

> I think for seven eighths of the film it's a great film, with great power, great emotion, and then the ending, of course, to me has always been weak. And we didn't have one at the beginning. I thought it would come during the making of the show. It didn't.[83]

The confidence Capra had in his filmmaking abilities after *Mr. Smith* had quickly withered away by the time he finished *John Doe*. Perhaps the failure of Willoughby and Ann's message to overcome the propaganda of the powerful D.B. Norton reflects Capra's own doubts that the myths he was creating on the screen were strong enough to combat the ideology of Hitler and Goebbels. Other critics see the plot of John Doe as an illustration of the battle Capra was having as an independent filmmaker in the studio system.[84] Either way, *Meet John Doe* feels intensely personal and remains Capra's most complex film.

Despite the unsatisfying ending, *Meet John Doe* was able to make a profit of about $900,000, with Capra's share amounting to $363,774.[85] Unfortunately, as a new company, all estimated profits of Frank Capra Productions, Inc. were taxable as excess profit, and had to be paid immediately. According to Capra, after borrowing the money to pay corporate taxes in advance, as well as paying personal income tax, Uncle Sam ended up with 90 cents of every dollar of profit they made. As a result, the company was dissolved on December 29, 1941, and plans to make a sequel were abandoned.

Even though *Meet John Doe* was not an unqualified success like many of Capra's other prewar films, it helped the director determine just how far he could push his ideological concepts before they no longer worked. Like *Mr. Smith Goes to Washington*, the film's most fascinating aspect is the main character, John Willoughby. We know even less about Willoughby's past than we do about Jefferson Smith's. He has no family ties and no real goals other than to play baseball. He is as blank a slate as the man he pretends to be. As a result, many Capra scholars assert that Willoughby may represent Capra himself. Both men appear on the cover of *Time* magazine, and both men doubt their actual independence in the age of media giants. One of the strangest aspects of John Willoughby, however, is that — unlike many of Capra's other heroes — John has no real ideals of his own. As pointed out by Charles Maland, the idealism of the John Doe movement actually originates from Ann's late father, from whom she borrows to write her stirring speeches.[86] In the end, it is John who becomes converted, out of his love for Ann and the belief in her sincerity. In this aspect, John Willoughby bears a greater resemblance to the female characters in *Mr. Smith* and *Mr. Deeds* who become converted by the idealism of the male heroes. The fact that the idealism of *Meet John Doe* originates not from the present characters but from a man long since dead, may also reflect Capra's belief that we must return to the forgotten ideals of the past to forge the strong identity needed to combat the evils of the present. The ultimate failure of the John Doe clubs, however, reveal Capra's sneaking suspicion that, in the end, these values may not be enough.

Arsenic and Old Lace
(Based on the play by Joseph Kesselring)
(Filmed December 1941-January 1942,
Released September 1944)

Despite the dissolution of Frank Capra Productions, Capra still remained one of the most sought-after directors in Hollywood. Rather than signing a lucrative Hollywood deal, the 44-year-old instead signed up for the Army. His impending service, however, weighed heavily on his mind. He was an independent director, with no studio home, and no real security. If he was truly serious about joining the Army, then he would have to figure a way to "make a cheap film for a fast buck to keep [his] family going."[87] He set his sights on *Arsenic and Old Lace*, a hit Broadway show that he knew he could film cheaply and quickly. When he found out the play had already been sold to Jack Warner of Warner Bros. Studios, Capra immediately set to work to convince Jack that *he* was the man to adapt the play for the movies. In order to get Cary Grant to play the lead, Capra knew he would have to decrease the rest of the budget as much as possible. To cut back on costs, Capra proposed that the whole picture be filmed on a soundstage (lowering costs for extras, transportation, and locations) and that it be shot in only four weeks. Jack Warner agreed to let Capra shoot the picture the way he wanted; unfortunately, he had agreed when he purchased the play not to release a film version until the play closed. As a result, although completed in 1942, the film was not released until 1944, when Capra was knee-deep in the production of his Army films.

Arsenic and Old Lace's delayed release and short production schedule cause many critics to ignore the film altogether, feeling it does not fit in with the rest of Capra's work. According to Charles Maland, the film "had almost none of the topical social and political interest" of Capra's earlier films.[88] Capra himself was relieved to make the film, as it had

> no great social document "to save the world," no worries about whether John Doe should or should not jump; just good old-fashioned theater — an anything goes, rip-roaring comedy about murder. I let the scene stealers run wild; for the actors it was a mugger's ball.[89]

Like *Broadway Bill*, *Arsenic and Old Lace* seems destined to remain one of Capra's lesser films, treated as sheer entertainment without any real substance. This is indeed unfortunate as there are a great many subtleties in this not-so-subtle film, subtleties which, when noticed, add to a greater understanding of Capra's work as a whole. Even though *Arsenic and Old Lace* was shot quickly and cheaply, so was *It Happened One Night*. It would take a lot more than a small budget and a tight production schedule to keep Capra from at least saying something about the nature of freedom and liberty in his films.

The film begins with an added scene of Mortimer Brewster (Cary Grant), Broadway critic and avowed bachelor, author of books like *The Bachelor's Bible* and *Marriage: A Fraud and a Failure*, ironically marrying Elaine Harper (Priscilla Lane) in a New York courthouse. On their way out of town for their honeymoon, the young couple make a stop in Brooklyn, where Elaine's father and Mortimer's aunts live. The two houses are separated by a spooky cemetery between them, with the Brooklyn Bridge rising in the background. As Elaine packs for the trip at her father's house, Mortimer visits with his two sweet elderly aunts, Abby (Josephine Hull) and Martha (Jean Adair), as well as his deranged cousin Teddy (John Alexander who, like Hull and Adair, also played the character on Broadway). The aunts are thrilled by Mortimer's decision to marry but are worried about what Elaine's father would think, as he hates Mortimer's "bachelor" books. Happy about his decision to marry Elaine, Mortimer vows to burn all the offending volumes, including the notes he left for his most recent work, *Mind Over Matrimony*. As he searches for the notes, he discovers, to his great surprise, a corpse hidden in the window seat. The surprise turns to shock when he learns that his aunts murdered the man, Mr. Hoskins, by serving him poisoned elderberry wine. They had temporarily placed him in the window seat in preparation for his funeral in the basement. His shock turns to alarm as his aunts eagerly explain that, over the years, they have murdered 11, possibly 12, lonely men in their house in the exact same way. The delusional Teddy Brewster, who believes he is Teddy Roosevelt, has conveniently been burying the men in the cellar under the belief that they are victims of yellow fever who died while building the Panama Canal. At this point Mortimer is morally torn between forgetting about these crimes and going on his honeymoon (which his aunts prefer), turning his aunts over to the police or having them committed to an institution. Instead, he comes up with a third idea: to send Teddy (who everyone in the neighborhood knows is crazy) to Happy Dale, the local mental institution and then frame *him* for his aunts' grisly murders. This requires Mortimer to juggle all the paperwork required to commit Teddy, as well as continually put off Elaine, without revealing to her what exactly is going on.

As if to make matters worse, while Mortimer is out running errands, Jonathan (Raymond Massey), his long-lost psychotic brother, shows up at the aunt's house with his partner and plastic surgeon, Dr. Einstein (Peter Lorre). The pair have their own body to dump, and Jonathan, his face transformed by Einstein to look like Boris Karloff (who hilariously originated the role on Broadway), plans to stay overnight so Einstein can change his face once again to avoid the police. While trying to hide their own dead victim, the two murderers are interrupted first by Elaine, then by Mortimer, who, after throwing Elaine out of the house to protect her, orders his brother to leave the house with Einstein and their dead victim.

At this time, Officer O'Hara (Jack Carson) conveniently stops in to pay the aunts a visit. Mortimer at first greets the police officer and aspiring playwright warmly, but when Jonathan reveals to Mortimer that he knows about Mr. Hopkins in the basement, Mortimer sends O'Hara away, promising to meet him later at a local bar to listen to him pitch his latest play.

While Mortimer is out finishing up the paperwork for Teddy and making up with Elaine, Jonathan tells Dr. Einstein that he plans to finally settle the score with Mortimer. When Mortimer returns, Dr. Einstein tries to save Mortimer's life by convincing him to forget about everything and to go off on his honeymoon with his pretty wife. Mortimer stubbornly refuses and is blindsided by Jonathan, who ties him up in order to torture him to death. Jonathan is interrupted by Officer O'Hara, who has returned to the house, angry about being stood up by Mortimer. Instead of freeing the bound-and-gagged Mortimer, O'Hara sees this as the perfect opportunity to play to a captive audience and begins to pitch his script. Just as Jonathan is about to attack the officer from behind, Einstein knocks him out and saves the officer's life. When more police officers show up at the house to address the neighbor's complaints about Teddy blowing his horn again, Jonathan wakes up from being knocked out and thinks the officers are there to arrest him. A scuffle ensues, and Jonathan is arrested. Lieutenant Rooney (James Gleason) arrives at the house and recognizes Jonathan as a wanted man, but refuses to believe Jonathan's claim that there are 13 bodies buried in the cellar.

Mr. Witherspoon (Edward Everett Horton) of Happy Dale arrives shortly thereafter. He and Mortimer convince Teddy to sign the paperwork so he can be taken away to the institution. When Witherspoon realizes that he cannot commit Teddy without the signature of a physician, Mortimer grabs Dr. Einstein just before he escapes out the front door. As Witherspoon goes to take Teddy away, the aunts realize they cannot in good conscience leave Teddy alone in the institution and decide to go with him. Before they are taken away, they reveal to Mortimer that he is not actually a Brewster, but the son of the family cook, who married their brother after giving birth to him. With this newfound knowledge and everything wrapped up nicely, Mortimer decides to go on his honeymoon, throwing his wife over his shoulder and carrying her triumphantly to her father's house.

The complex and well-constructed plot of *Arsenic and Old Lace* left little room for Capra to substantially change the story. Working with Julius and Phillip Epstein, the screenwriters who would also write the adaptation of *Casablanca*, Capra opened the play a bit by adding an exterior of the house location and by ending the film on a more optimistic note. (The original play ends with the aunts offering Witherspoon a drink of their poisoned Elderberry wine.) Capra and the Epsteins also include a funny running gag with a taxi cab driver standing outside the house throughout the entire film, waiting to take the couple off to their honeymoon. The most substantial change in the script, however, is the addition of Mortimer's wedding to Elaine. In the original version, Mortimer is simply delayed from going to see a play with Elaine. The addition of Mortimer and Elaine's wedding and promise of its consummation increases the conflict and adds sexual tension to the film, as well as providing Mortimer with the promise of a better future once he has taken care of his urgent family matters. Strangely enough, the Elaine character in the play is a much stronger, more sexually experienced, and more opinionated woman than the character in the film. In another strange twist involving the film, Elaine actually comes across the dead bodies in the cellar, whereas in the play she is protected from that knowledge. In the film, when Elaine tries to tell the police, Mortimer shuts her up by kissing her and whisks her out the door. After receiving the long-awaited attention from Mortimer, she conveniently "forgets" about the bodies and lets her husband take her away in

1. Pre-War Capra 49

his arms. These changes reflect Capra's belief that the attention to one's immediate family (in this case, Mortimer and Elaine) not only brings about a renewed feeling of hope and optimism in a world seemingly gone mad, but also allows one to forget the horrors that can take place in one's own backyard. *It's a Wonderful Life*, Capra's next narrative film, would explore this theme even further.

Once one sees the Brewsters' house as a metaphor for the dark side of American history and liberty, *Arsenic and Old Lace* takes on a much greater relevance. Capra, either subconsciously or consciously (my guess is the latter), understood that Kesselring's play is really about the nature of freedom in America. The contrast of the sweet dispositions of Mortimer's aunts with their horrific actions illustrates the problem of America itself. While America claims to be an optimistic beacon of liberty to the entire world, it can also be a place of extreme violence and prejudice. The string of murders committed by the aunts forces Mortimer, as well as the audience, to examine the potential dangers of liberty. When Mortimer confronts his aunts about their crimes, for instance, Abby uses liberty as an excuse, indignantly saying, "Mortimer, we don't try to stop you from doing things you like to do. I don't see why you should interfere with us." The concept of freedom occurs throughout *Arsenic and Old Lace*, as the play continually brings up both the just and unjust checks of freedom that exist in a democratic society, whether those checks are marriage (Mortimer and Elaine), institutions (the aunts and Teddy are taken to Happy Dale), prisons (where Jonathan is taken), or families (represented by Jonathan's binding and gagging Mortimer).

Capra must also have understood that Mortimer's attempts to resolve his feelings about his aunts and their actions also represent every American's struggle to balance American myth with actual history. The entire Brewster house, for instance, is steeped in both contradictions and history. At the beginning of the film, O'Hara's superior officer makes the contradictory statement that the whole area "just stinks with atmosphere." The exterior set also exudes history in its cemetery, which Capra makes sure to show (in close-up) was established in 1654. The contradictory set also places the dilapidated cemetery (a representation of the horrible finality of death) next to a church (a representation of the belief in life after death). In addition to the exterior set, the Brewster house interior and inhabitants are steeped with history. The sisters wear Victorian clothing, display all of their father's keepsakes, and refer to the dead in the present tense. While the house is believed to be the nicest in Brooklyn, it also houses 12 dead bodies in the cellar. Such contradictions represent the many contradictions of American history.

It is my opinion that Capra understood these contradictions when he made the film. In his autobiography, he takes credit for the design of the exte-

The shadow on the wall behind Jonathan Brewster (Raymond Massey) looks surprisingly like Abraham Lincoln.

rior set. He also chose Raymond Massey to play the villain, Jonathan, an actor more resembling Abraham Lincoln than Boris Karloff. In fact, Massey was well known for playing Lincoln in the film *Abe Lincoln in Illinois* just one year earlier. Massey's striking resemblance to the late president would cause him to be cast in the role four more times after *Arsenic*, both on television and in film. This resemblance is especially apparent in *Aresenic and Old Lace*, in a scene in the basement, when Capra projects Jonathan's shadow onto the wall next to Dr. Einstein. Why would Capra cast a man who looked like Lincoln as the villain Jonathan? If we view the Brewster house as an expression of the contradictions of American history, Lincoln becomes the obvious choice. While Lincoln did abolish slavery, he also expanded the role of federal government in the everyday lives of Americans by initiating both the draft and the federal income tax. As the sitting president during the Civil War, Lincoln also has more blood on his hands than any president, before or since. The other president occupying the house, Theodore Roosevelt, as channeled by Teddy, though beloved by the American public, also expanded the role of the military and established America's strong imperialist policies.

With these added touches, as well as its optimistic ending, Capra seemed to be preparing the audience for the coming war. Capra uses *Arsenic and Old*

Lace to tell Americans to learn some way to come to terms with the country's violent past and understand both the positive and negative consequences of liberty before protecting the country and its values from its enemies. In his play, when Witherspoon is poisoned once Mortimer has gone off with Elaine, Kesselring hints that the relationship between freedom and violence will never end in America — especially if everyone allows themselves to be distracted by the opposite sex. Capra's conservative ending, on the other hand, illustrates the antithetical view, proposing that one can only have a future when one separates oneself from the troubling questions of the past. Love and marriage (which leads to sex and children) not only provides America with a future, but also become the perfect distractions to prevent citizens from thinking too much about the inherent contradictions of the country's past. Conformity, not introspection, is required for a country about to enter into war.

This interpretation of Capra's last prewar film, I believe, is crucial to the understanding of his conservative mindset before embarking on his war career. It not only helps to frame the themes of Capra's war films and his masterpiece, *It's a Wonderful Life*, but it also proves that a thorough analysis of the lesser films of a talented filmmaker like Capra leads to rewarding and enriching insights. While many view *Arsenic and Old Lace* the same way they view his war documentaries—as unimportant additions to his more famous films—I whole-heartedly disagree, believing that Capra signature touches and ideas can be found in every film he produced and directed at this critical time. Capra was an extremely moralistic filmmaker who could not help but inject his values and beliefs in every film he made. Excluding these films from the discussion creates an incomplete picture of the filmmaker's life and work.

"One Man, One Film"

Throughout the 1930s, Capra had built a substantial career by making films praising the "common man"— and had made a lot of money doing it. From the profits of *Mr. Deeds* to *Mr. Smith* alone, he personally made $815,658.[90] In addition, he was a major factor in the success of Columbia Pictures in the mid-to late-thirties, which often used Capra's films in their block-booking deals with theater chains. In these deals, theaters would buy other, less popular films from Columbia in order to play guaranteed hits from Capra, including *You Can't Take It with You* and *Mr. Smith Goes to Washington*. From the beginning of his career at Columbia, when he was hired to direct only B-pictures, Capra made sure that he would maintain control of his films. Stung by his experience with Harry Langdon, Capra told Cohn he would only accept the job if he had complete control of the writing, directing, and editing of his films. Cohn assented, admiring the young man's confidence in his own abilities. This agreement with Capra, although different from other studio heads at the time, was borne out of sheer practicality. Cohn told the director that as long as his films made money, he could do whatever he wanted.[91] This caveat not only assured Cohn that Capra would take great care in making sure his films would be of the highest quality, but also kept Cohn from being needlessly bothered by tedious details during their production. According to Richard Schickel, Harry Cohn wanted his directors to be able to work independently. If a director asked the studio head for advice, he would be out. Cohn was not one to worry about anyone's reputation; he wanted directors to act with "guts."[92]

This degree of control was unusual at the time, as most directors in the studio system were controlled by either producers or studio heads who believed the films should serve *their* ideological vision. Capra thrived in the freedom of Columbia Pictures, as his authoritative personality would have made it difficult for him to have been successful anywhere else. In 1937, for instance, producer David O. Selznick wanted Capra to make films for him, offering a $200,000-a-picture deal. Capra turned it down, even though the deal meant he could have escaped Columbia. He simply was not interested in working for a man known for controlling the script-development process.[93]

Capra understood that his authoritative, "Sicilian" personality would not make a good fit in many places in Hollywood, where blindly following orders was the norm.[94] He described his controlling personality as follows: "I'm a bad organization man; I like to be my own man and I don't like somebody else telling me what to do, it was just the natural rebel in me that I couldn't take orders."[95]

When his relationship with Columbia ended, Capra decided to start his own company rather than work for anyone else. Much of his insistence on control originated from his healthy ego, which only increased as he became successful. He often said that he "knew more about films than the people who tried to tell [him] how to make them."[96]

Capra also understood that with great power came great responsibility. With Cohn's agreement came the unspoken understanding that any substantial failure would result in a loss of both control over his films and the choice of what films he could make. Because of this, Capra became obsessed with every aspect of the film's production, from the writing of the script to the audience previews. He explained his obsession as follows: "I never stopped sleeping, drinking, eating the picture, you couldn't stimulate me with anything else. You'd talk to me about something else and I wouldn't listen, I couldn't listen. All I was thinking about was the picture."[97]

Capra took the success or failure of his films extremely personally, which explains his obsession with winning an Academy Award. Liking his film was tantamount to liking him. While reading his biography, one gets the feeling that Capra beat himself up over his failures, even decades after the fact. "If a film failed," he tellingly wrote, "I failed."[98] This responsibility for his films would extend to his documentary efforts during the war. Although no one received official credit for any of his department's war films, Capra knew his name would always be associated with their production, and it was an association he took very seriously.

In the end, as long as the public enjoyed his films, Capra felt the validation he needed to continue working. Furthermore, the success of these films reinforced his belief in the cinematic and narrative techniques he used to make them. America was voting with their wallets, and they had told him they not only liked the stories he was telling but also the way he told them. Thus, Capra's name became a brand that could be used to sell a certain type of film, one that contained idealistic heroes who fought against fascism and greed with good old-fashioned common sense. Starting with *You Can't Take It with You*, Capra's name would be placed above the title of the film on the screen and in print advertising.[99]

This increasing identification between Capra and his films would perpetuate his belief in the "one man, one film" theory of making films. This belief, that films were entirely the result of decisions made by the director, would later be named the *auteur theory* by French New Wave critics. Starting in the 1950s, Capra asserted that he was solely responsible for the content of his past films. In an interview with Arthur Friedman, Capra stated that he had never worked on a picture in which he didn't "produce and direct it, and perhaps even write it."[100] Later, in 1968, Capra explained his feelings about the theory in a public appearance:

> I think every man's picture is in a sense an autobiography. The films you make — put them together and you've got the man's autobiography pretty well there somewhere, if he's the filmmaker and not just the employee. And so this feeling to make pictures about the common people was just my answer. As an immigrant kid coming over here I liked the common people, and you know, I wanted to sing their songs.[101]

Always an advocate for personal as well as artistic freedom, Capra, in his later years, urged the failing studios that they would only be successful if they allowed their directors to make the films *they* wanted to make, and in several speeches, he implored students in film schools to follow *their* visions. In an interview with Dick Cavett in 1972, when he shared the stage with up-and-coming directors Robert Altman, Peter Bogdanovich, and Mel Brooks, he explained that he would never allow a studio to take over a film of his and recut it, advising his fellow directors that they had "to find a way to get control of their films."[102]

Most film scholars agree with Capra's assertion that he was the sole author of his films during the studio system, an acknowledgment Capra shares with only a handful of studio system directors, namely Hitchcock, Lubitsch, Hawks, and Ford. Peter Bogdanovich reiterated Capra's sole authorship in 1974, writing:

> Frank Capra exemplifies his own artistic credo: one man, one film. No matter what the literary source, Capra's films are his. The same signature can be identified from *It Happened One Night* through *Mr. Deeds Goes to Town* and *Mr. Smith Goes to Washington* to *It's a Wonderful Life*.... In these films we are in the presence of one man — his obsessions, fantasies, dreams.[103]

Charles Maland agrees, writing the following in the opening page of his book: "When viewing Capra's films from the 1930s, one senses a firm hand guiding both the film style and narrative. One suspects the hand is Capra's. The suspicion is reinforced when one meets him."[104] And yet, strange as it may seem, Maland, like many other Capra scholars, continue to assert that Capra exerted relatively little control over the films he made for the U.S. Army, even though the research proves the exact opposite to be true.

However Capra felt about his pictures on the inside, it is important to note that he still recognized the importance for the crew to feel they were part of a collaborative process while he was shooting. In 1937, Capra's assistant director, Buddy Coleman, said that on the set he "never heard Frank refer to a production as '*my* picture, in which *I* did this or that'; it has always been '*our* picture, in which *we* did this or that.'"[105] And yet, everyone knew Capra was in charge; he was the one making the crucial decisions. When all was said and done, whether the films were failures or successes, Capra's name was attached to the picture, and whatever the result, he alone was responsible for the content on the screen.

Or was he? Was Capra truly an *auteur* who bucked the oppressive Hollywood studio system, or was he trying to rewrite history? Although the technical style of Capra's work can easily be attributed to Capra himself, the true authorship of the themes and structure of these films proves more problematic. The influence of screenwriter Robert Riskin, writer of *It Happened One Night*, *Mr. Deeds Goes to Town*, *Lost Horizon*, *You Can't Take It with You*, and *Meet John Doe* must be thoroughly discussed before any attempt can be made to link Capra's themes of his prewar films to the themes of his war documentaries. For although Riskin was the head of the Overseas Branch of the Office of War Information during World War II, he had no creative impact on the films Capra made during the war. If one is to link the attributes of Capra's narrative films to his war documentaries, it stands to reason that one must

Robert Riskin (left) and Frank Capra share a moment during the production of *Mr. Deeds Goes to Town*. (Columbia/Photofest)

first prove that Capra was the true author of those films, or else the argument would fall apart.

The working relationship between the two men was fairly routine. Riskin would write a long first draft, which he and Capra would revise and pare down for the next two and a half months at the La Quinta Hotel, located some 20 miles from Palm Springs. According to Chet Sticht, who would type script pages during these meetings, Riskin would effectively put Capra's ideas into words.[106] Riskin described the working relationship with Capra as follows:

> We have some awful battles over how the story should be developed, but we never argue about what constitutes a story. He's a great editor. He'll walk into the office, give his opinion of a scene, and in doing so toss off an idea from which I can take a dozen successful steps.[107]

In addition, Riskin admitted that his writing partner was a "positive genius in applying his 'magic touch' to the finished film."[108] Capra's version of events does not necessarily refute Riskin's: Generally, I'd be a little ahead of him on material; then we'd talk it over and he'd put it together in words. So we'd have a rough draft. We'd go back, and I'd do the casting and all the rest and he'd polish it up."[109] Capra, in return, credited Riskin with a great ear for the spoken word and claimed that the screenwriter's biggest contribution was the dialogue.[110]

According to screenwriter Phillip Dunne, a friend of Riskin, the fact that the two were so different may have contributed to their success. "Frank provided the schmaltz and Bob provided the acid," he said. "What they had together was better than *either* of them had separately."[111] Although they were successful collaborators, they remained separated by their political views. While Capra was a solid Republican, Riskin was described by his friends as a Roosevelt man, a New Deal liberal. In fact, it was not an unusual occurrence for Capra to work with people who had ideas unlike his own. He did not care for "yes men," and frequently surrounded himself with liberal writers like Riskin, Swerling, and Buchman. He would listen to their viewpoint and their discussions would sometimes make it into the film.[112] According to McBride, Capra's collaboration with these writers softened his Capra's conservative views. The audience of the time demanded he push his films towards the direction of social reform and anti-big business, and with Riskin's help, Capra was able to respond to that need. The sense of brotherhood and compassion came from Riskin, which gave Capra a greater sense of community in his films.[113] The films, therefore, became a mix of both political ideologies, which in turn appealed equally to both the left and the right.

On the surface, this collaboration seems to oppose the supposition that the five major films written or adapted by Riskin —*It Happened One Night, Mr. Deeds Goes to Town, Lost Horizon, You Can't Take It with You,* and *Meet John Doe*— were the result of a "one man, one film" production. In the hierarchy of even the most rigid studio system, however, it should be noted that the director outranks the screenwriter in every situation. Capra himself claimed that although he and Riskin collaborated well together, should an argument arise, Capra had the "final yes or no on everything."[114] If anyone outranked the director at the studio it was the producer, and Capra was named producer over all the films he made for Columbia (as part of his deal with Cohn). Only the studio head could outrank Capra, and Cohn asserted very little control over him due to Capra's excellent track record. In any case, the director is on the front lines of the production and sometimes has to improvise when the scripted scene does not work. The famous hitchhiking scene in *It Happened One Night*, for instance, was made up by Capra the night before it was shot.[115]

Furthermore, Capra was the type of director who viewed the script as something fluid, which allowed him to develop scenes and take advantage of opportunities on the set when they developed. He often remarked that this ability originated from his training on silent comedies, which usually had no scripts and whose gags were usually made up on the spot.[116] His training in silent comedy also helped to keep his films from becoming bogged down by dialogue, which he believed would ultimately bore the audience. To keep the film from becoming dull, he would continually add visual activity to punch up dialogue-heavy scenes.[117] One finds that these visual touches are often more memorable than the dialogue. We tend to remember the visuals of Capra's films first and foremost — Peter Warne eating a carrot while discussing the art of hitchhiking (allegedly the inspiration for Bugs Bunny); Deeds sliding down the banister in his mansion; Jefferson Smith fidgeting with his hat, and John Willoughby pretending to play baseball. The most striking moments in Capra's work, in fact, are the times when the film is completely silent.

Ultimately, though, what is or is not put on the screen is the result of decisions made by the director. Capra explained this process in an interview early in his career:

> When a script is completed, whether I wrote it or someone else writes it, it's mine, In the sense that I have to absorb it and like it in order to interpret it on the screen. Even though somebody else wrote it, it becomes yours before you're through with it.[118]

Quite simply, it would be unwise to grant Riskin too much credit for the success of Capra's films because Capra, not Riskin, directed them. The one film Riskin did direct in the 1930s, *When You're in Love*, was a critical and box-office disappointment. His second film, *Magic Town*, which was made after the war, fared no better. According to Capra, while Riskin was "brilliant" as a writer, as a director, he just did not "have the ability to get things done under stress."[119] In addition, three of Capra's most famous films of the time, *Mr. Smith Goes to Washington*, *Arsenic and Old Lace*, and *It's a Wonderful Life* were not written by Robert Riskin at all, yet all contain signature Capra elements.

These facts might have provoked Capra in later years to claim more responsibility for the films written by Riskin than was actually the case. Toward the end of his career, Capra increasingly insisted that it didn't matter who wrote the films because "they expressed dreams, hopes, and angsts that came out of [his] guts."[120] In the end, however, even Capra would agree that his collaboration with Riskin contributed greatly to the films' success. More importantly, these films (especially *Mr. Deeds*) provided Capra with a formula he could recreate with other screenwriters. Even after their partnership broke up, Capra would borrow the style, techniques, and themes of the films written by Riskin, and apply them to his later works. This is especially true of the war documentaries, which would borrow as much as they could from Capra's fictional films of 1930s. By that time, he had so absorbed the formula that it could easily be recreated, even in orientation films for the Army.

2
The Capra Formula

In order to trace the influence of major films like *Mr. Deeds Goes to Town, Mr. Smith Goes to Washington,* and *Meet John Doe* as well as the minor films *American Madness, Lady for a Day, Broadway Bill,* and *Arsenic and Old Lace* on Capra's war documentaries, it becomes necessary to define the Capra formula established by those films. Once the common techniques and themes are discussed, parallels between the two genres become more evident. Naturally, the editing of these films bears some study, as does Capra's choice of shots and use of visual metaphors. But his passion for the ideologies of religion and American history, as well as the pro-work, pro-action stance he takes in these narrative films also shapes the films he made during the war. Most importantly, the arguments these films made about the power of the individual, the dangers of mob mentality, and the importance of honest, straightforward speech are all relevant to the real-life battle America was waging against the forces of fascism, and are used to great effect in his documentaries.

The shot composition and visual metaphors of Capra's films are not especially groundbreaking as Capra is not known for being a visual director in the tradition of Hitchcock or Ford. Because Capra primarily used medium and long shots at eye level, many critics have incorrectly categorized him as just another director following the typical "invisible" studio style. Just because Capra did not fill his films with directorial flourishes does not mean that his films are directed the same way as any other director during the studio period. From the start of his career, he made the story, themes and acting a priority in order to sell the realism and messages of his films. As early as 1931, when he was working on *Dirigible*, Capra told a reporter that directorial touches and photographic splurges should be kept out of pictures. "Excellence in direction," he added, "is reached when the audience never thinks of the director's work."[1] At the end of his career, Capra reaffirmed his earlier statement in an interview with *Variety*, advising future filmmakers to focus on the "basic tale" and not to rely on gimmicks.[2] Starting with *Lady for a Day*, Capra regularly chose simplicity over ostentation. *Bitter Tea of General Yen* and *Amer-*

Frank Capra (far left) directs James Stewart and Jean Arthur on the set of the Academy Award-winning *You Can't Take It with You*. (Columbia, Pictures/Photofest)

ican Madness, the earliest of the films mentioned, engage in visual experimentation lacking in Capra's later, more popular films. In *Bitter Tea*, for instance, Capra employs surrealistic dream sequences, and in one instance, superimposes several riot scenes over a close-up of Megan to illustrate her confusion. In *American Madness*, the camera moves a great deal more than his later films; in the scene following the one in which Matt walks in on Phyllis and Cluett embracing, for instance, he employs a low-angle trucking shot to accentuate Matt's despair.

    The conservative use of the camera during his golden period should not be mistaken for a lack of talent or creative energy. It is clear from the darker scenes from films like *Bitter Tea of General Yen*, *Arsenic and Old Lace*, and *It's a Wonderful Life* that Capra could employ directorial flourishes as well as Hitchcock or Ford. In addition, the montage scenes in *Meet John Doe* and *Mr. Smith Goes to Washington* are as visually arresting as anything else put on the screen by less "invisible" directors. In his book *Another Frank Capra*, Leland Poague refuses to describe Capra's style as invisible, citing numerous examples in his films when Capra broke away from the traditional form of studio shooting. Many times, for instance, Capra violates the 180-degree rule (which forces the director to keep all the cameras and shots on one side of the action) and the 30-degree rule (which mandates that shots in a scene have a difference of at least 30 degrees between them). This failure to completely adhere to the invisible Hollywood style could be attributed to Capra's need to keep the pace of his films moving as quickly as possible, or could be the result of the constant re-editing Capra did after test screenings. Poague, however, believes that this breaking from the traditional classical style may have originated from Capra's desire to stand out among his peers.[3] It is my estimation, that after the failure of the ornate *Bitter Tea*, coupled with the subsequent success of his first Oscar-nominated film (*Lady for a Day*, which was filmed in a much simpler style), Capra chose to stick with the visual style of the latter in order to mimic its success. The subsequent success of the films that followed *Lady for a Day* reinforced that the conservative style worked best for the type of films Capra wanted to make — thematic, story-driven films populated by colorful characters. As such, Capra's most famous films tend to be classified as comedies because they are shot in a similar visual style to comedies of the era — brightly lit, medium and wide shots filmed slightly below eye level.

Any scholar of Capra, however, knows that his films cannot be so easily categorized. Unlike other famous comedies of the time, known for their light touch, physical slapstick and rapid pace, Capra's films contain elements of serious drama, darkness, and human emotion, especially towards the end. Charles Maland supposes that Capra's films have a dark undercurrent because throughout Capra's life, the successes in his career are often marred with personal disappointment and tragedy.[4] His sudden, near-fatal illness after the success of *It Happened One Night*, the death of his son the night of the *You Can't Take It with You* premiere, his firing by Langdon at the height of the comedian's success: all allow Capra to create films that are convincing in both their scenes of happiness and their scenes of agony and despair. It is in these dark, dramatic moments that Capra usually reveals his unique visual style. By saving his most visually exciting shots for his films' most dramatic moments, Capra not only confers these parts of the film with greater importance, but is also able to hold the audience's attention when the slapstick and witty dialogue has faded away. The switch is subtle, but remarkably effective. One is hardly aware that the shift has taken place until one finds oneself completely emotionally absorbed in the film's concluding moments. Thus, in the lighter parts of the film, Capra's simple visual style places the viewer in the passive role of observer, which allows him/her to comfortably ease into the story and become acquainted with its characters. Once this has occurred, Capra employs a stronger visual style, which places the viewer in a more active role just as the film's plot takes its most dramatic turn. One can see Capra toying with this formula in the more dramatic moments of *It Happened One Night*. Unfortunately, in *Broadway Bill*, the dramatic turn happens so close to the end and is so devastating, that the viewer is too emotionally drained to respond to the film's attempt at a happy ending. In Capra's best films, *Mr. Deeds Goes to Town, You Can't Take It with You, Mr. Smith Goes to Washington*, and *It's a Wonderful Life*, Capra balances his objective and subjective visual style and provides the audience with enough catharsis to buy into their happy endings.

Needless to say, one tends to study the most dramatic moments of Capra's films when seeking to define his visual style. This is especially true in Capra's conservative use of the close-up. As Ray Carney writes in his book, *American Vision: The Films of Frank Capra*:

> Close ups ... do occur at crucial moments in the later films (though far less often, to the point of rarity in *Meet John Doe* and films that follow it), but they are not routine events. They must be earned and achieved. They define special and increasingly rare occurrences in a formal world of medium and long shots and a dramatic and social world of powerfully encroaching others.[5]

In Capra's films, close-ups are mostly employed to create a connection between a character with the audience, to evoke a greater emotional response in the audience, or a combination of both. Capra explained the former in an interview for the American Film Institute: "You can have a character who represents the audience. He sees what is going on and is amazed by it, moved by it, stunned by it and he reacts."[6] Capra further explained that this technique is particularly useful in comedic scenes, as it can punctuate a line or a moment. This reactive role is usually the main character as it helps develop the connection between that character and the audience necessary for the later, more dramatic sequences. The reactive close-up, however, can also be used for secondary characters, like the cynical Happy Maguire in *Lady for a Day*, or the fussy Colonel in *Meet John Doe*. These characters often voice their opinion when the film is in danger of becoming too saccharin or preachy.

For the most part, Capra reserves close-ups for key dramatic scenes. As he said in an interview in 1976: "A close up is an emphasis. You want to get up close so you can see that person's face, the person's eyes. What are her thoughts at this moment. Close ups are for dramatic purposes—not just to speed up or not just for glamour."[7]

Close-ups of Apple Annie in *Lady for a Day*, for instance, are reserved only for Annie's lowest moments (e.g., finding out her daughter is coming to visit) and highest moments (e.g., seeing the real governor and mayor arrive at her party, waving goodbye to her daughter at the end). In *It Happened One Night*, the closest shots in the film are of Ellie's face, crying after a rejection from Peter—once sleeping outside on a farm, and once on their last night together in the motel room. A similar close-up is used of Alice after a long night in the stable in *Broadway Bill*. In *Mr. Deeds Goes to Town*, close-ups are reserved primarily for the scenes between Longfellow and Babe, when they first meet and right before Longfellow proposes. Dramatic close-ups are also shown throughout the trial scene and when Babe confesses her betrayal to Longfellow over the phone. In *Meet John Doe*, close-ups occur primarily in important relationship scenes between the two main characters, Ann and John. In *Lost Horizon*, most of the close-ups are reserved for the emotional reactions of Robert Conway, in his scenes with the High Lama and Sondra, as well as in the climactic scene wherein Conway takes one last look at Shangri-La before leaving the valley with his brother George. Capra employs close-ups in *You Can't Take It with You* of Alice and Grandfather during the trial scene, Anthony Kirby, Sr., in the Vanderhof home and the final board of director's meeting at the end of the film, and of each member of the household as the fireworks go off. Strangely enough, the opening shot of *Mr. Smith Goes to Washington* is a close-up of reporter "Nosey" (Charles Lane) on the phone telling someone about Senator Foley's death. From that point on, however, Capra reserves close-ups primarily for the most dramatic scenes involving Jefferson Smith: his visits to the Lincoln Memorial; when he receives a briefcase from the Boy Rangers at the Governor's dinner; when he is asked to take the stand at the hearing before the Committee on Privileges and Elections; and the final scene right after Clarissa shouts out to Jeff in an attempt to stop his filibuster.

In the scene before the committee investigating the allegations against Smith, Capra employs the close-up in a unique way regarding the antagonist of the story, Senator Paine. In this scene Smith finally realizes how entrenched Paine is in Taylor's machine, the senior senator having just lied shamelessly about Jeff in front of the committee. Smith rises from his seat in a medium-shot and walks over to Paine and stares at him. Capra then cuts to a massive close-up of Paine, who looks straight ahead, stone-faced. Because Capra frames this close-up in profile, the viewer is robbed of all connection with Paine: the character is emotionally inaccessible to the audience. The close-up grants Paine dramatic power, but also shows him as unapproachable and irredeemable. This technique is also used at the end of *Meet John Doe*, in a scene reminiscent of *American Madness*, when Ann pleads with John Willoughby not to kill himself on the roof of City Hall. John is shown in profile in close-up at the beginning of the scene, then turns towards the camera only *after* he has changed his mind about the suicide. Unlike Paine at the hearing, Willoughby is viewed as redeemable because he turns his head and connects with the audience, rather than staying in profile. The use of the close-up profile may also be the reason *Broadway Bill* does not provide enough catharsis for the audience to appreciate the happy ending. In a particularly moving scene in the stable after Bill's death, Capra cuts to a profile close-up of Dan in complete despair. When Alice comes over to console him, rather than turning towards the audience and providing the proper catharsis, Dan turns away from the audience towards Alice, robbing of the viewer of the emotional connection they desire. The shot cuts Dan off from the audience by making his grieving process private, which adds to the sadness of the scene, but does not adequately relieve it. In the same scene in *Riding High*, the remake of *Broadway Bill*, Capra wisely shoots Dan in a three-quarter view, bringing his face around toward the viewer just enough to maintain the needed connection.

The unapproachable close-up of Senator Paine (Claude Rains) confirms his betrayal in *Mr. Smith Goes to Washington*.

As a whole, Capra employs close-ups when his characters are either in love or in a state of hopelessness or despair. With the exception of *You Can't Take It with You* and the close-ups he uses for telephone calls, in most close shots, Capra rarely has the featured character speaking. Capra's close-ups, according to Ray Carney, are silent because they "communicate highly charged states of verbally inexpressible consciousness."[8] Without dialogue, viewers are forced to use their imagination to decipher the expressions of the actors in these powerful shots, increasing their involvement and their empathy. The use of silent close-ups also illustrate Capra's belief in the primacy of visuals over sound and dialogue during dramatic moments, which in turn forces the viewer to focus on behavior rather than on words to determine emotional truth. The silence also provides a sharp contrast to the highly verbal comedic scenes which are usually covered in wide and medium shots.

In most scenes, Capra creates a sense of separation in his characters not through close-ups (which are reserved for the most intense emotional parts of the film), but through "singles," shots that only contain only one character with no other characters in the background or next to them. In *Meet John Doe*, for instance, Capra frequently places John Willoughby in medium shots by himself, intercutting these shots with group shots of other characters in the scene. He employs this technique in the scene in which Bert Hansen and other John Doe club members meet John at the small-town hall, and the scene wherein John listens in on Norton and his cronies on the night of the convention. During the radio speech, medium close-up singles of John and Ann are used, intercut with group shots of the crowd listening. This technique continually sets John Willoughby apart from others, either because he is their leader (as in the radio and town-hall scene) or because he does not fit in ideologically with the rest of the characters (as in the dinner scene with Norton). In *Broadway Bill*, the ritualistic dinner scene is filled with single shots of Alice and Dan, which illustrates that their values are different from the rest of the people in the room. A similar technique is used in the first boardroom scene in *American Madness*, where Tom is framed in singles, facing the camera (and the viewer) while the investors are depicted in group shots. Capra also uses singles of the Colonel in various scenes in *Meet John Doe* as he is always outside the system, distrusting of the ideologies of Ann and Norton. His single shots (as with Happy Maguire in *Lady for a Day*), however, are usually medium or long shots, which makes him more distant from the viewer than the singles of John and Ann. In *Lost Horizon*, in a scene when Robert Conway observes Sondra teaching the children of the valley in an outdoor classroom, both Conway and Sondra are shown in isolated shots while the children are always framed as a group or in crowded medium shots. This technique elevates the status of these two Western characters over the native children, which in turn reinforces the imperialist theme of the film. In the montage sequence of Jefferson Smith taking his tour of Washington, D.C., he is primarily shown in singles, which accentuates the personal connection Smith has to both the living history and the ideas these monuments represent. Furthermore, because Jefferson Smith's desk is situated in the back of the Senate chamber, Capra could continually frame him in single shots against the back wall, without showing any senators behind or around him. This arrangement, which mirrors the placement of the vice president (Harry Carey) who sits with his back to the front wall of the chamber, allows Capra to frame these two men in isolated shots without seeing any other people in the background. When the shots of the two men are consequently cut together, a personal connection between the two men is created even in the crowded Senate chamber. Throughout the trial in *Mr. Deeds*, Longfellow Deeds and Babe Bennett are shown reacting silently to the trial in isolated shots, while the other shots in the scene are more jumbled and crowded with people. The same effect is created in *Broadway Bill* between Alice and Dan at the Higgins' dinner table, which foreshadows their future relationship. Thus, Capra often uses singles to subtly separate his heroes from the outside world, which is both different from them and less important.

The contrast between isolated shots and group shots is also illustrated in an earlier scene wherein Deeds gets a send off at the train station in Mandrake Falls. In the beginning of this scene, Longfellow is at ease among the folks of his home town and is included in the group shots with them. In the next scene, however, Capra contrasts the sense of community shown in the group shot of Mandrake Falls with a "single" of Deeds looking out of a window in a train car heading off to New York. Deeds has moved from a place where he is accepted to a place where he sticks out, where he is unique. Capra uses this effect in reverse in *You Can't Take It with You*, intercutting the group shots of the Vanderhof family with single shots of visitors like Mr. Kirby and the IRS man. This reverse effect also creates a sense of separation between the individual and the group, only in this instance the separation is used to illustrate that the individuals in these shots think differently from the family. Although Capra preferred to use the subtle technique of single shots versus group shots to symbolically separate the more important characters from the rest of the players, this technique also fits completely with his subtle style, which emphasizes acting and theme over visual flair.

In cinema language, placement of the camera at eye level, below eye level (low angle), or above eye level (high angle) affords the character depicted in the shot a certain amount of power. Low-angle shots, where the camera is placed below the subject's head, for instance, increases the power of the subject as it forces the viewer to "look up" to him/her, as a child looks up to a parent. High-angle shots, however, places the viewer above the character on screen, which diminishes the character's power. Most of Capra's films are shot at eye level, where the camera is placed near or slightly below the same height as the eyelines of the characters, placing the viewer and the characters on equal footing. Both *You Can't Take It with You* and *It Happened One Night* are shot almost entirely in this manner. In his other films, Capra creates "natural" high- and low-angle shots through staging. The set of *American Madness*, for instance, places the boardroom and Dickson's office at the top of a grand staircase, which leads to natural high- and low-angle shots. In addition, characters lying down or sitting, like Semple's nephew in *Mr. Deeds* or Jefferson Smith in his scene with Taylor, are naturally placed in positions of diminished power and are photographed from above. Characters who are standing while others are sitting — such as Cedar and Deeds in the courtroom, Smith in the Senate Chamber, and Willoughby during his speeches — are naturally shot in low angles which endows them with greater power and importance. Capra intentionally cast tall men, like James Stewart and Gary Cooper in his "hero" roles because their above-average height (6'3") forces the camera operator to shoot them at slight low angles when standing in a group. Capra's villains, played by the likes of Claude Rains and Edward Arnold, are usually much shorter than their co-stars, which not only forces them to look up to the hero in their scenes with them, but also places them below the height of the camera. As a result, the two most dramatic close-ups of these two men (Arnold as Norton in *Meet John Doe*, and Rains as Paine in *Mr. Smith*) are shot in high angles, which diminishes their power even though the framing increases their importance. Extreme high angles, where the camera appears to be floating above the action, are used infrequently in Capra films. Capra uses extreme high angles in *Mr. Smith* when Jefferson Smith enters the Senate Chamber on his first day and when he walks into the Lincoln Memorial. This technique reinforces both the reverence and humility Jeff feels when entering these sacred American institutions. At the end of *Meet John Doe*, an extreme high angle is employed when Willoughby steps out onto the City Hall roof on Christmas Eve, which accentuates his feelings of hopelessness and despair.

Directors who oversee a large number of films develop a visual toolkit — similar techniques upon which they rely for dramatic emphasis in every picture. Capra was no exception, using similar visuals in all of his films of the '30s, visuals he would later implement in his war documentaries. The ringing bells in *Lost Horizon* which symbolize liberty and freedom, for instance, changed into the clanging Liberty Bell in *Mr. Smith*, an image also used at the end of every *Why We Fight* film. *Mr. Deeds Goes to Town*, *You Can't Take It with You*, *Mr. Smith Goes to Washington*, and *Meet John Doe* all use similar shots of their villains making plans around a large business desk surrounded by their cronies. Jefferson Smith, Tony Kirby, Jr., and Longfellow Deeds, on the other hand, conduct business differently, usually a one-to-one basis with the person with whom they are working.

Throughout his films of the thirties, Capra also shows a penchant for silent, picturesque faces to represent the common man. This technique started in his very first film *Fultah Fisher's Boarding House* (1922), for which he sought out ruffians — men with scars, pock marks, and actual peg legs — from the wharves around San Francisco to fill the scene. Later, in 1944, he confessed that he chose these types of men to cover up his inexperience with professional actors.[9] If he could not direct actors to play ruffians, he would cast real ruffians to create the sense of realism polished actors could not. Capra seemed to rediscover this technique in his Oscar-nominated *Lady for a Day*, with the casting of Apple Annie's friends, who were obviously chosen for their common looks over their acting ability. By using ordinary, even slightly deformed faces in his films, Capra perhaps felt that he could ground the artifice of studio-made films with an element tangibly real — ugliness. In *Lady for a Day*, Annie's friends serve as stand-ins for the audience, cheering on the actions of Dave the Dude, observing the situation from afar, and making comments about what they see. Such casting seems to add credibility to the story by incorporating some much-needed realism to the fairy tale. Illustrating his obsessive need to please the ordinary people in his audience, Capra often places these common people in the position of judges, who silently watch the events of the film unfold. The final close-up in the funeral scene in *Broadway Bill*, for

Apple Annie's ordinary-looking friends observe and comment on the events of *Lady for a Day*.

instance, is not of Dan or Alice, but a nameless man with a common face. The inclusion of the staring face of the old black man at the Lincoln memorial in *Mr. Smith*, the farmers who show up at Longfellow Deeds's mansion, the wannabe John Does and Grubbel (Frank Austin) in *Meet John Doe*, and the common rabble in the drunk tank in *You Can't Take It with You*, not only adds a sense of realness to the Hollywood films, but also either validates the proceedings or forces the hero to acknowledge their existence. In an interview at North Carolina State University, Capra explained his use of picturesque faces in his films:

> I like people, and I get right into them. I use people a great deal for background. I shoot many scenes in crowds because I think people are more interested in other people than they are in anything else. They love the faces; they don't know who the devil they are, but they like them because they are people.... That's why I direct my attention to the people or to the actors that are representing people, and they become credible, and they know who they are and then the audiences care for them. The biggest thing is that I want them to care about these people.[10]

The cragged faces of these silent witnesses show the human toll of the Great Depression. Capra uses these faces not only to force the viewer to confront the poverty and inequality they represent, but also to show that he understood and acknowledged their suffering.

Lastly, Capra uses shadow and light in key scenes in his films, with shadow representing hopelessness and despair and light representing wisdom and goodness. *Meet John Doe* even evokes the dark/light imagery in its dialogue. John, for instance, asks his listeners to help their neighbor immediately, urging them not to wait until the game "is called on account of darkness." In Connell's speech in the bar with John, the disillusioned editor calls Washington, Jefferson, and Lincoln "lighthouses in a foggy world." Capra primarily uses the light/dark metaphor in key scenes of his films through the use of dramatic, low-key lighting. This type of lighting, however, is used sparingly as most of Capra's films were shot high key (mainly for practical purposes as Capra normally shot with three cameras at once). Low-key lighting often requires more time to set up as well as precise blocking for both the camera and the actors. As such, anytime Capra employs dark shadows and dramatic lighting effects, he does so intentionally, not only to set a certain mood, but also to enhance the light/dark, good/evil, wisdom/ignorance, hope/despair metaphors of his films. Robert Conway and his friends, for instance, move out from the dark cave and into the light of Shangri-La in *Lost Horizon*. Light emanates from the High Lama when he speaks to Conway in the darkened room. When the lights go out in the opening Baskul scene enveloping the hanger in darkness, Conway, the righteous leader, picks up a brightly lit lantern and leads them to safety. Jefferson Smith refers to the light of the Capital dome shining through his office window, and the words "government of the people, by the people, for the people shall not perish from the earth" glow in the Lincoln memorial when Smith visits the sacred landmark. Light also seems to emanate from Annie's daughter's picture in her run-down apartment in *Lady for a Day*. In *Arsenic and Old Lace*, Mortimer runs over to Elaine, who is bathed in the light emanating from her bedroom window, reinforcing to Mortimer that starting a new family with her is the only way out of the darkness in which his family has placed him.

Capra uses shadows in his films for the opposite effect. Shadowed elements in the immediate foreground add a feeling of foreboding to scenes in *American Madness* and *Bitter Tea of General Yen*. Mr. Smith, John Doe, and Mr. Deeds are all shown in silhouette at the lowest point of their battle with the forces of evil. In these scenes, at the Lincoln Memorial, on the roof of City Hall, and at the sanitarium, respectively, Capra's heroes appear overcome by darkness. Capra also uses silhouettes to create suspense and pique audience interest, which he does in the motel scenes in *It Happened One Night*. In *Lost Horizon*, silhouettes are used twice before Maria, the villain of the film, appears. George is in silhouette before he meets Maria for the first time and

Longfellow Deeds (Gary Cooper) is shown in silhouette at his lowest point in *Mr. Deeds Goes to Town*.

Chang is in shadow right before Maria appears later in the film. The villainous Jonathan Brewster is introduced as a shadow through the window of the front door in *Arsenic and Old Lace*. This use of light and shadow, as we shall see, would also play a crucial role in the *Why We Fight* series and other war documentaries produced by Capra.

Although the editing style of Capra's films is fairly straightforward, one must not discount the director's passion for the post-production process. Capra's first creative job in the Hollywood industry was, in fact, editing writer/director Bob Eddy's slapstick comedies before being promoted to gag writer.[11] He explained his passion for film editing as follows:

> Now I loved film editing — I get a sensuous feeling out of film when I feel it in my fingers. I know what can be done with film: I know what the juxtaposition of scenes can mean for the finished film, how when you have twenty scenes and you put it together there's probably only one or two ways in which that film can come alive and the rest of the ways you can put them together mean dullness. I think that editing is the greatest fun of filmmaking.[12]

Editing appealed to the controlling aspects of Capra's personality, and as such, he would play an important role in the editing process not only in his narrative films but also in the *Why We Fight* series. While Ray Carney believed the narrative editing in Capra's films was mainly routine,[13] the editing process was enormously important in these films because Capra, unlike Hitchcock or Ford, tended to shoot a great deal of coverage. As such, his films were usually shaped in the editing room. From the beginning of his career, Capra understood that editing controlled the flow of the film, because more than any other part of filmmaking, it directed the attention of the audience. As he said years later:

> Every cut must have a purpose. One of the principal things about it is to get the smooth flow, the filmic flow, the dynamic of film. You can edit a film so that it flows very smoothly from one cut to another. You don't know where you have a cut; you just don't know.[14]

Throughout the postproduction process, Capra searched for the elusive flow that would create the perfect audience reaction, repeatedly tweaking the editing of his films based on the audience's reaction to the preview screenings.[15] When finishing *Mr. Deeds*, for instance, Capra previewed the film six or seven times, and changed the film "where the laughs were too long or too short or if something was dull."[16] Such constant tweaking probably resulted in the jump cuts (cutting from one shot to another with less than 30 degrees of difference between the two) Leland Poague observed while watching several of Capra's films. This style of editing not only accelerates the film's pace, but as Poague pointed out, also breaks from the traditional "invisible" style of most studio films of the time.

In his autobiography, Capra claims he became interested in the pacing of his films while directing *American Madness* in 1932. On this film (his first with Robert Riskin), Capra noticed that scenes slowed down when projected in front of a large audience. To compensate for this, he cut out long walks, prolonged entrances and exits, eliminated dissolves, and sped up the pace of the scenes during shooting.[17] When shooting, he also asked the actors to play the scene 60 percent faster than they did in rehearsal. At that pace, a scene that usually played for one minute would be shot in only 40 seconds. The accelerated pace, Capra claimed, forced the audience to pay attention. The speed created an urgency to the scene, and as a result, the audience "couldn't take their eyes off the screen" because they were afraid of missing something."[18] Capra also uses rapid cutting and pace to increase the audience's attention at the climaxes of his films. In *Broadway Bill*, the climactic final horserace cuts between horses, jockeys, and observers at a pace equal to most modern films. Capra scholar Charles Maland remarked that in the final 100 seconds of *Mr. Smith Goes to Washington*, Capra cuts 20 times, much higher than the pace of studio films at the time.[19]

One can also see the progression of the editing of Capra's films by analyzing the montage sequences of his films of the thirties. The montages of *It Happened One Night*, *Mr. Deeds*, *Lost Horizon*, and *You Can't Take It with You* are fairly conventional, primarily using newspaper headlines and stock shots to convey a lot of information visually in a short amount of time. The montages in *Mr. Smith* and *Meet John Doe*, on the other hand, are more technically complex and visually sophisticated than their predecessors. According to Leland Poague, this also marks a distinct break from the typical "invisible" style of most studio films.[20] Although these montage sequences were created by Slavko Vorkapich, Capra claimed that he would lay out the sequence shot by shot in storyboards for Vorkapich, then allow the Russian editor to shoot the footage himself.[21]

The impressive montage in *Mr. Smith Goes to Washington* (showing Jefferson Smith's quick tour of Washington) includes many images that will resurface in the *Why We Fight* series, as it intercuts shots of its main character with patriotic images, historical landmarks, and iconic statues to a medley of recognizable folk tunes—"Yankee Doodle," "My Country 'Tis of Thee," "The Star-Spangled Banner," "When Johnny Comes Marching Home," "Taps," "Red River Valley," and "The Battle Hymn of the Republic"—all in the span of about three minutes. The superimpositions and cross-dissolves in this complex montage are sometimes three images deep and the footage is pleasantly varied, switching from wide shots to tight shots of minute detail, like the quill pen in the hand of Jefferson's statue. Not only does this montage travel quickly through the important moments of American history, it also uses close-ups and point-of-view shots of Jefferson Smith to give these overused symbols greater relevance and intimacy. According to Carney, the elaborate Washington montage of *Mr. Smith*, which was edited in the Soviet Eisensteinian tradition by Vorkapich, is so overwhelming it ends to "dwarf the human figure" and make the individual seem "not to matter very much."[22] In addition, the loud patriotic scoring of the sequence "drowns out the aural imagination of the sound of the mere individual human voice."[23] This devaluation of the individual seems to run counter to Capra's ordinary filmmaking practices, but this particular montage sequence in *Mr. Smith* is necessary because it briefly places American ideology above both character and story. As a result, the viewers, whose senses are overwhelmed, can do nothing but passively let the images and music wash over them, and remain awestruck and speechless—the exact state of Jefferson Smith during the scene. As we shall see later, Capra would use this same montage technique in his war documentaries, especially in battle scenes, to create a sense of awe in the soldier and to evoke emotional reactions in the viewer rather than encouraging discourse and analysis.

The *Meet John Doe* montage right before the Christmas Eve suicide attempt, although much shorter than the one in *Mr. Smith*, is equally complex. Rather than overwhelming the viewer with symbols and ideology this montage uses giant newspaper headlines, multiple superimpositions, layered dialogue, and metaphorical images, to visually illustrate the subconscious of John Willoughby. Although this sequence is more abstract than the one in *Mr. Smith*, it shows a level of sophistication in editing unseen in earlier Capra films. Both of these sequences, however, illustrate that Capra was well aware of the technical and narrative possibilities of editing at the time the *Why We Fight* series was made.

The montage sequences in *Meet John Doe* and *Mr. Smith Goes to Washington* also call attention to the director's use of traditional American music in his films. Capra rarely uses music in his films, except in the opening and closing credits and montage sequences which primarily used "Americana" music in the background. "For He's a Jolly Good Fellow" is used in both *Mr. Deeds* and *Meet John Doe*, and the opening sequence of *Meet John Doe* contains a medley of Stephen Foster's "Hard Times, Come Again No More," "Take Me Out to the Ball Game," "Roll Out the Barrel," and "Oh! Susanna." This technique emphasized the "common man" approach of these films, not only because Capra was using songs that any American could easily identify, but also because these songs were closely tied to the American culture in the times in which they were written. It comes as no surprise that this same folk music technique is used in Capra's war documentaries, especially as they used the same composer, Dimitri Tiomkin, who wrote the musical scores for *You Can't Take It with You, Mr. Smith Goes to Washington*, and *Meet John Doe*.

Spontaneous folk music also plays an important part in identifying common, everyday Americans in Capra films. As Capra commented in an interview in 1981:

> My music is not philharmonic, not heavy. It's music by the people, for the people, and of the people. The little people make the music — they play, they sing, they dance. The songs are not difficult — parade music and popular standards.[24]

Thus, the crowd is legitimized as "common people" at the John Doe convention because they sing "Oh! Susanna" and "My Country 'Tis of Thee," as are the bus passengers in *It Happened One Night* who enthusiastically sing "The Man on the Flying Trapeze." Longfellow Deeds breaks into a makeshift version of "Old Folks at Home" (also known as "Swanee River") with Babe Bennett in the park, and Tony Kirby dances spontaneously with Alice outside with a bunch of kids in formal attire. Longfellow Deeds unashamedly plays the tuba, and John Willoughby, the Colonel, and Grandpa Vanderhof all play the harmonica. The music in Capra's films brings a folksy quality to the idealistic proceedings and also creates a sense of play and community for the characters. In *Meet John Doe*, by playing his "doohickey," the confused John Willoughby feels comforted after his radio address, and in *You Can't Take It with You*, Anthony Kirby and Grandpa Vanderhof bring their two families together with a rousing harmonica duet of "Polly Wolly Doodle." By employing familiar music in his films, Capra ingratiated himself and his movie stars with the ordinary American audiences who watched them, making his heartfelt ideological messages more palatable.

When analyzing the role Capra's popular films of the thirties had on his war documentaries, however, we must look beyond the technical aspects and common elements of his work and delve into the films on a deeper level. Biographer Charles Maland believes that understanding Capra's core belief system and personality is the key to understanding his films. Unlike other directors of the 1930s, Capra saw filmmaking as a moral responsibility.[25] The spectres of fascism and communism threatened the democracies of the world during the Great Depression, and the leaders of government, industry, and entertainment, whether conservative or liberal, saw it as their patriotic duty to revitalize the American mythology.[26] Capra rose to the occasion, compelled to defend democracy and capitalism against those who preferred to overturn the whole system during hard times. After all, the American dream had worked for Capra; he had risen up through the ranks to become one of the most successful men in Hollywood. Capra's films acknowledged that times were hard, but rather than condemning the system, Capra used the plots of his films to show the ways the system could be reformed. By following the rules of common sense, decency, and Christianity and by having faith in the work ethic of the average American, Capra believed the system could work and America could return to its former glory. This belief first pops up in the boardroom scene in *American Madness*, when bank president Tom Dickson, who lends money based on character and faith, defends his lending process to the board of directors by quoting Alexander Hamilton. Capra asserts in this film, as well as many of his other films of this period, that if America returned to the beliefs of the founding fathers, who had faith enough in individuals to preserve their liberties, then our country could be great once again.

Because of his unique ability in the mid-to-late thirties to choose his own scripts as well as because of his close association with his screenwriters, Capra could easily inject these and other beliefs into his films, including the films he made during the war. Thus, through his popular fiction films and his war-orientation films, Capra, perhaps more than any other director before or since, was able to transmit his own value system to the millions of Americans who came to be known as the "Greatest Generation." This value system, which revered history, praised religion, democracy, and hard work, as well as glorified the imaginative man of action who spoke plainly, was perpetuated and reinforced in Capra's fiction and nonfiction films and was ultimately used as justification to send millions of Americans overseas to fight a war against the dangerous fascist ideology of the Axis powers. Thus, it is absolutely crucial when writing about Capra's films, whether fiction or nonfiction, to specifically define the world view he presents in his most watched films. As such, the next part of this chapter will show key examples of Capra's ideology in his most popular fiction films leading up to the war. In Chapter 5, we will delve deeper into the world view presented in Capra's war documentaries, most especially the *Why We Fight* series, for the first time comparing them to the ideology of his fiction films. This comparison, it is hoped, will yield greater insight into Capra's influential work.

As early as 1928, public relations guru Edward Bernays understood that in order to persuade the public to follow a particular idea, politicians cannot simply explain to the people why they should follow them. This old-fashioned approach ultimately ends up only antagonizing people and assaulting their resistance.[27] When Capra decided to make message movies, whether as a result of his "conversion" experience or not, he followed Bernays's rule for creating propaganda. He realized that in order to reach an audience, it is better to dramatize than to preach to them directly. Starting with *Mr. Deeds* (and perhaps as early as *American Madness*), Capra learned that a message movie must prioritize entertainment over its message in order to be successful. According to Capra, without entertainment, moralistic films become too heavy, and when that happens you "can't sell the American people anything."[28] This approach is perhaps best illustrated in one of Capra's all-time favorite scenes. In *Meet John Doe*, Connell meets Willoughby in a bar to tell him that Norton is planning to use the popularity of the John Doe clubs to run for president. When Connell talks about how much he loves America, however, Capra inserts several gags with Connell's cigarette, which he is having trouble smoking because of his obvious inebriation. Capra explained the scene in an interview in 1977: "When you get into that hairy stuff, you've got to do it a certain way, you laugh at it but you listen. It's touching that way, being drunk, having trouble with that cigarette..."[29]

According to Ted Sennett, author of *Laughing in the Dark*, this toning down of message, as well as the fast pace and great performances, prevent Capra's films from "drowning in the milk of human kindness."[30] Capra sincerely hoped that by winning over the American people through laughter and entertainment he could also leave them with a final message of hope and patriotism. As a result, he not only saved his most powerful and uplifting statements for his films' dramatic climaxes, but also abruptly ended the film directly afterward, hoping the message as well as the uplifting sense of satisfaction one received from the film would be fresh in the minds of the audience as they walked out of the theater and reentered the real world.

Although Capra admitted in his book to being a "Christmas Catholic" in the twenties, his nearly fatal illness and the visit from the "little man" (whether real or imaginary), stirred up religious feelings that would permeate his films of the thirties and forties.[31] Capra considered himself a Catholic in spirit, one who believed that the Cross would survive even if the "anti-moral," the "intellectual bigots" and the "Mafias of ill will" destroyed religion.[32] The ideas of Christianity, in other words, were greater than the institutions that upheld it. Although he was not one to regularly attend Mass, Capra still believed in the transformative power of religion. In his autobiography, for instance, he describes the experience he felt attending Mass:

> It may happen to you only once in a hundred masses—but it will happen. You walk back from communion with the host on your tongue—a nobody, you kneel, drop your head in your hands. Slowly the wonder of it fills you with joy—the dissolving host in your mouth is the living Christ! The priest, the church, all the bowed heads around you, disappear. You hear nothing, see nothing, feel nothing. Your mind empties itself of all thought, your body of all substance. You are a spirit suffused in a glorious light, and out of its glory a word infuses your spirit: "Courage!" You have glimpsed the eternal![33]

Thus, to Capra, true religious feeling comes from a highly personal place, not from churches and priests. Although Capra plainly believed that religious institutions were a positive influence in the world and important in a free world, he also believed that the concept of faith and the ideals of Christianity were best understood on a personal level. In Shangri-La, one needs only to believe the High Lama's story and exercise moderation to live a long and happy life. Nothing else is necessary. As a result, Capra's films rarely use priests as characters or churches as locations. In a telling interview, Capra explains why in *It's a Wonderful Life* George Bailey, at his lowest point in the film, says a prayer in a bar and not a church:

> [George] says a prayer. "Oh God, I'm at the end of my rope. Show me the way!" It's a short prayer but we believe it. He's desperate and has nowhere to turn. If we showed him on his knees in church or in a private corner, the audience wouldn't take to it. But in a bar, right after gulping down a shot of whiskey, we are inclined to believe it.[34]

Similarly, in *Meet John Doe*, the John Doe Convention takes place in a ball field and not a church, and while a priest shows up to say a prayer at the opening night, his speech is more of a burden than a blessing, as it gets in the way of Willoughby's more important confession. The Vanderhofs say a prayer of thanks before dinner, and Jefferson Smith reads from the Bible during his filibuster, but none of these characters are shown going to church or worshipping with others. Like Capra, theirs is a personal faith, a faith that is revealed through the practice of loving one's neighbor and doing good. This belief in the triumph of goodness can be found in Capra's earliest films with Harry Langdon, a character whose basic decency ends up protecting him from the evils of the world. This non-specific approach to Christianity appealed more to mainstream American audiences who came to theaters with different ideas about the practice of religion. In addition, this "generic" approach to Christianity in his films allowed Capra to connect with his audience on a basic level, without promoting the more rigorous Catholic ideology with which he was most familiar.

Despite this compromise, the major philosophy introduced in Capra's films still remains true to the basic teachings of Jesus in the New Testament. The fundamental core of both the John Doe and the Longfellow Deeds speeches is "Love thy neighbor as thyself" from Matthew 22:39. Capra wrote in *The Name Above the Title* that this rule, Christ's spiritual law, was the "most powerful sustaining force in anyone's life."[35] Such devotion to the golden rule was not unusual during the Great Depression. Like John Willoughby, the populist star Will Rogers discussed the problem of applying the "Love thy Neighbor" principle at the very time when the country needed it most: "Our Savior had a plan; He left it up to us and He knew it would help us. He said, Love thy neighbor as thy self, but I bet there ain't two people in your block that's speaking to each other."[36] Those words, which sound as if they come right out of a Capra film (Capra was a professed fan of Rogers) point to the lack of faith Americans seemed to have in one another during the Great Depression. The "Love thy Neighbor" rule is not an abstract Biblical concept, but a practical and necessary belief in the inherent goodness of humanity. In *American Madness*, Tom Dickson explains to the cynical board of directors that by helping one person you end up helping everyone because such help generates increased trust in the system. At the end of the film, Dickson is rewarded for his trust in his fellow man, as Matt and others in whom he put his trust actually turn the negative tide of the bank run. "Love Thy Neighbor" is also the basic rule behind Jefferson Smith's camp, where kids of all different backgrounds get to know one another. It is the rule Smith believes guides the country's laws. In part of his filibuster speech, he says: "I wouldn't give you two cents for all your fancy rules if behind them they didn't have a little bit of plain, ordinary everyday kindness. And a little looking out for the other fella, too."

As Jefferson Smith approaches exhaustion, confronted by mounds of letters urging him to end his filibuster, he makes one desperate attempt to redeem Paine. He says:

> All you people don't know about lost causes. Mr. Paine does. He said once they were the only causes worth fighting for. And he fought for them once, for the

only reason any man ever fights for them. Because of just one plain, simple rule: Love Thy Neighbor. And in this world today full of hatred a man who knows that one rule has a great trust. You know that rule, Mr. Paine. And I loved you for it just as my father did.

According to Maria Elena de las Carreras Kuntz, in her article "The Catholic Vision in Hollywood," Capra was a firm believer in *communion*, which in theological terms means that "our relationship with God does not excuse us from our responsibility towards our neighbor, for whom we should care, especially for one in need."[37] Kuntz adds that Capra seemed to believe in the inherent good of the common man, as long as they are led by some sort of mediator, who, like Christ, contributes to the "creation or reaffirmation of a communal spirit."[48] These mediators are the heroes of Capra's stories — Tom Dickson, Jefferson Smith, Longfellow Deeds, John Willoughby, Grandpa Vanderhof — men who stick to the "Love Thy Neighbor" principle even when all hope seems lost.

The Christ analogy is pushed even further with Longfellow Deeds, Jefferson Smith and John Willoughby. All three characters appear to be virgins, as they are embarrassed and confused by sex. Longfellow Deeds is the son of Joseph and Mary Deeds, and like Smith and Willoughby, is unjustly persecuted by people who want to stop his message of hope and kindness. All three films mention their heroes being "crucified." In *Mr. Deeds Goes to Town*, Babe screams that she is "crucifying" Deeds with her "Cinderella Man" articles. Senator Paine says to Taylor that he will not be a part of "crucifying" Smith in *Mr. Smith Goes to Washington*. In *Meet John Doe*, when Ann listens to the crowd turning against Willoughby at the disastrous convention, she shouts that he's being "crucified." On the rooftop in *Meet John Doe*, Ann even calls Christ the "first John Doe." Not that Capra would ever confess that his characters were meant to be seen as Christ figures, as he tended to avoid any talk of distinct theological connections to his films. In 1978, when he was asked if John Willoughby was a Christ figure, Capra replied that he never meant to endorse any particular faith in his films. "We all," he added, "can worship in the ecumenical church called humanism."[39] Despite these denials, the connection between Capra's films and Christian doctrine are too obvious to dismiss. More importantly, this use of the Christian faith to promote the concept of helping one's neighbor, even to the point of sacrificing one's life, would be used by Capra as a justification for sending men to war in the *Why We Fight* series.

Furthermore, Capra uses the New Testament to champion the weak and oppressed, whom, he believes, would create a better, more democratic world if placed in positions of power. This empathy for common men and women appealed to the majority of Americans at the time, who felt better about their lot in life after seeing Capra's films. As Charles Maland commented, in a world where upward mobility is difficult, it was better to encourage people to seek fulfillment in human relationships than to link happiness to wealth and material goods.[40] While the common people in Capra's films seem sincere and grounded, most of the wealthy are depicted as lonely, unhappy, and incapable of fun. As such, in order to guarantee that his heroes would connect with the audience, Capra made sure Jefferson Smith, Longfellow Deeds, and John Willoughby all started off as common, ordinary men before being plucked from obscurity and given power. In the end, their common roots, their experience with the ordinary and everyday prevent them from being corrupted by the selfish men in power. This belief in the unlikely, humble hero comes straight out of the Beatitudes, found in the fifth chapter of Matthew, which Capra admitted on several occasions were the underlying ideas of his movies.[41] The most famous of these Beatitudes, "Blessed are the meek, for they shall inherit the earth" (Matthew 5:5), is invoked in both *Lost Horizon* and *Meet John Doe*. In *Lost Horizon*, the High Lama sees this New Testament prediction as inevitable. "When the strong have devoured each other," states the religious leader to Robert Conway, "the Christian ethic may at last be fulfilled and the meek shall inherit the earth." *Meet John Doe* takes a less passive stance. At the end of his radio broadcast, John Willoughby says, "The meek can inherit the earth when the John Does start loving their neighbors." Unless the common man, the meek, the John Does, unite, they will constantly be the prey of selfish men in power. This belief in the common man reaffirms the importance of democracies, wherein leaders among the common people, men like Jefferson Smith, John Willoughby, and Longfellow Deeds, have a right to be heard. The perfect world of Shangri-La is possible in a democracy if and only if the people fight for it; it is impossible in the fascist world where the thoughts and ideas of the common man are crushed by the ruling authority.

It is important to note, however, that Capra's belief in the superiority of the values of common Americans is not a complete condemnation of the upper class as a whole. After all, Capra himself was a member of this much-maligned elite group. It is, in fact, possible to be rich and be liked in a Capra film. Alice Higgins, J.L. Higgins, Ellie Andrews and her father Alexander Andrews, Anthony Kirby (Senior and Junior), all come across well in their films because (unlike Capra's villains) these people, at some point, admit to the superiority of the virtues of the middle class.[42] In addition, these characters are willing to make sacrifices for their families, step outside their comfort zone, and spend time with "regular" folks.[43]

From Mr. Deeds to John Doe, Capra's heroes believe deeply in the unique history of the countries in which they live. Tom Dickson quotes Alexander

Hamilton. Jefferson Smith is known to cite Lincoln and Jefferson by heart. Grandpa Vanderhof quotes Lincoln. Even Robert Conway, the English hero of *Lost Horizon*, holds a fondness for history as he is the only one of his party who asks questions about Shangri-La and how it came into being. Capra himself was extremely fond of history. Ever since his fifth grade teacher, Jean McDaniel, got him interested in the subject, he enjoyed reading American History books, especially those involving the Revolutionary War.[44] Like Vanderhof, who believed the spirit of his wife still lingered in his house, Capra and his heroes regard history as an active, living force. This force demands reverence and awe for those who believe, and provides guidance, strength, and inspiration in return.

Capra's heroes, however, are less knowledgeable about history once their thoughts and words are analyzed more thoroughly. As Leland Poague points out in *Another Frank Capra*, although Jefferson Smith can recite Lincoln and Jefferson by heart, he, strangely enough, knows very little about how Congress works.[45] In *You Can't Take It with You*, Grandpa Vanderhof quotes from Lincoln's second inaugural address: "With malice towards none and charity to all," and contrasts it to the present by saying, "Nowadays they say, 'Think the way I do, or I'll bomb the daylights out of you.'" By idealizing the past, Grandpa (and perhaps even Capra and Riskin) fail to take into consideration the more complex reality of men like George Washington and Abraham Lincoln, who actually did command troops to fight and kill men who disagreed with their beliefs.[46] Smith, Deeds, and Vanderhof know little about the real practical facts of history, because such knowledge would make them more worldly and less naïve. Instead, history is used by these characters merely as a jumping-off point for their imaginations and as foundations for their passionate views on liberty. Their knowledge of history is less academic and more religious in nature, as they use the subject mainly as a source of inspiration.

Capra was no stranger to this "religious" feeling in the face of history. When he visited the Senate Chamber to research *Mr. Smith*, for instance he wrote the following in his autobiography:

> I'm a silly goose about things patriotic, so it was a natural—I got a bad case of goose pimples. There it was, spread out below me, as silent and awe-inspiring as an empty cathedral—the Senate![47]

Compare the above passage to the speech made by Mr. Deeds as he describes what he sees when he looks at Grant's tomb:

> I see a small Ohio farmboy becoming a great soldier. I see thousands of marching men. I see General Lee with a broken heart surrendering. And I can see the beginning of a new nation like Abraham Lincoln said. And I can see that Ohio

boy being inaugurated as president. Things like that can only happen in a country like America.

Like Capra, Deeds uses landmarks to make an emotional and imaginative connection with history, not an intellectual one. Historical landmarks are hallowed places where patriotic men go to pray. This is why Jefferson Smith goes to the Lincoln Memorial, not to a church, to seek inspiration when he first arrives in Washington as well as after the disastrous hearing, when he feels his lowest. Capra confessed to making the same trip to the memorial when he had doubts about whether he should make *Mr. Smith Goes to Washington*, an idealistic film about America in the middle of the Great Depression. He left the "most majestic shrine we have in America" convinced that "it was never untimely to yank the rope of freedom's bell."[48] To Capra, this kind of reverence for American ideals spurs men to action because men who see history as a living force take personal responsibility for the country. As Connell explains to John Willoughby after finding out about Norton's misuse of power in *Meet John Doe*, "I get mad for a guy named Washington, and a guy named Jefferson, and Lincoln."

The visits to Grant's tomb and the Lincoln memorial in *Deeds* and *Smith*, however, are not about the connection to buildings, but the connection with the men who are honored there. According to Ray Carney, Grant, Lincoln, Washington, and Jefferson are particularly singled out in Capra's films because they stand out as pragmatic, individual performers in United States history. "It is their individuality that Capra's heroes admire and emulate," he writes, "not their institutional abstractness."[49] Capra sees history as the biography of great individuals, and is eager to perpetuate the mythic elements of their singular, independent achievements. In fact, in an interview with Leo Foreman of the *New York Herald Tribune* in 1935, Capra claimed he was going to direct a picture about George Washington.[50] These men, most especially Washington and Lincoln, appealed to audiences of the 1930s because they ushered the country through times of great crisis, keeping our democratic ideals intact.[51] History, then, became a tool in Capra's films to promote the ideologies of certain "chosen" people, special individuals who stood out above the crowd through their hard work, humility, imagination, and stubborn adherence to their ideals. It comes as no surprise then, that Capra would rewrite elements of his own history to better conform with this standard, transforming himself from a mere director of motion pictures to a visionary, capable of changing the world.

Capra understood that the pure ideals of America's past can be used to spur men to action only if they are connected to individuals. The Lincoln Memorial is inspiring because it combines the ideals Lincoln stood for, represented by the words written on the walls, with a representation of the man himself. This is why, in his first trip to the Lincoln Memorial, Jefferson Smith looks back and forth between the statue of Lincoln and the words on the wall. It is the *combination* of word and flesh that spurs men to action. In *Meet John Doe*, the ideas of Ann's father must be combined with the person of John Willoughby to form a third entity, John Doe, who acts as a symbol to inspire the masses. It takes the physically broken body of Jefferson Smith, combined with the reminder of his father's ideals, to finally convert Senator Paine, causing him to confess. Past ideals, without a visual manifestation to reinforce them, become stuck in history books. Consequently, heroes without ideals are uninspiring and lifeless. In his idealistic films of the '30s, Capra attempted to manifest the ideals of the founding fathers in the bodies of his fictional heroes. These films created a new set of founding fathers—Jefferson Smith, Longfellow Deeds, and John Willoughby, men with vague pasts and ordinary sensibilities, on whom he could not only project but modernize the ideals of Washington, Lincoln, and Jefferson. Deeds's trip to Grant's tomb and Smith's trip to the Lincoln Memorial are ways to establish this link. Capra's young heroes are also granted legitimacy through the acceptance of elders in traditional positions of authority. The judge in *Mr. Deeds*, the Vice President in *Mr. Smith*, the High Lama in *Lost Horizon*, Connell in *John Doe*, all recognize the uniqueness of Capra's heroes and support their idealistic endeavors to the best of their ability.

Capra also reinforces the connection of the founding fathers to his heroes through clever editing and the use of *mise-en-abîme* composition. When Jefferson Smith goes on the warpath in *Mr. Smith*, for instance, he punches a member of the press corps in front of a painting of Washington. When the man comes to, Smith has already left, and only the painting of the first president remains. In the Millville City Hall scene in *Meet John Doe*, a picture of Abraham Lincoln, the "everyman president," hangs on the left behind Willoughby with a picture of Washington on the right, as he listens to Bert Hansen and his friends explain the impact of his radio speech. This connection in Capra's work between visual and verbal, high ideals and individual action, past and present, all attempted to make the American ideals presented in the Declaration of Independence and Lincoln's inaugural addresses relevant to an audience angry and embittered by the Great Depression. In the following decade, Capra would use similar techniques to convince young men that these ideals were worth sacrificing their lives to protect.

The optimistic ideals of Willoughby, Smith, Deeds, Conway, and Vanderhof are what separates them from their fellow men, those who are most selfish, jaded, serious, and unimaginative—that is, until they are either reformed or confronted by Capra's heroes. The starry-eyed innocence of

Capra's protagonists, however, is only possible because these men have not, or will not, trade their purity for power.[52] It is no wonder that the powerful villains in Capra's stories act like responsible, pragmatic, realistic, and boring adults, while his heroes take on the attributes one most associates with children — imagination, playfulness, optimism, and innocence. Longfellow Deeds, for instance, enjoys hearing his voice echo in his mansion, sliding down the banister, and playing in the rain. John Willoughby acts like a kid on his first day in the hotel room, looking out the window, ordering room service, and asking if anyone's ears popped in the elevator. In *American Madness*, Matt is introduced telling jokes while he opens up the vault, and Tom Dickson starts off his first scene playfully pushing down the hat of the bank's security guard. At the beginning of *Broadway Bill*, Dan confesses the urge to, "sit under the moon and throw rocks at a window." In *You Can't Take It with You*, Alice's mother (Spring Byington) is filled with childish curiosity when she notices the gun worn by the agent who visits their house. Senator Paine refers to Jefferson Smith as a "boy" a number of times in *Mr. Smith Goes to Washington*, at one point warning the junior senator that he's been "living in a boy's world." Taylor refers to Smith as a "drooling infant" while Saunders compares him to a "boy going off to his first day at school." In an interview in *Film Comment* in 1972, Capra confessed that this treatment of Jefferson Smith was completely intentional, as he imagined Jeff as a child in one way and a man in the other. As a man, he doesn't like to see evil invade the Senate, but as a child he is able to "speak the truth."[53] This technique of infantilizing his heroes may be a holdover from his days as a writer for the silent "Our Gang" shorts and Harry Langdon features. According to Ray Carney, the heroes of Capra's most popular films are basically variations of these earlier characters:

> They are somewhat childlike, sheltered, starry-eyed unsophisticates who represent a comic state of social disengagement or otherworldliness that separates them from, and elevates them above, the more practical and hard-headed characters around them.[54]

Capra's childlike protagonists are set apart from the ordinary, everyday, world, which not only becomes a rich mine for comedy but also places his heroes in the perfect position to criticize the absurdities of modern life. However, Carney warns film scholars against equating the childlike qualities of these men with ignorance and simplicity. Capra's heroes are far from simple; their distance from the adult world simply allows them to break away from traditional modes of thinking, forcing them to use their imaginations to solve traditional problems in a new and exciting way.

The imagination of Capra's heroes, which often takes the form of improvisational imaginative play, is one of the greatest tools of conversion in

Capra's stories. Grandpa Vanderhof's playful questioning, for instance, prods men like Poppins and Kirby to "examine their most deeply held convictions or assumptions," which, in turn, leads to more critical self analysis.[55] John Willoughby spends a large part of the film playacting as John Doe, and wins over his bodyguards by engaging an imaginary game of baseball in his hotel room. Ellie gets closer to Peter after pretending to be married in front of detectives. Deeds and Babe bond over an improvised "Old Folks at Home" duet; Alice and Dan sing an improvisational song about split pea soup and succotash; and Conway woos Sondra by building a makeshift sculpture out of her clothes. Capra explained the practical reasons for showing his characters in engaging in improvisational play in an interview with Richard Glatzer:

> Sometimes your story has to stop and you let the audience just look at your people. You want the audiences to like them. The characters have no great worries for the moment — they like each other's company and that's it.... When the audience rests and they look at the people, they begin to smile. They begin to love the characters, and *then* they'll be worried about what happens to them.[56]

I believe the playfulness of Capra's characters has a deeper, more profound significance than simply creating a bond between characters and the audience. In Capra's films, imagination becomes an expression of both childlike sensibilities and individual freedom. One of the reasons *Lady for a Day* is not as effective as Capra's later films is because Dave the Dude has little fun going along with the premise. When Dave is trying to teach his gangster friends to act like gentlemen and politicians for Annie's reception, for instance, he comes across more like a frustrated producer than an inspiring hero. Dave is too limited by both his finances (which are quickly dwindling in order to keep up the character) and the short time frame to truly enjoy himself. In his later films, Capra finds ways to free his heroes from heavy responsibilities so they can actively participate in the fun. His heroes are either jobless (John Willoughby, Dan Brooks, Peter Warne and Grandpa Vanderhof), rich (Longfellow Deeds, Ellie Andrews, and Anthony Kirby, Jr.), or eager to start a new adventure (Mortimer Brewster, Robert Conway, and Jefferson Smith.) Men like John Cedar, Anthony Kirby, Sr., and George Conway are either too obsessed with their jobs or feel too responsible to take time to live in the "present." Men who are able to play are men who live in a state of complete freedom with the courage to act in whatever manner they choose. This courage makes them tools of conversion, men who, in their "freeness," inspire people to actively engage in life and their community. It is no wonder (as we will discover in Chapter 7) that images of play are often associated with America and Allied soldiers in Capra's war documentaries, while Axis soldiers are often portrayed as serious, unimaginative automatons who blindly obey their leaders.

2. The Capra Formula 85

A special reverence is held for children, most especially boys, in Capra's most successful films. These children tend to be depicted as wiser than the adults. In *Mr. Smith*, the governor of Smith's state chooses the Boy Ranger's leader as senator only after a hearty endorsement from his children. Richard Jones, a young pageboy, fills Smith in about the geography of the Senate, people, and procedures on Smith's first day on the job. In turn, an endorsement from children in a Capra film justifies the undertakings of the hero. When Smith proposes his bill for the boy's camp, he is cheered by a group of boys in the visitors' section, and Cedar has to peel a young boy off Longfellow Deeds's back when he boards the train to New York. Tony Kirby, Jr., and Alice Sycamore gain the appreciation of children by "loosening up" and dancing to the improvisational music the kids are playing in the park. When John Willoughby is greeted by a crowd outside his hotel room, children line up in the front row. Capra's heroes stick out from the rest of the world because they seem to be the only ones who are cognizant of their impact on the younger generation. John worries about going along with Ann's idea because if he gets caught in a racket, the kids will be disappointed. Jefferson Smith evokes kids as the salvation of the world twice in his filibuster speech.

> It's a funny thing about men, you know. They all start life being boys. I wouldn't be a bit surprised if some of these senators were boys once. And that's why it seemed like a pretty good idea to me to get boys out of crowded cities and stuffy basements for a couple of months out of the year, and build their bodies and minds for man size jobs because those boys are going to be behind these desks some of these days. And it seemed like a pretty good idea getting boys from all over the country, boys of all nationalities, and ways of living, getting them together.... But of course if you've got to build a dam where that boys camp ought to be to get some graft to pay off some political army or something, well that's a different thing.... Oh, no, if you think I'm going back there and tell those boys in my state and say, "Look, aw, fellas, forget about it. Forget all this stuff I've been telling you about this land you live in is a lot of hooey. This isn't your country, it belongs to a lot of James Taylors." Oh, no, not me! And anybody here that thinks I'm gonna do that has got another thing coming!

Capra, like Jefferson Smith, understood that America must protect the ideologies of its children if it expects these children to carry the ideals of the founding fathers into the future. Capra's heroes are willing to sacrifice their own comfort and dreams to protect the optimistic ideals of children, which is why Jefferson Smith refuses to surrender to Paine and Taylor, and why Ellie and Peter give their last dollars to a starving boy and his mother on the bus. If one loses children to cynicism and doubt, one loses the country. (This belief will reemerge in the war documentaries Capra makes in the next decade, prominently featuring images of suffering children in order to inculcate in its audience the need for sacrifice and commitment.)

The youthful nature of Capra's heroes is also illustrated in their individual speech patterns. Like the young boy ranger who stumbles through his address at the Governor's dinner for Jefferson Smith, Capra's heroes often have difficulty expressing themselves. This inability to speak effectively plagues Matt, Deeds, Smith, and Willoughby, but also endears them to the audience because they seem all the more real because of it. When Smith stumbles through his speech to the Senate, when Doe tries to explain his dream to Ann, when Deeds fails to properly articulate his romantic feelings towards Babe, and even when Bert the soda jerk explains the formation of the John Doe club, the dialogue feels improvised, unrehearsed, and emotionally true. According to Carney, men like Jefferson Smith speak with "unsystematic, unformulateable feeling" because much like children, they are faced with the difficult task of translating their abstract, highly personal imaginations into words.[57] This childlike inability to communicate and express one's emotions becomes a source of frustration for the hero, which ultimately leads to strong physical action (such as hitting) and unstable mood swings, personality traits shared by Jefferson Smith, Longfellow Deeds, and John Willoughby.[58] The strong female characters in Capra's films—women who have already successfully navigated the waters of adulthood—thus become burdened with the responsibility of teaching these men to communicate with the adult world through spoken language.[59] It is no coincidence that these characters—Ann, Saunders, and Babe—engage in professions where writing and effective communication skills are essential.

Unlike the dialogue of the antagonists of these films, which is usually dry and businesslike, the dialogue of Capra's heroes is usually flowered with slang, idioms, and jokes. Smith, for instance, in the middle of his stirring filibuster speech, elicits a laugh when he turns to the senator next to him and asks, "How am I doin'?" In the beginning of *Mr. Deeds*, Longfellow makes a joke about Cedar's business card, the humor of which is lost on the stuffy lawyer. Although Tony Kirby, Jr., is dressed in a business suit (like one belonging to his father) in his first scene in *You Can't Take It with You*, he comes across much differently than Kirby Sr. He cannot hide his boredom while his father discusses business affairs, and he uses words like "cockeyed" which makes his serious father laugh out loud. In *American Madness*, Capra contrasts the language of the extremely likeable Matt with the smooth, dignified speech of Cluett. When Matt confronts Cluett and Phyllis in Cluett's apartment, Cluett says, "You would do well to mind your own business." Matt responds, "I'm wastin' my breath talkin' to you, Cluett."

The "good guys" are also easily identified in Capra's films because more often than not, they use slang and idioms to get their point across. According to Charles Maland, Robert Riskin was responsible for this type of dialogue in Capra's films, as he understood slang better than the director.[60] In *Meet John Doe*, Ann tells Norton he would be a "dumb cluck" not to run with the John Doe story, and tells Connell, "If it was rainin' a hundred dollar bills, you'd be looking for a dime you lost someplace." John Willoughby calls the hotel "nifty" and plays a "doohickey"; Longfellow Deeds describes the New York City Aquarium as "swell," and Jefferson Smith cannot help but say "gee whiz" when describing the majesty of the Lincoln Memorial to Saunders. Dan Brooks playfully calls the Higgins house a "mausoleum" and asks for a "slug of whiskey" before dinner. *Lady for a Day*, partly because it was adapted from a story by Damon Runyon, is filled with characters who use slang to express themselves. Even characters about whom the audience may have doubts, men like Happy Maguire, Colonel Pettigrew, Diz, Connell, "Corny" Cobb, and Henry Bernard, predictably end up on the "good" side because of their penchant (in early scenes) for using slang and common expressions. One exception to this rule is Mr. Jones, the dubious American entrepreneur who has a penchant for speaking slang in *The Bitter Tea of General Yen*. Another exception is Oscar Shapely in *It Happened One Night*, who continually uses slang as he tries to pick up Ellen Andrews. According to Carney, Shapely is immediately considered inappropriate for Ellen because, unlike Peter's language which feels extemporaneous, Shapely's lines are repetitive and mechanical, and consequently insincere.[61] This tactic of using extemporaneous, slangy speech to ingratiate oneself with the common people, however, was not unusual in the 1930s, as politicians like Huey Long would often use colorful, passionate language to separate himself from other bureaucrats. In the field of entertainment, the popular Three Stooges shorts and Marx Brothers features regularly contrasted the improvisational and slangy language of their stars with the stilted, formal language of their upper crust foils. Will Rogers, perhaps the most famous man in America in the early '30s, regularly addressed the problems of America in his newspaper articles and his radio addresses in the folksy, down-to-earth language of ordinary people. This populist approach to speechwriting, in fact, dates as far back as the Jacksonian era, where politicians used the everyday speech of rural Americans to attack the elite and condemn any trace of aristocracy.[62]

The use of "folksy" speech in Capra's films is meant to contrast with the smooth-talking elite, those men who do not believe in the equality of the human race. Like the Populist movement of the '30s, Capra embraces the 19th century Jacksonian belief that the common man was superior to the urban intellectual, who often treated "country folk" with unwarranted condescension. Starting with the film *Ladies of Leisure*, Capra began to make a connection with the proletariat by proving that sophisticated city people with their large vocabulary and formal language were actually hypocrites, using the air of respectability to suppress anyone outside their circle. As a matter of fact, the villains in Capra's films use words as their primary means of attack. Leland Poague points out that in *Mr. Smith*, James Taylor is not so much a character as a sign of power exercised "chiefly as and through language."[63] All Capra's villains seem to do is make speeches, wishing to exert control either through smooth talk or by shouting at their underlings over the telephone. Big-city wheeler-dealers like Norton, Cedar, and Taylor, therefore, would rather use their intellect and words to manipulate the working man into giving up his liberty for their own selfish ends than engage in physical violence. Rather than breaking Smith's legs for disobeying him, Turner instead chooses to break Smith with words, by forging documents, starting a smear campaign in the press, and delivering an avalanche of letters to the Senate chamber. Cedar goes after Deeds in the courtroom, hoping to overcome his adversary with words and arguments. The language and words of the upper class, therefore, becomes just another form of fascism, either luring the common man into becoming his slave or overwhelming him into submission. Capra and Riskin both understood this fear and reflected the conflict between the upper and lower classes in the dialogue of their films, contrasting the slangy, stumbling lines of their heroes with the well-calculated, articulate words of their villains. In *Meet John Doe*, good guy Bert tells his wife that if "Sour Puss" is right, he's a "banana split," while bad guy Norton smoothly tells Connell that he is supporting the John Doe clubs for the "satisfaction of knowing that my money is spent for a worthy cause." The language of these two people could not be more different.

The contrast between the formal and the informal was further reinforced by casting. Capra found that actor Edward Arnold, who played the villain in three consecutive Capra films, was perfect for these roles because of his "phony laugh" and his penchant for blowing lines as a power play to get more attention than the other actors.[64] The theatrically trained British actor Claude Rains, in turn, made a perfect foil to the awkward, stuttering James Stewart in *Mr. Smith*. As Carney writes in *American Vision*, the choice of Rains to play Senator Paine was a stroke of genius on Capra's part, as Rains "represents, in every cadence and inflection of his voice, in every gesture and stance ... an essentially British theatrical form of expression, opposed in its very essence to everything for which Smith stands."[65] This use of British actors to play charming, well-spoken villains is still employed today, especially in animated films wherein the smooth voices of George Sanders (*The Jungle Book*), Peter Ustinov (*Robin Hood*), Jeremy Irons (*The Lion King*), and Peter O'Toole (*Ratatouille*) would be used as a contrast to the predominately American voices of the heroes.

All of Capra's most popular films, therefore, use the dialogue of their characters as the primary indicator of their allegiances. With the exception of *Lost Horizon*, which featured a British protagonist, well-spoken, polished lines were reserved for self-serving, manipulative villains, while genuine heroes spoke simply with genuine humility and true emotion. It was up to ordinary citizens to recognize the charming yet selfish intellectuals as the deceitful snakes they really were and to use good old-fashioned common sense to combat them in courtrooms and Senate chambers. By winning these smaller battles, ordinary people would also be protecting small-town Christian values from the self-serving, relativistic values of the city. This conflict between the two classes would be illustrated in many Depression-era films, including *The Grapes of Wrath*, but would also carry over into television, with popular shows like *The Andy Griffith Show*.[66] Capra plays out this class conflict three times in a row in the beginning of *Mr. Deeds Goes to Town*, when Longfellow Deeds sees through the machinations of the opera company, the lawyer representing his uncle's common-law wife, and, finally, the villain Cedar. A sample of the dialogue from one of these exchanges illustrates the contrast between those profoundly different men:

> CEDAR: I don't wish to press the point, Mr. Deeds, but if you'll give me your power of attorney, we'll take care of everything. It will save you a lot of petty annoyances. Every shark in town will be trying to sell you something.
> DEEDS: Oh, yes, there have been a lot of them around here already. Strangest kind of people, salesmen, politicians, butchers, all want something. I haven't had a minute to myself. Haven't seen Grant's Tomb yet.
> CEDAR: But you see, youre uncle didn't bother with that sort of thing. He left everything to us. He traveled most of the time, and enjoyed himself. You should do the same thing, Mr. Deeds.
> DEEDS: Besides wanting to be my lawyer, you want to handle my investments, too?
> CEDAR: Yes, that is to say...
> DEEDS: Outside of your regular fee, how much extra would it cost?
> CEDAR: Oh, nothing. No extra charge.
> DEEDS: But that involves a lot of extra work for you...
> CEDAR: Yes, yes, but that's an added service a firm like Cedar, Cedar, and Buddington usually donates.
> DEEDS: Buddington ... funny, I can't think of a rhyme for Buddington yet.

And then later in the scene:

> CEDAR: I think you ought to give this matter some thought, Mr. Deeds.
> DEEDS: Huh?
> CEDAR: I mean, about the power of attorney...
> DEEDS: Yes, yes, I will. I'll give it a lot of thought. There's a fella named, uh, Winslow here a little while ago, wanted to handle my business for nothing too. Puzzles me why these people all want to work for nothing. It isn't natural. So I guess I better think about it some more.

In these scenes and others like it, Longfellow's dialogue is honest, straight-forward and specific, while the dialogue of the urban sophisticates who want to use him is vague, generic, and condescending. In addition, the climaxes of Capra's films usually include a scene wherein the main characters, inspired by their female colleagues, must express their goals in sincere and passionate language in order to get what they want. Dave the Dude pleads his case at the police station, which ultimately leads to the involvement of the mayor and the governor. Peter's passionate speech about his love for Ellie convinces his editor to advance him a thousand dollars so he can propose to her. Deeds, newly inspired by Babe's declaration of love, defends himself in his court hearing, and John Willoughby tells off Norton and his cronies on the night of the John Doe convention. In perhaps one of the most moving scenes in film history, Jefferson Smith, his voice cracking and barely audible, defends his ideals in his passionate improvisational filibuster on the floor of the Senate. With these endings, Capra illustrates his belief that while the controlling forces in America are usually better at communication and manipulation, the common man can triumph over them by learning to speak their ideas passionately and sincerely, as their ideas are, by their very nature, more in tune with the will of the people.

Through the language of his heroes, Capra takes sides in the great class struggle of the 1930s, showing a preference for small towns over cities, working men over executives, straight truth over cloying flattery, and slang over sophistication. Although this preference seems odd coming from a wealthy, college-educated director from Los Angeles, it was not uncommon for Hollywood directors to make films intentionally designed to appeal to the working class. The movies were art for the masses, and Capra understood that for his ideas to be heard, they must be expressed in the language of the people.

It comes as no surprise, then, that Capra reveres men of action over men of intellect. This anti-intellectual bent may have reflected Capra's own personal attitude towards intellectuals on the East Coast, who not only showed a disdain for Hollywood, but also saddled Capra with the unflattering "Capracorn" label. He may have also inherited this stance early in his career from producer Mack Sennett, who notoriously distrusted anyone who was literate.[67] In interviews throughout his life, Capra continued to attack the intellectual elite, claiming they were more connected to Europe than their own country.[68] In an especially telling interview towards the end of his life, Capra claimed that, in times of stress, ordinary people who knew how to plant a seed or sow the grass would survive, while "all the intellectuals will be knocked off or starve."[69] Although Capra was a college graduate, he preferred to number himself among the working class, making sure to recount in his autobiography the physical labor he engaged in throughout his life, including working four jobs in high school to earn extra money.[70]

Like Capra, the heroes in his stories are not afraid of getting their hands dirty, but rather than working for money, they work to achieve their dreams. Robert Conway stays up late writing telegrams on the plane even after barely escaping China alive; Ann learns that John Willoughby is homeless because he injured his arm pitching a 19-inning game; Dan Brooks works all night, braving a severe thunderstorm in order to keep Broadway Bill dry. Longfellow Deeds does not leave his house for two weeks when working on his loan program to farmers, and Jefferson Smith comes back to his office late at night to work on his bill after attending a party, and pushes himself to physical exhaustion during his filibuster. Even though Alice is the only one in the Vanderhof family who seems to work a legitimate job in *You Can't Take It with You*, all the members of the family are industrious, busy working on their own individual passions. In Capra's films, love, family, and success only come to his heroes after work is completed. In *Mr. Deeds*, Longfellow cannot have a relationship with Babe until after he devotes himself fully to the work of loaning out money to farmers. Happiness in Shangri-La only comes to the Westerners *after* they actively involve themselves in the physical work of improving the city. (George, unlike the others, never engages in any physical activity in Shangri-La so he is naturally the most discontent.) In addition, Saunders only declares her love to Smith as he approaches exhaustion during his filibuster. In Capra's world, one must work before reaping any rewards.

In addition, unlike the work of the villains in these stories, the work of Capra's heroes is mostly physical and done for the benefit of *all* the people, not just a selected few. D.B. Norton, Anthony Kirby, Sr., Jim Taylor, and John Cedar do their work wearing well tailored coats and ties in private boardrooms, around desks and dinner tables, while Capra's heroes, disheveled and unshaven, perform their duties in full view of the public. The aggrandizement of hard labor and practical work was not only found in the films of Frank Capra, however, but was used throughout the 1930s as a way to invigorate a disheartened and disgruntled work force who felt they were not receiving their just due. According to John Savage's book, *Teenage*, Roosevelt's New Deal claimed to renew America by rejecting the 1920s principle of crass materialism and replacing it with "a pioneer vision of hard work for the collective good."[71] The theme would also carry over into many of Capra's war documentaries, wherein young G.I.s were shown how physical labor would be the best antidote in stopping the spread of the Axis powers.

What is unusual about Capra's films, however, is that the villains of these stories, men like Cedar, Taylor, and Anthony Kirby, Sr., are usually the ones who have specific goals to accomplish in the films. According to Leland

Poague, Capra's heroes, although hard working, are typically dreamers and visionaries who are not particularly goal oriented.[72] They are less active than "acted upon." As a result, the plot is usually driven by these lawyers and businessmen, who, although they do not expend much physical energy, use the system they control to attack the heroes and force them to defend their ideals. The villains, therefore, take on the role of aggressors, so the heroes can be depicted as righteous defenders. Although these men seem to stop at nothing to achieve their ends, their complicated schemes are usually self-serving and void of any kind of lasting ideology. In *Lost Horizon*, for instance, George's primary problem is that he thinks too much about his own desire to leave Shangri-La, while the other Westerners think less and work more, creating a home there by taking on projects to better the lives of the natives. Paradise, therefore, is not a life of ease and comfort, but doing what you love in the service of others. Unlike George, Henry Barnard (Thomas Mitchell) understands that lesson in Shangri-La, abandoning his selfish gold scheme in favor of modernizing the plumbing for all the people of the valley.

Capra believed taking action required people to vigorously fight for what they believed. In 1971, he would tell a group of directors that for a director to go as far as he could, he "has to say no; he has to argue, he has to fight."[73] Fighting sometimes meant getting your point across with your fists. Capra proved time and time again early in his life that he was not afraid of confrontations, even if they turned physical. Although he claimed not to go looking for fights in high school, as a poor immigrant outsider, he was often forced into fighting to preserve his self-respect. "If somebody said a word about my clothes," he wrote, "I'd kick him right in the ass or right in the balls."[74] Capra believed physical action was in many cases required to resolve conflict. This belief was shared by many men and boys during the Great Depression, those who lived vicariously through fictional men of action like Popeye and Superman. Even Little Orphan Annie was known for beating up bullies who crossed her or her friends. Capra's heroes are no different, rejecting passive alternatives to fighting and often resorting to violence when they have been tricked or humiliated. Peter Warne beats up Danker when he tries to steal the couple's luggage, Jefferson Smith hunts down and punches out the reporters who humiliated him, and John Willoughby punches out Norton's nephew. Twice in *Mr. Deeds*, Capra intentionally stretches out the humiliation of his title character, once in the restaurant and again in the climactic trial scene. By forcing the audience to witness the painful suffering heaped upon someone they know to be decent and kind, Capra increases the longing for catharsis, which he relieves only through an act of violence. This same technique would be used in *Why We Fight*, when he overwhelms the viewer with images of innocents unjustly destroyed, hoping that the images will compel the viewers to take up arms against those responsible. After the restaurant scene in *Mr. Deeds*, when Longfellow is told the next morning that socking people in the nose is no solution for anything, he responds that "sometimes it's the only solution." One can imagine this response applauded by audiences of the time, as they were finally seeing the intellects, the men usually in power in the real world, get their comeuppance on the big screen. It comes as no surprise then that Capra's heroes suffer no consequences for these sudden, violent actions. Senator Smith receives no censure for attacking reporters on the streets of Washington, and Longfellow Deeds is declared in the courtroom to be the "sanest man" the judge ever met, even after Deeds concludes his closing statement by punching John Cedar. The masculinity of Capra's heroes, therefore, is not determined by their sexual prowess (Jeff and Clarissa, Peter and Ellie, for instance, do not even share one onscreen kiss) but by their ability to hold their own in a fight. They are clearly more fighters than lovers. This belief that one often has to resort to violent action to resolve conflicts with people who wield their power in irresponsible ways, would become one of the justifications Capra uses for going to war in the *Why We Fight* series. Capra's heroes prove that sometimes the only way to stop a bully is a "sock in the nose."

This belief in the fighting spirit of ordinary Americans, the righteousness of common sense and small-town values over the selfish intellectualism of the cities, the reliance on good old-fashioned hard work to solve our country's problems did not begin with Capra's films, but comes from the long lasting spirit of populism that has its roots with the founding father, Thomas Jefferson. In a sense, Longfellow Deeds's plan to redistribute money to a large number of small, independent farmers is very similar to Jefferson's vision of America nearly 150 years earlier.[75] Although raised in the city of Los Angeles, Capra, like Jefferson, believed in the purity of rural America, where success was measured by hard work and determination. In an interview late in life, Capra shared his feelings about big cities, saying: "I saw the very seamy side of the city—the alleys—so I wasn't particularly impressed with the city. I thought people in the country were more honest, and had more love for each other than people in the city."[76] It is no coincidence, then, that many of Capra's most popular heroes come from small towns whose citizens love and cherish them. The beginning of *Arsenic and Old Lace*, written specifically for the film, shows a fight break out at a baseball game, equating the big city of Brooklyn with violence and disorder. It is no surprise then, that Abraham Lincoln, who rose up from humble beginnings in Kentucky and Illinois, is the president most often seen in Capra's films. Lincoln, an outsider who traveled to Washington in the midst of the country's greatest crisis, and whose plain talk, strong work ethic, and adherence to a strict moral code brought the nation together, became the perfect role model for Deeds, Smith, and Willoughby. Capra even cast tall actors in these "Lincolnesque" roles to accentuate the connection. Lincoln, more than the current president, Franklin D. Roosevelt, whose blue blood roots and intellectual demeanor disqualified him as a representative for the populist cause, became the "go-to" founding father for Capra, as he was not only a martyr for his cause but a man respected by the majority of Americans despite their political affiliation.

The populist stance of Capra's films was a "win-win" for Capra as it allowed him to make political statements without offending members of either political party. Perhaps it was because Capra, a professed Republican, often chose Leftist partners to help him write his stories. It is more likely, however, that Capra's films satisfy both Democrats and Republicans, because the populist ideology contains elements of both political parties. Democrats see in Capra's films a reinforcement of some of their core beliefs— the importance of free speech, the need to protect the "little guy" from the greedy, the condemnation of big business, and the redistribution of wealth in order to help people out in times of trouble. Republicans, on the other hand, can point out that Capra's films also condemn taxes, lawyers, big government, and handouts to people who don't deserve it, as well as show the inefficiency and corruption of bureaucracies. Capra's ideology, being tied to the populism of past figures like Jefferson and Lincoln, was just vague enough to give all Americans what they wanted without offending anyone — a rare feat at a time when partisan battles and angry rhetoric filled newspapers and congressional chambers.

It is important to note, however, that Capra's ability to attract mainstream American audiences in a time of political discord, through the use of humor, plain-speaking common sense, and populist ideology, was not altogether new. Radio, film, and newspaper star Will Rogers was the first to ride the populist train to great media success. Capra was well aware of Rogers's popularity and personal magnetism, having met him at the Hal Roach studios in the mid-twenties. In his autobiography, he also claims that Rogers not only let the young writer use his dressing room as an office, but also recommended him for a job with Mack Sennett. From the 1920s to the mid–1930s, Will Rogers's simple wit and common-sense approach made him one of America's most popular personalities. Star of radio, stage, screen, and print, Rogers wrote over 667 weekly articles in his syndicated column from 1922 to 1935, and was the biggest box-office draw in 1934.[77] His untimely death in a plane crash in 1935, however, left the populist ideology without a spokesman. Capra thus took up the gauntlet, replacing Rogers as the face of populism, hoping to share in his idol's popularity. *Mr. Deeds Goes to Town*, the film that would establish the Capra common-sense, small-town ideology, would arrive in theaters less than a year after Rogers's tragic death.

2. The Capra Formula 95

While Capra's populist bent condones the righteous action of the individual, he is much more skeptical about the action of groups, which are easily manipulated and can quickly devolve into dangerous mobs. This concern was shared with many Americans in the late '30s, who saw ordinary people in Germany, Italy, and Japan bow to the demands of fascist leaders without offering much resistance. As early as *American Madness*, Capra showed the dangerous changeability of people gathered together as a group. The mob in *American Madness*, as well as in *Broadway Bill*, illustrates the tendency of mob behavior to grow out of individual action. In these films, the greedy actions of individuals snowball into a mass movement, automatons devoid of common sense and logic. Mobs, therefore, can easily occur in America as a byproduct of individual freedom. Other Capra films, like *Lost Horizon* and *Bitter Tea of General Yen*, illustrate the potential danger and destruction of panicking mobs. Even the supportive crowd at the end of *Mr. Deeds*, when Deeds is declared sane, jump over tables to get to him, carry him out of the courtroom against his will, and rip his clothes. The senators in *Mr. Smith* all seem to act in the same way, whether they are booing, cheering, ignoring, or laughing at Jefferson Smith. In these films, Capra saw the mass as diametrically opposed to the individual. Thus, when asked what he was fighting against in *Mr. Deeds* and *Mr. Smith*, Capra responded: "Massism — mass entertainment, mass production, mass education, mass everything. Especially mass man. I was fighting for, in a sense, the preservation of liberty of the individual person against the mass."[78] In addition to showing the negative impact of this massism on one's individual liberty, two of Capra's films also illustrate how quickly large groups can devolve into rioting free-for-alls. The prisoners in the drunk tank with Kirby and Vanderhof go from dancing together in the jail cell to nearly ripping one another apart over the banker's discarded cigar. In *Meet John Doe*, through the direct intervention of Norton and his cronies at the John Doe convention, ordinary men and women change from a pleasant group singing "My Country 'Tis of Thee" to a demented mob yelling for John's destruction.

This belief, that people were much less effective as a group than they were on their own, also seeped into Capra's professional life. Edward Bernds, the sound man for *Mr. Smith Goes to Washington*, recalled a moment during production when Capra got angry at the extras who were wandering off the set. Furious, the director shouted, "These are the people, the fellows you want to do things for. I wonder — maybe the mob is so lazy, so stupid, so wrongheaded that only harsh leadership of energetic, able men is practical."[79] Groups, in other words, require leaders in order to motivate them to positive action. It is no wonder that Capra at one point had a picture of Mussolini, a man whose leadership at first seemed good for the Italian people, on his bedroom wall. (In fact, according to Joseph McBride, in 1935, Mussolini wanted to finance a $1 million film that he would write and Capra would direct. Harry Cohn went so far as to send someone to discuss the offer with the dictator, but ultimately turned it down because of Il Duce's association with Hitler.)[80]

Thus, Capra believed that whether large groups would have a negative or positive impact on the world depended entirely on the intentions of the leaders they blindly followed. Leaders like Smith, Deeds, and Willoughby, all of whom speak plainly and openly, encourage cooperation over competition, and stay mostly apolitical. Intellectual, smooth-talking men like Norton, Paine, and Taylor use their power to control the press, serve their own self interest and hidden agendas, and win the public over by making promises they never intend to keep. The danger of the group, as Capra sees it, is that they are equally likely to support one of these leaders as another. The only exception seems to be children, who can easily spot the difference between the two types of leaders, and stand behind idealistic men like Jefferson Smith even in their darkest hours.

Although the treatment of people in Capra's films reflect the growing fear many Americans had of another world war erupting in Europe, they also showed that groups of people can also be easily molded into a force of good if they are led by the right person. These leaders, in the tradition of American heroes like Washington and Lincoln, speak emotionally and honestly, work hard mainly in the service of others, are not afraid to fight to defend their "boyish" ideals, and support the policy of "Love Thy Neighbor." Men, in other words, a lot like Frank Capra — at least the person Frank Capra wanted to be.

The Fight for Freedom

During the course of writing this book, I have slowly discovered what I believe to be the key element in most of Capra's films: the struggle between the righteous individual and the fascistic powers that mean to control him/her. Starting with *The Bitter Tea of General Yen*, Capra began musing on the importance of liberty in everyday life. Many of his films begin with his hero or heroine unwillingly being placed in a position of confinement, or loss of freedom. Meagan comes to China to marry a virtual stranger in *Bitter Tea*; Ellie Andrews is held prisoner on her father's yacht; and Dan Brooks is held prisoner by his father-in-law, who wants him to be something he is not. In *Lost Horizon*, Conway is trapped in the middle of a terrible riot in China, and John Willoughby begins *Meet John Doe* with a broken arm (which he slangily calls a "broken wing"), which prevents him from working as a pitcher. In the beginning of these films, all of these characters long for something more: to break free from the confining status quo so they can realize their true potential. This breaking out of one world, however, only makes them more vulnerable, as they end up under the thumb of another, greater power, who once again threatens their liberty. In *Bitter Tea*, Megan is kidnapped by General Yen. In *It Happened One Night*, Ellie Andrews trades her dictatorial father for the confident but controlling Peter Warne. In *Lost Horizon*, Conway escapes from China, only to be kidnapped again by Chang and taken to Shangri-La. In *Broadway Bill*, Dan's lack of funds exposes him and Bill to the manipulative forces of the racing world. In *Meet John Doe*, John Willoughby makes a deal to get his arm fixed, but as a result, has to let Ann, Connell, and Norton tell him what to do. In *Arsenic and Old Lace*, Mortimer willingly gives up his freedom in order to marry Elaine, but becomes trapped in the Brewster house by the murderous acts of his aunts and brother. Even if Capra's heroes start off free, they are eventually threatened with the loss of liberty by some controlling power, who wants the hero to give up the very part of them that makes them special. In *Mr. Deeds Goes to Town*, Longfellow moves to New York, where his individualistic actions make him a target for both Babe and John Cedar. In *Lady for a Day*, Annie changes everything about herself in order to impress her future in-laws. In *You Can't Take It with You*, Grandpa Vanderhof is threatened with the loss of his house by both Anthony Kirby, Sr., and the federal government.

To combat these controlling forces, Capra's heroes must undergo a certain amount of risk. If they fail, their endeavors put them in danger of permanently losing their freedom. In *Bitter Tea*, Meagan puts her life on the line for Mah-Li. Ellen risks abandonment by declaring her love for Peter in *It Happened One Night*. Longfellow Deeds is threatened with being committed to an asylum because he risks his inheritance on a farming scheme. Dan Brooks bets his entire future on Broadway Bill — even though losing would mean returning to work for J.L. Higgins and never being allowed to race again. Grandpa Vanderhof risks losing his house to win his granddaughter back and convert Anthony Kirby, Sr. Jefferson Smith is threatened with censure, humiliation, and the loss of his dream when taking on Turner, while John Doe is threatened with exposure as a fraud, which would forever end his dreams of playing baseball. Capra's heroes suffer for trying these risky schemes, but without the attempt, they could never achieve the level of freedom they ultimately enjoy. Thus, Capra believes that risk taking is integral in the fight for one's freedom, even if it means losing everything. Capra's fight for independence and control over his films within the oppressive studio system proved that he practiced what he preached.

Many times, the heroes' belief that they can win the fight against the oppressive forces that threaten to take away their liberty is based on false hope. In *Bitter Tea*, Meagan puts her trust in Mah-Li and is betrayed. Broadway Bill's popularity at the racetrack is based on gossip and rumor, and Dan thinks he has the chance to win even though his jockey is bought and paid for. Deeds believes Babe loves him, which encourages him to act freely when, in reality, Babe pokes fun at his behavior in the press. Jeff moves forward with his bill under the mistaken belief that Paine is behind him. John Willoughby goes ahead with the John Doe clubs without realizing Norton is using the clubs to jump start his own political career. What Capra, then, seems to be saying with these films is that the reasons people undertake the fight for their freedom are less important than the fight itself. Although the heroes are deluded in the belief that they are supported in their fight to win their independence and validate their value systems, their actions inspire others to join their cause and enact real social change. This stance of Capra's is disconcerting as it seems to show that the director would have no ethical problem deluding young men who were drafted to fight in World War II. As long as the cause was right, the reasons given do not have to necessarily be true.

Capra resolves the confrontation between individuals and the dictators who seek to control them in a myriad of ways. Sometimes, the two opposing forces reach a mutual agreement, with what amounts to a slight conversion of the authority figure, as it does in *It Happened One Night*, *Broadway Bill*, and *You Can't Take It with You*. In these films, the fascist powers, which all happen to be fathers, come to respect and even admire the freedom and self sufficiency of the impetuous individuals they face. In *The Bitter Tea of General Yen*, the tyrant figure, seeing himself as no longer relevant in the modern world, kills himself. The newly freed individual, Megan, is allowed to live the rest of her life as she wishes, but has come to admire and perhaps even love the man who imprisoned her. In *Lost Horizon* and *Lady for a Day*, the main characters actually give up part of their individuality and let themselves be "handled" by the ruling authority, but they do so in order to create a better world for the next generation. In other films, the opposition between the individual and the "dictatorial" figure is not so easily resolved, and usually ends in the triumph of one power at the expense of the other. In these films, *Mr. Deeds Goes to Town*, *Mr. Smith Goes to Washington*, and *Meet John Doe*, the two forces remain enemies, and the heroes become martyrs who suffer unduly for their cause. *Mr. Deeds* is the only film in which the individual is truly victorious, perhaps because John Cedar is a much weaker foe than either Norton or Taylor. In *Mr. Smith Goes to Washington*, the martyrdom of Jefferson Smith converts Paine, a man who has lost himself in the system, but the film does not resolve Smith's conflict with the more imposing fascist, Jim Taylor. In *Meet John Doe*, Capra's last film before the war, John Willoughby's only victory is that he manages to keep from killing himself. At the problematic end of the film, which we have already discussed, Norton is unmoved by Willoughby's heroic determination to live. While the film ends on a hopeful note, the viewer is left with the feeling that, although the John Doe movement may carry on, it will never reach the great heights it achieved with the backing of Norton. The conflict remains unresolved, as it does in both the *Why We Fight* films and *It's a Wonderful Life*.

One can see Capra's preoccupation with the fight against fascism as a symptom of working in the studio system. When Capra was getting along with Cohn at Columbia, his films tend to endorse the idea that individuals with ideas must either learn to work within the system or try to convert those in power to their way of thinking. As Capra grew apart from Columbia in the late 1930s, his films seem to accept the idea that long-term conversion is basically impossible for those in power because they would have to admit they had weaknesses. The only real way to get one's voice heard is to gather together a core group of supporters who believe in one's cause and work against these powers on a grass roots level. This solution is partially illustrated in *Mr. Smith Goes to Washington*, as Saunders uses the Boy Rangers to spread the word of Jeff's innocence, as well as in *Meet John Doe*, where John Willoughby walks off with a handful of supporters. In fact, the very production of *Meet John Doe* could be considered a test of this solution, as Capra made the film outside the studio system, with a handful of his most talented friends and supporters. Thus, the ending of *Meet John Doe* was difficult for Capra and Riskin to write because they had no way of knowing if such a plan would actually work. Either the film would be a success and prove that small groups can make a difference, or it would fail, and a new solution to the problem would have to be discovered.

We know now that *Meet John Doe* would prove to be a disappointment for Capra. Although his reputation was not hurt by the well-made but ultimately flawed film, Capra's dream of owning his own production company abruptly ended. As a result, Capra would retreat back to the studio system, this time to Warner Bros., to make a film almost entirely for the money. Like Mortimer Brewster, who married Elaine even though it went against all his earlier beliefs, Capra compromised his freedom for stability and the promise of a new life, hoping to put his past behind him. This attempt of Capra's to reexamine how he fit into the system may have also prompted his enlistment in the army. Capra seemed to understand at this point in his life that a strong authoritarian force was necessary in order for him to reach a large audience. In his *Why We Fight* films, Capra devised a new solution to the problem — that sometimes it becomes necessary to give up one's individual liberty to a higher authority, if and only if that sacrifice will protect one's family from a harsher, more authoritarian regime.

And so, when Capra left Hollywood to produce documentaries during World War II, he took along with him all the tools that made him a success. His theories about fascism and individuality, his philosophy and idealism, his shooting and editing techniques, his ability to sell lofty ideals in practical terms, all served him well in his new role in the Special Services, where he would produce a library of propaganda films unequalled in American history. These films, like his fictional films of the '30s, helped define America during a critical point in its history, while attempting to persuade thousands of troops to give up their lives in the service of their country.

3

The Roots of Why We Fight

Before embarking on a thorough analysis of Capra's war documentaries, however, it becomes necessary to delve into the reasons he joined the army in the first place. Analyzing these motivations will give greater insight into Capra's attitude during the production of these films as well as provide clues to understanding the filmmaker himself. It was hypothesized at the end of the previous chapter that Capra joined the army in an attempt to reinvent himself after the failure of *Meet John Doe*. In addition, Capra seemed to be finally coming to terms with the necessity of working under someone's control in order to reach a mass audience, having already done so with *Arsenic and Old Lace*. His one-film deal with Warner Bros., unfortunately, proved to be only a temporary fix for Capra. With the outbreak of war, Warner Bros. was forced to cut back production, which meant the elimination of production deals with any director outside the system.[1] Had Capra not joined the army, he may have found himself without a studio home throughout the war, not unlike being the only person left standing in a game of musical chairs.

In his autobiography, first published in 1971, Capra proffered two additional reasons why he joined the service at the time. First, he felt he had successfully "climbed the mountain" of Hollywood and was becoming bored with his success, no longer challenged to create anything new. Capra confessed to being "an uphill man." "When my motor races uphill," he wrote," my interest rises. When it idles on the flat, I'm bored."[2] Second, he admitted that his great success had taken a toll on his soul. He had made a living making films about the poor and downtrodden and felt like a phony and a hypocrite, living "like the Aga Khan."[3] This guilt, this feeling of undeserved success, which originated in Capra after the immense popularity of *It Happened One Night*, is not at all unusual in high achievers, especially in Hollywood, where fame and fortune is both illusory and arbitrary. Joan Harvey, a psychologist who studied this phenomenon, wrote that a person who suffers this guilt also "fear[s] that sooner or later some humiliating failure [will] reveal his secret and unmask him as a fraud."[4] By joining the army, Capra could escape both the Hollywood lifestyle and the feelings of guilt and unworthiness that went

Capra was both intimidated and influenced by the propaganda films of Leni Riefenstahl (pictured right, with Hitler) when he made his *Why We Fight* films. (Synapse Films/Photofest)

with it. To Capra, the army "was a welcome out for [me]; a clean, respectable way to turn down enslaving million dollar contracts that form, courtesy, acclaim, and forward momentum were forcing [me] to accept."[5] In addition, joining the army during the war "gave one a superior aura of patriotism and self sacrifice — qualities one rarely has the chance to flaunt in the faces of his peers."[6]

Furthermore, Capra had always been a supporter of the U.S. military. Previous to his World War II career, Capra joined the army during World War I after graduating from Cal Tech (then called Throop Polytechnic), teaching soldiers ballistic mathematics in San Francisco.[7] Another time, with the help of his cameraman Joe Walker and a hired machinist, Capra produced several inventions in a small store on Santa Monica Boulevard for use in the military. Two of these inventions — wind cups that would spin aircraft wheels prior to landing and a selenium-celled see through grid for antiaircraft gunners — were donated to Howard Hughes for use in the military, free of charge.[8]

Despite this service to the military, Capra still found himself on the wrong side of the government throughout the 1930s. When he was president of the Screen Actors Guild in 1938, the Guild voted to support the writer's strike of the *Hollywood Citizen News*, which had fired five staff members in retaliation for an attempt at unionization. Frank Capra, along with director John Ford, was photographed joining the picket line in May of that year. This action, along with the fact that Capra was foreign born, made him a target of the House Un-American Activities Committee (HUAC), which had been created nine days after Capra was photographed supporting the strikers. In addition, U.S. Army Intelligence was looking into the political views of the director in 1938. At that time he was working on *Mr. Smith Goes to Washington* which had been written by Sidney Buchman, an active member of the Communist Party.[9] Such negative interactions with the federal government compelled Capra to constantly defend his patriotism and citizenship. As penance for the previous instance, Capra decided to direct a short play on *America Calling*, a special patriotic NBC radio show which aired on December 14, 1938 — the same year Capra became the highest-paid director in the industry.[10]

Frank Capra's devotion to America was further questioned with the release of *Mr. Smith Goes to Washington*, which premiered in Washington, D.C., in October of 1939. As mentioned earlier, although Capra and many critics believed the film showed the triumph of democracy, many in Washington misunderstood the film and interpreted it as a Hollywood criticism of how the government was run in the nation's capital. Senator James Byrnes of South Carolina called it "the kind of picture that dictators of totalitarian governments would like to have their subjects believe exists in a democracy."[11] Joseph Kennedy, the U.S. ambassador in London, took matters a step further, wiring Harry Cohn, the head of Columbia Pictures, and warning him that releasing *Mr. Smith* would be a blow to our allies and may be construed as propaganda favoring the Axis powers.[12] In addition, big producing companies were offering Columbia $2,000,000 if the studio would withdraw *Mr. Smith* from circulation in an attempt to appease Congress and prevent punitive action against the industry.[13] Punitive action came in the form of Senate Bill No. 280, known as the Neely Anti-Block Booking Bill, which was passed shortly after the film was released. The bill, which author Gerald Gardner believed was pure revenge for *Mr. Smith*, made the compulsory block-booking deals illegal, effectively destroying the distribution system of the major studios.[14]

Capra had further incentive to prove his loyalty to the United States two years later, in 1941, the same year he decided to re-enlist in the U.S. Army. This time, the controversy revolved around the citizenship status of his sister, Ann, who moved to America with Frank in 1903. Although Ann thought she became a citizen when she married her first husband, she learned when registering under the Smith Act that she was still considered a citizen of Italy. This categorized her as an enemy alien, subject to travel and curfew restrictions as well as possible deportation. According to McBride, his sister's experience reminded Capra of his own tenuous immigrant crisis in World War I.[15] At that time, Capra found out he was not a naturalized U.S. citizen when he enlisted in the army. He had mistakenly thought that when his father became a naturalized citizen, he had become naturalized as well. He was allowed to join the army with his application for citizenship pending, and finally received his citizenship papers on June 4, 1920.[16]

Earlier that same year, Capra again felt compelled to make a public profession of his patriotism on the radio, this time appearing in a scripted interview show aptly titled *I'm an American!* which aired on March 23, 1941. When asked for his views on the war, Capra, although he had told the interviewer earlier that he was against war, stated in the on air interview that "our obligation to the world is to show that democracy will work. We may have to do this at the risk of our lives."[17]

Thus, Capra's enlistment in the U.S. Army was caused by a combination of guilt, boredom, and insecurity, and he consequently gave up a lucrative career in Hollywood for a peak monthly salary of $333.33.[18] Whatever the reason for enlisting, Capra joined the ranks of John Huston, John Ford, W.S. (Woody) Van Dyke, and William Wyler, as one of the few major directors who chose to enlist at a time when the movie business was booming. And so, Frank Capra arrived in Washington February 15, 1941, ready to employ his acclaimed filmmaking talents on behalf of an adoptive country skeptical about his patriotism.

Capra, like fellow director John Huston, joined the army hoping to be sent to a photography unit on the front lines. Huston, after weeks of "begging to be sent where the action was," would travel to Alaska to make *Report from the Aleutians*, and later to Italy to direct the acclaimed *Battle of San Pietro*.[19] Frank Capra, however, would never get his wish.[20] His one and only instance came when he was working on the film *Tunisian Victory* in 1943. While staying with Huston in London, Capra received his first and only up-close view of war, when bombs were dropped on the city from German planes. McBride mentions in *Catastrophe of Success* that although at the time Capra may have been preoccupied with the film (or perhaps could not have expressed his full range of feelings), his comments about the attack he communicated to his wife "conveyed not dismay but excitement that he finally was an eyewitness to war."[21] (As we shall discuss in Chapter 6, however, this brief encounter with the effects of the war may have actually had a greater impact on Capra than McBride acknowledges.) In spite of this one particular incident, Capra would spend most of the war stationed in America, working with footage shot by men who witnessed the true reality of war through their lenses. He would, however, use this footage to produce 17 films in only three

3. The Roots of Why We Fight

years, including the groundbreaking seven-part series *Why We Fight*, which is considered the most famous film achievement of the U.S. War Department.[22]

Of course, Frank Capra could not predict these results when he walked into the Army Signal Corps office in February. Within six days of his arrival, Capra learned that he had been transferred to the Information Division of the Special Services. Darryl F. Zanuck, head of Twentieth Century–Fox, was already working for the Signal Corps, and Colonel Schlosberg told Capra that one filmmaker in his outfit was enough. "You Hollywood guys just won't fit in with the Army way of producing films," he explained.[23] Capra claimed to know very little about how to make a documentary, stating in his autobiography that, at the time, he saw documentaries as "ash-can films made by kooks with long hair."[24]

In actuality, Capra had made one documentary early in his career. According to Joseph McBride, on November 6 and 7, 1921, Capra shot a short documentary film for the Italian Virtus Club in San Francisco to commemorate the two-week visit of the Italian ship *Libia*. The film was shown at the People's Theater on December 3, four months before Capra claimed in his autobiography that he shot his first film, *Fulta Fisher's Boarding House*. This detail refutes Capra's claim in *The Name Above the Title* that he simply walked on a set and started directing his first film without any previous experience.[25] Regardless, Capra's skills were proven in directing fiction films, so he wanted to employs his skills shooting on the front, not overseeing the production of propaganda.

The U.S. Army, it appears, had different plans for him. In his first meeting with General George C. Marshall, the army chief of staff, the general explained his purpose for having Capra transferred to the Morale section of Special Services. The general felt strongly that young Americans, even those who grew up in the isolationist atmosphere of the previous decade, could be good soldiers if they knew why they were in uniform and understood the cause for which they were fighting. The enemy soldiers were already highly indoctrinated and highly trained, and if American soldiers were to meet them on the field of battle, they must believe in the Allied cause as much as the Axis believed in theirs. Capra was won over by the general's passionate belief in his cause and in the director's abilities, and quickly went to work on what was to become the *Why We Fight* series. He entered his small office (furnished with five empty desks) intimidated, confused, and without "the foggiest idea" of how to make the documentary films General Marshall wanted.[26] It was an auspicious beginning to what would become the most challenging and far-reaching government projects ever undertaken by a film director. By the war's end, Capra would be left confused about his role in the war as well as emotionally and creatively drained, returning to an industry that had moved on without him.

Frank Capra realized in a short amount of time that making films for the government would be much different than making films in Hollywood. This distinction became crucially important while Capra made his documentary films for the military. Not only would he have to work within the limitations of this new production environment, he would also have to fight the natural skepticism and resistance both the American public and Congress held towards anything that smelled remotely like propaganda. Although the roots of Capra's documentary films would mainly come from his fictional films of the 1930s, government-produced films, American newsreels, and Nazi propaganda films all played an important part in their construction as well. It is important, therefore, to analyze these outside influences so we can separate their influence on the *Why We Fight* films from the influence of Capra's popular narrative films before the war.

Government Films before 1941

The division to which Capra first reported had, in fact, a long history of film production previous to World War II. Although historians cannot pinpoint the precise creation date of the U.S. Army Signal Corps, their earliest training and education films date back to 1909.[27] The role of the Signal Corps expanded during World War I, as the need for more training and orientation films increased with the enlistment of new troops. They supervised the production of 62 training films, maintained a visual historical record, and provided footage to newsreel companies and government-sponsored documentaries throughout the course of the war.[28]

America's entry into World War I also witnessed the first use of motion pictures in war. In 1917, one week after the U.S. entered the Great War, President Wilson created the Committee on Public Information (CPI) under journalist George Creel.[29] The CPI conducted propaganda through films, posters, pamphlets, and lectures, all aimed at squelching any anti-war sentiments and convincing the public that the war and the sacrifices of our soldiers were necessary to preserve democracy.[30] Before the war, most Americans viewed propaganda in a fairly positive light, seeing it simply as the spreading of opinions through publicity.[31] In addition to its propaganda activities, the CPI managed the footage shot by Signal Corps cameramen in both the U.S. and France, and distributed most of the footage to newsreel companies for a low price. The remaining footage was made into feature-length films by the CPI.

The three most important feature film documentaries produced by the

CPI during World War I are considered to be *Pershing's Crusaders*, *America's Answer*, and *Under Four Flags*. At first, the films were distributed to patriotic societies and played in theaters free of charge. This system was not only expensive, it did not allow large groups of people to see the films. CPI thus became an exhibitor for their own films, sending as many as eight road companies to promote and advertise exclusive and "official" showings, much like the agit-prop trains used by the Soviets after the Bolshevik Revolution. By the time the CPI was abolished by Congress in June of 1919, *Pershing's Crusaders* and *America's Answer* had played over 4,000 theater bookings and had made about $180,000 each in film rentals. *Under Four Flags* fared less well, with 1,800 bookings and over $60,000 in rentals.[32] The *Allied War Review*, a weekly series made in partnership with the CPI and our Allies, had almost 6,000 bookings and made over $334,000 total.[33] Overall, the CPI's division of films made $850,000 and had a circulation that reached about one-third of the U.S. population.[34]

The films of the CPI are virtually nonexistent now, as they contributed little to the development of film art. Although they incorporated actual war footage shot by the Signal Corps, CPI's films were considered too propagandist in nature, and like much of the Creel Committee's output, left a bitter taste in the mouths of many Americans. This opinion was not unusual at the time, as the use of propaganda to sway public opinion fell into disfavor immediately following the war. There was a fear that with the new modes of mass communication large governments had enough resources to enable them to easily manufacture the consent of the public.[35] The fear became a legitimate concern once knowledge leaked out about the half-truths and manipulations put out by Germany in their propaganda during the war.[36] Creel attempt to separate his material from Germany by refusing to call his efforts "propaganda," as "that word, in German hands, had come to be associated with deceit and corruption."[37]

Distaste for CPI, however, was not only due to the negative conception of propaganda tactics used by our enemies. There were legitimate complaints about the type of propaganda put out by the CPI as well. According to J. Michael Sproule, author of the book *Propaganda and Democracy*, American troops became disillusioned with the official view of the war while in Europe, as they discovered that the stories of the atrocities committed by German soldiers had been greatly exaggerated.[38] According to Allan Winkler in his book *Politics of Propaganda*, George Creel also made the mistake of overselling the war, stirring up "hatred of all things German," and generating false hopes of peace that were crushed in the years following the Treaty of Versailles.[39] As a result, the CPI experiment, although a success during the war, was a ultimately a failure in the long term, creating serious doubts among Americans and scholars about the use of propaganda to manipulate public opinion during a war. Capra would have to fight many similar battles during his wartime career. The failure of CPI's overt propaganda tactics, as well as the chaos of postwar Europe, left many Americans feeling that the Great War had been a costly mistake. Europe had not been fixed by America's involvement in the war, and had "swiftly slid into its historical vices of authoritarianism and armed rivalry," while America reverted back to its isolationist roots.[40] The ideas in the Creel films became outdated almost as soon as they had been released.

Nearly a decade after the Great War ended, Edward Bernays published a book resurrecting the idea of propaganda, claiming that it was necessary for governments in the modern world in order to maintain the "intimate relationship with the public."[41] Governments (like any business, including movie studios), he claimed, depend upon the acquiescence of the public in order for them to be successful.[42] Propaganda, therefore, aids in the transmission of ideas to the public in order to ultimately gain their interest and approval. The "astounding success" of the propaganda techniques used by the government during World War I opened Bernays's eyes to the possibility of creating a better relationship between the public and the government.[43] This could only occur, however, so long as the information related to the people was entirely truthful. Bernays kept the idea of propaganda, a word he often interchanged with public relations, alive at a time when the practice was at its lowest reputation. Throughout his book, he cites the many benefits of propaganda, claiming the practice could be used to benefit women's groups, universities, new inventions, and minority interests. Without the benefit of mass communication, many groups would be unable to reach a large enough population to espouse their ideas. Propaganda, therefore, is a necessary byproduct of the invention of mass communication. In order to make one's voice heard, one must understand not only how to communicate one's ideas through newspapers, radio, and film but also be able to manipulate the audience into agreement. According to Bernays, those who can use the media to manipulate the "habits and opinions of the masses" are the true ruling powers of our country.[44] In that case, the phenomenal success of Frank Capra in the next decade surely qualified him as a member of this "invisible government," as Bernays at the time called the "American motion picture the greatest unconscious carrier of propaganda in the world."[45]

Although the U.S. Signal Corps was not abolished with the CPI, it did see its overall production scaled back after the First World War, even as it increased its sphere of influence. In 1925, the Signal Corps was placed in charge of all army publicity and, by 1929, was in charge of all photographic and cinematic work by the army. It continued to make training and orienta-

3. The Roots of Why We Fight

tion films in the thirties, but the films produced were regarded as inferior in quality. Frank McCarthy, an aide to General Marshall in 1941 (and later a producer of the 1970 film *Patton*), felt the Signal Corps films before Capra's involvement were "a terrible bore, doctrinaire, with no creative quality at all. They imparted information, but had nothing that would grab a soldier and involve him emotionally."[46] General Marshall shared this opinion of the Corps' training and orientation films, and believed that Frank Capra would be the one to correct the sins of the CPI and the Signal Corps and make films of lasting importance.

A more substantial attempt to make government-produced documentary films was initiated in 1936 by the Roosevelt administration, which, early on, saw the importance of mass media to reach the American public. That year saw the release of Pare Lorentz's *The Plow That Broke the Plains*, a government-sponsored documentary film made for the Resettlement Administration. Lorentz, a novice film producer and director, made the 30-minute film for $19,260 on a budget of $6,000. He intended to use it to explain the causes of the Great Drought in the Midwest.[47] Its critical success, as well as the success of Lorentz's second film *The River*, showed that America could produce documentaries as well as any of its European neighbors, and prompted Roosevelt to form the U.S. Film Service in 1938. These two short films chronicled the destruction of the environment due to unrestrained capitalism, overproduction and waste. *The Plow That Broke the Plains* details the loss of the Great Plains due to the overproduction of wheat during the 1920s, and the inevitable decline that followed, turning the region into an uninhabitable Dust Bowl. *The River*, made for the Department of Agriculture, illustrates the flooding and the subsequent destruction of the Mississippi River by the lumber industry and the manufacturing interests set up along its banks.

As a whole, both films resemble Russian films more than anything Capra would produce over a half a decade later. The films move at a fairly steady and even pace, mixing beautifully photographed landscape shots with haunting, empty, silent shots of the aftermath of natural disasters (a trick Capra would employ in his *Why We Fight* films). As most of the shots in these documentaries were filmed expressly to be used in the films, many feel posed and staged. As in Russian films, *The Plow That Broke the Plains* and *The River* focus more on nature and society than on individuals. As such, most of the people in these films are seen in long shot and medium shots, with their faces either shadowed or turned away from the camera. In addition, the people featured in these films display little emotion; they stoically accept their fate as victims of these natural disasters, resigned to a life of misery and poverty. The films are elegantly scored, and the music is definitely prioritized over the narration, which is used sparsely in *The Plow That Broke the Plains*. The narration of *The River* is more poetic, and uses elevated language, repetition, and long lists to add drama and flavor to the piece. As in *Why We Fight*, animated maps are used to illustrate geography and to provide proper context. The editing is evenly and slowly paced, except for a few quick montage sequences. In *Plow*, Lorentz intercuts newsreel footage of cannon fire, explosions and war with headlines and scenes of wheat production to dramatize the agricultural overproduction that occurred during the war and the years that followed. In *The River*, shots of people preparing for a flood are punctuated by shots of lightning and the sounds of thunder. These explosive scenes briefly energize the somber mood of the film, a tactic used not only by Capra in his documentaries during World War II, but also by German filmmakers in their propaganda campaign films.

The creation of the U.S. Film Service by Roosevelt under the National Emergency Council united the country's documentary directors and provided a place where other government departments could bring their film ideas. The American documentary had finally become recognized, after years of existing on the fringe of the art world. Prompted by this endorsement, Mary Losey formed the Association of Documentary Film Producers in 1939 in an attempt to organize nonfiction filmmakers, who, up until this time, had been working in isolation.

The Film Service produced several notable documentaries, such as *Power and the Land*, *The Land*, *Fight for Life*, and *Ecce Homo*, but two factors caused its quick decline. For one, these films, which had been made by the government and not the studios, could not be distributed and reproduced in mass quantities like Hollywood pictures could. This difficulty is addressed in a review of *The River* by Gilbert Seldes in *Scribner's*:

> [*The River*] stands, therefore, totally out of line of commercial films, and this may have some effect on its distribution. (The reluctance of exhibitors hindered the showing of Mr. Lorentz's earlier documentary film, *The Plow That Broke the Plains*.) I have so often advised readers to protest against the films they do see, that I now feel free to urge them with all the vehemence and authority I may possess to demand the showing of this picture at their local movie houses.[48]

Seldes would never get his wish. Without the popular support needed to keep it funded, the Film Service was left to wither away to nothing. More importantly (and perhaps not surprisingly), the fact that these documentaries were funded by the Roosevelt Administration caused both the public and Congress to be dubious about their motives.[49] In a *New York Times* report on the difficulties of getting the public to see *The Plow That Broke the Plains*, a distributor was quoted saying: "If any private company or individual made this picture, it would be a documentary film. When the government makes it, it automatically becomes a propaganda picture."[50] As such, the films were labeled "New Deal Propaganda," and the Film Service was unceremoniously dissolved by Congress on June 30, 1940.

The failure of the U.S. Film Service, however, would pave the way for the success of Capra documentaries only a few years later. Service documentary filmmakers Robert Flaherty and Joris Ivens would work for Capra's unit, and footage from *The River* and *The Land* would make it into some of his war films.[51] The documentaries of the U.S. Film Service also showed that it was possible for the government to produce critically lauded films when skilled filmmakers were employed to make them. In addition, these documentary films, like the unmediated images in *Life* magazine, showed images of the country not presented by Hollywood or manipulated by advertisers. The American public was now able to see "the many faces of their country as never before."[52] Finally, the failure of the distribution and exhibition of the films and their lack of popular support made it clear to the Roosevelt Administration that if they wanted to get their ideas out to the American public, they would need the assistance of Hollywood.[53]

Newsreels in the 1930s

The newsreel, or filmed version of the news, would also greatly influence Frank Capra when making his wartime documentaries. These films, which played before the feature, were *the* major source of information about world affairs for Americans, as citizens with poor reading skills preferred them to magazines and newspapers.[54] Although newsreels took too long to produce to be timely, they encapsulated and summed up events tidily for quick absorption. This was a new and growing trend in mass media in the 1930s. (The circulation of *Reader's Digest*, for instance, a magazine filled with easily digestible concepts and optimism, jumped from 250,000 to seven million in the 1930s.)[55] Despite the popularity of newsreels, most studios felt that filming news was unnecessary, preferring to spend more time developing their profitable narrative feature films instead.[56] Consequently, little care was taken in their production. Studio newsreels were considerably uneven, often cramming six to seven unrelated stories into one reel, sometimes mixing tragic stories with lighthearted fare. The newsreel genre changed substantially in 1935 with the introduction of the *March of Time* series. This innovative series, developed by Time, Inc., as a kind of mass-media experiment to supplement their magazine, would alter the way newsworthy events were communicated to the public, as well as influence Capra in his army career. Unlike the studio newsreels, the *March of Time* films would take a journalistic approach to their subject matter, tackling a single issue or event in a 20-minute film. This approach would provide audiences with more depth and clarity about particular issues, helping them synthesize past events into an easily understandable whole they could remember. As it took a relatively long time to produce quality work, timeliness took a back seat to quality and coherence. The *March of Time* series' use of narration, structure, and reenactments would create a template for future documentary films, not only influencing Capra, but also William Wyler, John Huston, and John Ford in their historical campaign documentaries.[57] Although modern audiences may cringe at the use of reenactments to flesh out stories, the *March of Time* films did not consider this "fakery" a betrayal of the truth. According to A. William Bluem, the *March of Time* films "stretched the limits of journalism by implicitly arguing that the picture as well as the word was, after all, only symbolic of reality."[58] Thus, the use of reenactments was not an uncommon practice in documentary filmmaking at the time, nor was it considered unethical. Documentary filmmakers Joris Ivens, Pare Lorentz, and Robert Flaherty all blurred the line between staged shots and reality.[59] What mattered most was not whether these films showed actual reality in every shot, but whether, within the "conscience" of the filmmaker, the films faithfully *reflected* the reality of the events they were showing.[60]

Within a year, the *March of Time* films were playing in more than 5,000 theaters in the United States, and 709 in Great Britain, reaching a monthly audience of about 15 million people.[61] By 1937, the monthly audience reached 22 million.[62] Leaders in Hollywood were impressed. David O. Selznick, producer of *Gone with the Wind*, was quoted as saying that the "*The March of Time*—with its courage and novelty—will prove to have been the most significant motion picture development since the invention of sound."[63] The *March of Time* series would receive a more substantial endorsement from the motion picture industry by winning a Special Award Oscar at the 1936 Academy Awards—the same year Frank Capra would win his second Oscar for directing.

By the late 1930s, the *March of Time* dealt more frequently with politics and war. From the summer of 1939 to the winter of 1941, 84 percent of the films dealt with military or political subjects.[64] In those years, the films took on a decisively interventionist, anti-fascist point of view, often warning Americans of the dangers of isolationism.[65] This trend would culminate in *The Ramparts We Watched*, a feature-length film produced by *March of Time*, which used the failure of President Wilson's initial anti-war policy during World War I as a warning to its 1940 audience of the dangers of letting a war in Europe continue without U.S. involvement. Like most newsreels of the time, the *March of Time* films focused more on the war in Europe than on the Japanese aggression in Asia. Richard W. Steele, in his book *Propaganda in Open Society*, however, observed that very little of the European war footage used in these newsreels actually showed *people* in combat situations. Instead, most newsreels of the time showed a "struggle of things rather than of people"— guns being fired, bombs dropping — as well as "pictures of troops and material in transport, 'atmosphere' glimpses of the various fronts, political and military leaders addressing their people." Steele claims that such treatment of the war "conveyed a sense of the 'urgency of the situation' without suggesting its bloody consequences."[66] Capra would adopt similar tactics for the battle scenes in his war documentary films, but would show the human cost of war with graphic footage of wounded and dead soldiers and civilians.

Besides confirming that film was the best way to impart news to the less literate population of America, the *March of Time* series, like most newsreels of the 1930s, proved it was possible to combine raw footage, persuasive narration and "true in spirit" reenactment into an entertaining, informative, and coherent retelling of current events. Furthermore, the ethical limitations imposed on print media could be stretched more in films for the sake of emotional impact, as long as the heart and conscience of the filmmaker remained true to the subject matter. This belief that historical events could be rearranged, manipulated, and edited to make them more coherent and compelling to a modern audience, would reach its pinnacle in Frank Capra's war films, establishing a new form of journalism based on sound and visual images rather than the written word.

Triumph of the Will *and* Nazi Propaganda Films

Of all the documentary and newsreel films produced in the 1930s, none influenced Capra more than Leni Riefenstahl's *Triumph of the Will* (1935). This filmed "record" of a Nazi rally at Nuremberg, was deliberately planned and staged to convince the German public, as well as the rest of the world, of the power of Nazism.[67] Unlike the heavy-handed techniques of the Soviet propaganda films, which tended to attack other government systems rather than explaining the strengths of their own, *Triumph of the Will* uses heroic imagery, a Wagnerian score, traditional symbols, moving cameras, large-scale events, and skillful editing to instill a sense of awe in the viewer.[68]

Soon after Capra joined the Army, he requested to see the *Triumph of the Will* in order to gain a better understanding of the propaganda films made by the enemy, but was denied security clearance. So, in April of 1942, Capra, Anatole Litvak (*Why We Fight*'s other director) and writer-producer Edgar "Pete" Peterson, went to New York's Museum of Modern Art to see the film and other Nazi propaganda films from their collection. Capra was both impressed and horrified when he watched Riefenstahl's film, remarking in his autobiography that "Satan couldn't have devised a more blood chilling spectacle."[69] Newsreels and "New Deal documentaries" had their moments, but *Triumph of the Will* had taken documentary propaganda to a new level, making it not only a film, but a "psychological weapon aimed at destroying the will to resist."[70] He left the viewing, impressed by Riefenstahl's mythic imagery, her use of music, and her arrangement of spectacle, but also depressed and paralyzed, wondering if his team would be creative enough to mount an effective counter attack. According to Peterson, right after the screening, their only solution was to go out and get drunk.[71]

Triumph of the Will is much different from the war documentaries Capra would produce. Riefenstahl's film focused on a single event, the Nuremburg rally, and she staged most of the footage for ultimate effect. Furthermore, the film's purpose was to overwhelm the viewer's emotions rather than informing them or persuading them through logic or discourse. Because of this, the film employs a great many shots filled with masses of people and seems to constantly be in motion. As film scholar Siegfried Kracauer observes, the apparent nihilism at the heart of the film is perhaps the most terrifying aspect of *Triumph of the Will*. He writes:

> It is a frightening spectacle to see many an honest, unsuspecting youngster enthusiastically submit to his corruption, and long columns of exalted men march towards the barren realm of this will as though they themselves wanted to pass away.[72]

In fact, the film seemed to take pride in showing the robot-like devotion of Nazi soldiers. *Triumph of the Will* proved that individuality is not necessary in countries devoted to a single-minded goal.

Triumph of the Will not only showed Capra the creative and powerful possibilities of propaganda, it also provided him with the basic strategy for his war documentaries. The more he watched Riefenstahl's film, as well as other Nazi propaganda films, the more he realized that he could use footage from them in his own documentaries. The Nazi footage could be used to condemn the mob psychology of the Nazis as well as convince Americans of the seriousness of the European situation. "Let their own films kill them," Capra told Peterson. Capra's idea to use footage of *Triumph of the Will* as an argument *against* Nazism soon became a standard practice in all the American war film agencies. Various branches competed for access to both the MOMA print and a print confiscated by the U.S. Customs Service. Hollywood studios also wanted segments to use as cutaways in their films.[73] In fact, parts of *Triumph of the Will* were used so frequently in American documentaries and films, Riefenstahl's imagery is perhaps better known in postwar America than in Germany, where the film was banned from public screening for over two decades after the war.[74]

In terms of influence, the German campaign films, *Baptism of Fire* and *Victory in the West*, are arguably more important to discuss, as their techniques more closely resembled the techniques Capra used in his war documentaries. As in America, there was intense pressure in Germany to make films about the war as quickly as possible, in order to mold public opinion about recent events. As such, these two feature-length documentaries creatively mixed newsreel footage with music and narration to tell the story of German victories in Europe. *Baptism of Fire* (a version of another film *Campaign in Poland*), released in April 1940, dealt with the Polish campaign in the East, and *Victory in the West*, which chronicled the success of the French campaign, was released in January of 1941. Much of this footage would actually be used in Capra's war films, so the films themselves certainly must have had an impact on Capra while he was producing his documentary films. Like Capra, the German filmmakers of these campaign films understood that in order to be perceived as factual, they must include as many newsreel shots as possible. In addition, the *Why We Fight* series would employ many of the same editing techniques used in these films. They move quickly; the announcement of an action is immediately followed by a visual accounting of its result. Battle scenes are quickly cut, and emphasize shots of firing guns without giving the audience any sort of understanding of time and space. This practice, Kracauer observes, helps "to confuse the spectator by a blurred succession of pictures so as to make him submit more readily to certain suggestions."[75] When seeing similar sequences in the *Why We Fight* series, one wonders if Capra was trying to elicit a similar response in his American audiences. Perhaps he may have already understood this technique, as the endings of his narrative films usually mixed fast-paced editing with heavy-handed ideology. Strangely enough, the German filmmakers in these films present Nazi Germany similarly to the way Capra would portray America: peace-loving, religious, and home loving. The films also present the prewar period as a "dramatic struggle between the powers of light and darkness," heavily contrasting the "good" Germans with their "evil" enemies— the degenerate French and the arrogant English.[76]

For all the influence these films had on Capra during the making of his war documentaries, there are some important differences. Unlike Capra, who usually did not shy away from showing corpses in his films, the campaign films show little of the human costs of war. They also show relatively few shots of citizens, preferring instead to focus on the German army and the German soldier.[77] Furthermore, unlike the *Why We Fight* series, which includes several maps and explanations of battle, the German campaign films are less instructive, preferring instead to focus on propagandistic images. This technique, observes Kracauer, not only makes the audience "realize that the Nazis, far from giving information, are merely seeking to impress them," but also illustrates the underlying contempt the Nazi leaders had for the mind of the individual.[78] This tactic exemplifies another important difference between these films and the *Why We Fight* series: the films' intentions. Capra's films were mainly about the enemy and America's allies and were directed toward soldiers. Their primary purpose was to inform and motivate. The German films, on the other hand, were mainly about German soldiers, and their intention was to convince civilian audiences of the superiority of the Nazi army. In many ways, the only Capra film even remotely similar to *Victory in the West* and *Baptism of Fire* was the campaign film *Tunisian Victory*, which would include none of the footage from these films.

The Signal Corps films, "New Deal" documentaries, the *March of Time* newsreels, and even German propaganda films all presented clear evidence that film was the best medium for educating the "Average Joe" and convincing him to fight. Before Capra enlisted, orientation for new soldiers about the war consisted of a series of lectures told to the men by a corps of speakers. This method, which started in 1940, proved to be confusing and boring to soldiers tired from basic training.[79] On the floor of the senate, General Marshall admitted their failure, stating that he "personally found the lectures of officers to the men ... unsatisfactory because of the mediocrity of [their presentation]."[80] Marshall, a known lover of movies (he often went to Fort Myer in Virginia to see movies with the troops), realized films would be a more effective medium than lectures to orient the troops, but understood that he first needed the right man for the job.[81]

4

Mr. Capra Goes to War

It becomes necessary, before one can connect the fictional films Capra made in Hollywood with the documentary films he produced for the Army, to describe the similarities and differences between the working environments of the two entities as well as the expectations of each.

As stated earlier, Capra was already familiar with the military when he volunteered to make films during World War II, having served during the previous war as a teacher at Fort Mason in San Francisco. Even before the war, those who knew him in college said he seemed to be more interested in the military than anything else. His graduation yearbook for Throop Polytechnic Institute noted that Capra "planned to join the Army and try to remain there the rest of his life."[1] Even after he started his lucrative film career, Capra shot combat, bomb, and plane footage with the assistance of the U.S. military in San Diego for his film *Flight* (1929).

Although Capra's experience with the military prior to World War II was a fairly positive one, entering the army at the age of 44, after a string of blockbuster hits and a cover photo on *Time* magazine, was quite a different experience. The biggest adjustment Capra had to make involved issues of power and protocol. When he butted heads with Colonel Schlosberg of the Signal Corps over the use of German and Japanese newsreels, for instance, Capra warned the colonel that "in the world of film" he always sat "at the head of the table."[2] Later, Capra would get into trouble for visiting the Soviet Embassy in order to negotiate for some footage of lend-lease material being used by Russian soldiers. When asked by whose authorization he consorted with representatives of a foreign power, Capra simply answered "his own."[3] Capra describes his early impatience with military bureaucracy in his autobiography as follows:

> I hated being a second class citizen; hated having to get an okay to make a long distance call, or send a telegram; hated having to remain within fifteen minutes of Washington without an approval from the Adjutant General—which took about five days. I hated having to swallow the galling figment that someone else's opinion was superior to mine because he outranked me. But I hated becoming a slave of a master race even more.... So come Army charters, or clod-pated

(From left to right): Capt. John Huston (rear), Lt. Col. Frank Capra, Sam Spewak, Capt. Anthony De Wolfe Veiller, and Jack Beddington discuss the war documentaries they are making for the U.S. Army. (U.S. War Department/Photofest)

colonels, or gentlemen generals, I would make films that justified this war to our soldiers.[4]

Although Frank Capra never became completely accustomed to military life, he did learn to accept it as a means to an end. As mentioned earlier, Capra's retreat back into the arms of the studio system after the failure of *Meet John Doe* may have already proven that his youthful wish for independence was quickly becoming a notion of the past. For the most part, however, Capra was left alone by his superior officers, and had a greater amount of freedom from the military bureaucracy once his 834th Signal Service Photographic Detachment was moved from Washington, D.C., to the vacant Fox studio in Hollywood. As Edgar "Pete" Peterson commented, they "never could have made those pictures in Washington."[5] Furthermore, he had a great working relationship with his superior officer, Chief of Staff George Marshall, who often invited Capra to eat dinner at his house in Washington.[6] General Marshall was considered a great delegator, one who usually left a person alone to do his job once he placed him in a position. Marshall's strong presence did not intimidate Capra, as he usually did his best work under the management of strong authoritarian figures like Columbia's Harry Cohn, drawing strength from the confidence they placed in his abilities.[7] Marshall appreciated the talent and wealth of experience Capra brought to the table, and granted him free reign to do what was necessary to complete the films. Even though policy statements in Capra's army films had to be checked for accuracy by the Office of War Information as well as presidential advisors, Capra was often allowed to make the best guess he could about national policy if no clear-cut answers were available.[8] And although his unit's work was scrutinized by officers at every stage of production, according to Paul Horgan, who worked in Capra's unit, no one above Capra "ever suggested an artistic or technical change."[9] In some ways, in fact, Capra thrived in the military, the strong elements of his personality muted by public service. He showed no sign of his usual ego and swagger, and was often described by those who worked for him as a team player.[10]

Capra's unit initially fell under the Department of Public Relations of the War Department, but became the 834th Signal Service Detachment under the jurisdiction of the chief of the Special Services Division of the Office of Supply in June of 1942. The Roosevelt Administration had learned a valuable lesson from the failure of the Committee of Public Information, which had complete autonomy during World War I, by making all film units during the Second World War subordinate to the United States military.[11] At first, the unit remained separate from the Army Signal Corps, which was directed only to supply technicians and assist the 834th upon request. In September of 1943, the 834th detachment was assigned to the Army Pictorial Service of the Signal Corps, but still produced films upon the request of the Special Services. During World War II, such rearranging and moving of departments was not at all unusual.

Soon after his wife had finished unpacking at their rented house in Maryland, Capra moved the unit back to Hollywood. Darryl F. Zanuck, who understood the difficulty of trying to make films in Washington, D.C., rather than California, let Capra use the old 20th Century–Fox studio, a "ghost studio" of rundown buildings on Western Avenue, to produce the films.[12] Even though this move would make it harder to know what footage was available for use (footage was stored in New York and Washington) it allowed Capra to work on his own turf and hire civilians with experience in the film industry, including talented long-time friends William Hornbeck (an editor for Mack Sennett) and composer Dimitri Tiomkin.[13] This inability to have direct access made it difficult for the writers of the film, who often had to write without knowing if there was footage available to illustrate what they were writing. (This problem was fixed in October 1943, when the unit was transferred yet again to the

SCPC [Signal Corps Photography Center] headquartered in the old Paramount studios in Astoria, New York, where it stayed until the war ended.)[14] The production of the films, once Capra's unit moved to the studios in Hollywood, allowed the crew to adopt methods similar to the assembly line filmmaking of the studio era, with some crucial differences which affected the content and quality of the pieces.

From the start, the *Why We Fight* series was imagined as seven one-hour episodes that would describe the events leading up to the U.S. involvement in the war. The episodes were to be completed as soon as possible under the management of Frank Capra. The output expected of the 834th unit was much greater than Capra was used to. Compared to other directors of the studio era, Capra's output after *It Happened One Night* was extremely low, averaging about one film a year. (It must be noted, however, that this output may have been greater had it not been for the production delays of *Lost Horizon*, its subsequent international press tour, and the bitter legal battle between Capra and Cohn which prevented Capra from working. That being said, Capra only made eight films between 1934 and 1941, whereas other major studio directors like John Ford and Michael Curtiz were credited as directing 20 and 30, respectively, in the same time period.) This newly increased output forced Capra to assume more of an executive producer role and adopt more of an assembly line approach to the films.

Furthermore, although Capra was working in a studio like atmosphere, the old Fox studio had very little equipment when Capra and his crew arrived. Capra was forced to beg, borrow, and steal furniture and editing equipment. Old 35mm projectors were shipped to the studio from Washington, D.C., along with the only operator in the world who could get them to work.[15] In addition, Capra was working within a very tight budget — around $400,000 for all seven *Why We Fight* films, or about one-fifth the cost of *Mr. Smith Goes to Washington*.[16] In order to stay within budget, Capra decided to primarily use found footage like field photography footage, newsreels, and enemy propaganda to make the films. As will be discussed later, this type of footage came with its own set of issues.

The production of the documentaries was fairly straightforward. As executive producer, Capra outlined the "scope and thrust" of each of the films, and worked with the writers and the research department on the scripts.[17] These scripts were based on a "Bible" prepared by the Army, which highlighted the main points of the films, and were reviewed by Capra, who had the final say.[18] Shot lists were then prepared and the film archives were searched to illustrate the scripts.[19] Once the shots were put together, Capra would watch the rough cut with someone reading the narration out loud. He would then give suggestions to the editing crew, headed by William Hornbeck, sometimes working on the editing himself. The editing phase, naturally, took the longest, with Capra refining the final cut.[20] It was during this phase that Capra exerted the most control of the films. Richard Griffith, a film critic who was in charge of research for the *Why We Fight* films, stated that the excellence of the series was based on Capra's skill of analytical construction. Even though Capra only personally directed the first three films in the series, Griffith noted that as executive producer, he had a hand in shaping all the films produced by his unit. He stated:

> Many times when a film had been virtually completed by others of his staff, [Capra] would take it away to the cutting rooms for a few days. Screened again, it would seem on the surface much the same, yet invariably it had acquired a magical coherence and cogency which testified eloquently to Capra's editing capacity.[21]

Capra would then fly to Washington with the finished film and screen it at the Pentagon, then at the White House for the president and the secretary of war. Paul Horgan, who accompanied Capra on these trips, remembers the discussions at the White House following the screenings as fascinating because he could feel U.S. policy being formulated during the talks as a result of the films.[22]

Although Frank Capra was the public face of the *Why We Fight* series, per army regulations, he did not receive credit for the films nor did anyone else who worked on them. In his autobiography, Capra credits the success of the series to director Anatole Litvak, writer and narrator Anthony Veiller, writer Eric Knight (K.I.A. in 1943), Edgar Peterson, and editor William Hornbeck. Capra's original unit started with eight officers and 35 enlisted men, who were primarily Hollywood technicians specifically asked to enlist for the job. Most were over the age of 35; the 25 enlisted editors, supervised under Hornbeck, had an average of 11 years experience in editing at the major studios.[23] Capra populated his crew with industry professionals because he felt that making informational films would not be that different from telling a narrative story.[24] Other personnel included writers Leonard Spigelgass, Ted Paramore, Sam K. Lauren, Theodore Geisel, Carlton Moss, John Sanford, Jerome Chodorov, Julius and Philip Epstein, historians Paul Horgan and Richard Griffith, writer/researchers William Shirer, John Whittacker, James Hilton, editors Henry Burman, Leon Levy, John Hoffman, composer Dimitri Tiomkin, production manager Sam Briskin, and narrator Walter Huston.[25] Chodorov, Sanford, and the Epstein brothers (with whom Capra had worked on *Arsenic and Old Lace*) were dismissed early from the writing staff mainly for political reasons. In his autobiography, Capra claimed it was because their early outlines were filled with communist propaganda. All four men were accused publicly in the late 1940s by the HUAC of being communists. Based on letters between Sanford and Capra, as well as Capra's autobiography, Capra justified dismissing these men because he was worried that their employment in the detachment would cause Congress to cut appropriations for the army films like they did for government films.[26] Other crew members who joined the staff but ultimately ended up leaving included documentarians Joris Ivens and Robert Flaherty, who found they could not fit into the mass-production atmosphere.[27] The Walt Disney Company produced the animated segments.[28]

Interviews with employees of Capra's unit all agree that Capra was in complete control of the unit, especially at the beginning of production. According to Paul Horgan, Capra's leadership was implicit, coming from his character, his kindness, and decency. His hard work also served as an example to his team, as he always seemed to be working harder than anyone else. Horgan said, "People worked way, way into the nights. Everybody was his ally, uncritically devoted to him."[29] Ted Geisel (later known as Dr. Seuss) was also impressed by the down-to-earth director, observing that Capra's greatest strengths during that time were his patience and his ability to teach.[30]

It is important to note that throughout the production of these war-orientation films, Capra left the old Fox studios for an extended period of time only once, in the summer of 1943, when he traveled to London to work on *Tunisian Victory* with the British Army Film Unit. Although he witnessed a bombing while stationed there, Capra never realized his dream of going out into the field and seeing true combat. (After Capra returned from London in November of 1943, he started working for the Army Pictorial Service [APS] as commanding officer of the Special Coverage Section, Western Services. He was assured after the remaining *Why We Fight* films and *The Negro Soldier* were finished, there was no work left for him to do, and he would be able to visit the front lines and work directly in the field with combat photographers like John Ford and John Huston. Instead, the APS never placed him in the field; Capra was instead commissioned to make two more orientation films—*Two Down and One to Go!* and *On to Tokyo*.)[31]

Strangely enough, Capra made all of his war-orientation films without ever seeing the results of combat. This, of course, was not unusual for Capra, who, throughout the thirties, made fiction films praising the virtues small towns without ever actually living in one.[32] Perhaps because of this lack of first-hand experience, the war in Capra's documentaries still retains a touch more excitement and idealism than say, a film like John Huston's *Battle of San Pietro*. Unlike reporter Ernie Pyle, whose writing became more bitter and honest the longer he saw the brutal battles of the Pacific Theater, Capra's films continued to focus on the idealistic reasons for fighting the Axis powers.[33] Like many of those on the home front, Capra's life during the war was not much different than his life before. While some men became soldiers during the war, Capra remained a filmmaker.

The distribution and intended audience of Capra's war films was also different from his Hollywood films. Capra once said that "a paying audience in the theater is the only way you get the truth about your film."[34] The reaction of the audience was very important to Capra, as he was known to record the reactions of audiences at previews and tweak his films accordingly. Because of the quick turnaround necessary for the war films, this strategy could not be implemented. Capra was only able to preview his films for the brass at the Pentagon and the president at the White House. There were also key differences in the purpose and audience expectation in both films as well. When he made films in Hollywood, Capra competed with the product of other studios and was forced to appeal to the widest audience possible — people who would go see his films for entertainment during their free time. Capra, in fact, prided himself on his mainstream sensibilities, feeling "sure that anything he enjoye[d] [would] be enjoyed also by 10,000,000 other people."[35] Capra's army films, on the other hand, were mainly shown to men on duty as part of basic training. In addition to close-order drill, military protocol, and physical conditioning, new recruits went through seven hours of indoctrination during this training, which included watching whatever episodes of *Why We Fight* that were completed at the time, before moving on to the second phase of instruction and then specialized training.[36] Attendance for the films was compulsory.

Most infantry, the typical audience member of Capra's war films, were fairly uneducated white men around the age of 26, as blacks and women were denied combat duties, and educated white men got technical or desk jobs.[37] A large share of these infantrymen scored low on the AGCT test, and only four out of ten had finished high school. Almost a third had no education beyond grade school, although the average education was one year of high school, three full years more education than the soldier of World War I.[38] The morale of the average draft soldier was low in 1941, mainly due to the Selective Service Act of 1940, which extended the service of draftees to two years rather than one.[39] In an August issue of *Time*, it was reported that the average soldier possessed "little pride of outfit, little joy of service," having grown up during the isolationist atmosphere of the 1930s.[40] These were the men to whom Capra would have to sell the war.

In addition to distributing the films to soldiers, the Office of War Information (OWI) also distributed Capra's war films to the American public. The theater owners and exhibitors in the War Activities Committee pledged 16,000 theaters for the purpose of showing war-information films free of charge, but the OWI pursued other venues as well, showing films to students, civic groups, and at American Legion posts.[41] As a result of their distribution, the total attendance of the seven films by July 1945 was 45,582,127.[42] In addition to showings in America, the OWI overseas branch, headed by Robert Riskin, translated Capra's films so they could be played throughout Europe.

The most obvious difference between Capra's narrative films of the '30s and his war documentaries was the fact that Capra shot very little of the footage used in the films. From the start, the fact that Capra had to use footage from either foreign documentaries or footage shot by Signal Corps cameramen, eliminated one of Capra's greatest strengths as a director: his ability to work with actors. With the exception of the voice-over talent, it would be impossible to draw any kind of performance out of the people photographed or ask for a second take. This difference cannot and should not be underestimated. Capra's fiction films were able to dramatize the fight for freedom through a central character (usually played by either Jimmy Stewart or Gary Cooper) whose onscreen charisma could arouse both passion and compassion in the audience. Furthermore, these characters provide a continual and lasting connection, both visually and aurally, with the audience. The only lasting connection the audience has in Capra's documentaries is with the narrator (who sometimes changes during the course of a film), who has no real stake in the story and who can only connect with the audience through his voice. In addition to the main character in his narrative films, Capra often included a cynical character with whom even the most cynical viewer could identify. In Capra's films of the 1930s, these audience "surrogates" were often the female characters, who are initially skeptical of the "too good to be true" heroes. Consequently, the conversion of these jaded surrogates at the climax of the film helps to sell the wildly idealistic notions of Capra's heroes to the public. The absence of this questioning character hurts Capra's documentary films as it makes their upbeat message and patriotic ideals a harder sell. Sometimes in the films, the narrator attempts to serve as both the hero and the audience surrogate by asking hard questions and then answering them, but this attempt is a poor substitute for the real thing. Capra would later solve this issue in his informational science films by including two live characters who would play the two parts and engage in lively, scripted discussions.

Not only did the use of found footage eliminate characters with whom the audience could identify, this practice also kept Capra from controlling the composition or angles of the shots. Thus, Capra could only exert directorial control over the type of shots that were picked. More than any of Capra's fiction films, these films would be created almost entirely in the editing room. When Capra started the *Why We Fight* films, he was forced to use German and Japanese footage to tell the history of the conflict, not just for budgetary reasons, but also because it was the only footage that was available at the time.

American newsreel companies had long been prevented from covering German affairs, which made it extremely difficult to cover events like Kristallnacht, which was intentionally not filmed by the Germans.[43] The Nazis, however, were very prolific filmmakers, especially when it came to shooting war footage, having two full divisions dedicated to shooting motion picture films during the war.[44] Even with the O.S.S. stealing as many enemy newsreels for Capra's unit as they could, Capra was forced early on to be creative with the footage he was using. In addition to using footage from *Triumph of the Will* and German newsreels, Capra also used material from the previously mentioned German propaganda films *Feldzug in Polen* (*Campaign in Poland*) and *Sieg im Westen* (*Victory in the West*), sometimes manipulating footage to place over scenes where no footage was available.[45] During the course of production, writer Eric Knight became afraid that too much of a reliance on German propaganda films, rather than inspiring troops, might lead to defeatism and despair. Because of this, Capra decided to balance the use of these films with other segments about America and the free world, creating an "us versus them" strategy which would be used throughout the *Why We Fight* series.[46] Even though Capra assured General Marshall that all footage in *Prelude to War* was authentic (except for the animation and newspaper headlines), he frequently showed footage of Hitler out of context and out of proper chronology.[47]

In addition to films shot by enemy photographers, Capra also creatively used material from feature films already shot by Hollywood. For *Battle of China*, Capra used a hundred feet of film shot in China by MGM for *The Good Earth*.[48] Footage from *Sergeant York*, *Air Force*, *All Quiet on the Western Front*, and *Wake Island* was used and passed off as reality.[49] As no footage was possible for scenes of the Revolutionary War, Capra used footage from D.W. Griffith's *America* and John Ford's *Drums Along the Mohawk* for historical content.[50] In some instances, as in *Tunisian Victory*, scenes were shot and integrated into sequences because the original footage was either substandard or lacking.

By the end of Capra's army career, more footage from the front became readily available, but this footage too had its limitations. First of all, only the Army Signal Corps and the Field Photography Unit were permitted to photograph the war.[51] Civilian reporters were only allowed to be news correspondents. As a result, much of the best footage, like the footage from Ford's *Battle of Midway*, could be kept by the military for use in particular documentaries or to support certain causes. As most cameramen were low ranked, any minor lieutenant could prevent them from shooting at any time. As *Variety* reported at the time, as a result of this interference, war photographers "missed thousands of opportunities for spectacular and historic footage."[52] Sometimes, footage that was already shot was censored or destroyed because it was deemed too graphic or harmful. In the documentary film *Shooting War*, for instance, cameraman Walter Rosenblum tells the story of an officer who tossed a duffel bag containing all the footage of the Normandy invasion over the side of the boat so the shots of dead soldiers would never be seen by the American public.[53] Self-censorship was also an issue, as many photographers resisted the urge to shoot dead soldiers. In another interview in *Shooting War*, war photographer Russ Meyer confessed he censored himself when shooting G.I.s killed in action as he was concerned that their families "would see somebody in the newsreels."[54] War photography could also be staged, especially if it contained shots of commanding officers, who often hired advertising agencies to make sure they looked good on camera. The 50 cameramen who shot Eisenhower and his generals going ashore in Normandy after the D-Day landings, for instance, were told which profiles they were allowed to shoot.[55]

Footage shot on the front lines also carried with them a certain look, which was based on the limitations of the equipment and the training of the cameramen. By late 1942, the military was officially training combat cameramen. The cameramen, many of them were already experienced photographers, were trained at the Hal Roach studios in Hollywood.[56] Most of the instructors for these cameramen worked in the film industry, and were trained to shoot the Hollywood way. The principles of "approach" and continuity were so ingrained in the photographers' heads, they were able to practice those techniques instinctively during battle. They were advised not to pan and to shoot only when close enough to use their revolvers.[57] Unlike the big studio cameras Capra used in Hollywood, the standard-issue camera for war photographers was the Eyemo, which had to be hand cranked, and had only one two-inch lens. In order to get close-ups, the cameraman had to move in on the subject, which could be very difficult in the middle of battle.[58] The camera was mainly hand held, and most footage contained medium or long shots. Such wide compositions were due to the limitations of the camera and because most of the shots were intended for newsreels which traditionally used these types of shots to encompass large amounts of action.[59] The fact that the cameras were hand cranked made it possible for footage to be shot in slow motion, but also prevented them from recording synchronized sound. As a result, the footage shot was not completely realistic as it contained no dialogue, no soldiers swearing, and no sounds of battle. Capra and his team would be forced to recreate the reality of battle in post production, using various sound effects to heighten the drama of battle scenes.

The fact that the most of the footage used in the war documentaries of the 834th unit was not shot by Capra specifically, however, does not completely negate his authorship of the films. After his experience with *Lost Hori-*

zon, Capra was accustomed to whittling down a large amount of footage into a cohesive narrative through an extensive, painstaking editing process, which he controlled. In addition, the sequence of shots within a film is nearly as important as the composition of the shot itself. Furthermore, Capra was able to structure these films and create metaphors and relationships between shots through pacing, narration, and music, over all of which he had complete control. Although the intent of these films was different from his narrative films, Capra found that the formula for success he had created with fiction could be implemented in propaganda films as well. When asked in an interview if making the *Why We Fight* films was that much different than making narrative films, Capra answered by saying that his background in making dramatic films was actually a great help. He added:

> I didn't have a documentary mind, I had a dramatic mind, here was the world stage, here were the actors, here were the plots, here were stories, and I told them dramatically. You had the world's greatest heroes and the world's greatest villains competing. You had a chance to dramatize it with film. I think what was different about those documentaries was that history was dramatized, and I think that was their main attraction.[60]

As such, the elements of Capra's style employed in his narrative films—the promotion of religion, history, patriotism, and hard work, the use of shadows, close-ups, and music, as well as the elevation of boyhood ideals and the plain spoken word, would all carry, over in one form or another, into his army films. Regardless of the differences in the audience or in the method of their production, Capra was still able to make the films of the 834th unit an extension of his own particular style of filmmaking, a style that would even influence the way we view the war today.

Capra's unit produced 17 war documentaries in three years. Among these were the seven *Why We Fight* films, the *Know Your Ally* and *Know Your Enemy* series, *Tunisian Victory, The Negro Soldier, Here is Germany, The Stillwell Road, Two Down and One to Go!, On to Tokyo!* and *Your Job in Germany*. Close attention will be paid to the first three *Why We Fight* films and *Tunisian Victory* as they were overseen directly by Capra. In addition to these films, *War Comes to America, Two Down and One to Go!*, and *Know your Enemy: Japan* will also be discussed as they, of all the war scripts in Capra's files, are the only ones which bear his name.[61]

The *Why We Fight* series, as mentioned earlier, was based on a series of 15 lectures about the war which started in 1940. The purpose of these lectures (and later the *Why We Fight* films), was to help the individual soldier understand his motivations, as well as to help define both his enemy and his allies. When Capra was tasked to make the films, he wrote in May 1942 in a memorandum to Lowell Mellet, chief of the Bureau of Motion Pictures of the OWI, adding that the films must also inspire soldiers to win the war and win the peace. He believed the films could create a will to win by:

1. Making clear the enemies' ruthless objectives.
2. Promoting confidence in the ability of our armed forces to win.
3. Showing clearly that we are fighting for the existence of our country and all our freedoms.
4. Showing clearly how we would lose our freedom if we lost the war.
5. Making clear we carry the torch of freedom.[62]

To win the peace and prevent further war, Capra felt the films should:

1. Explain and expose aggression and conquest
2. Show the necessity for better understanding between nations and peoples
3. Show the necessity for outlawing conquest and exploitation by the few
4. Show the necessity for eliminating economic evils
5. Proclaim the four freedoms
6. Promote democratic peoples [63]

The goals clearly fit into the ideology established in Capra's fiction films. He decided early on to set up the war as a battle between good and evil, with evil associated with aggression, manipulation of the masses, and slavery and good associated with courage, individualism, and democracy. As in his fiction films, Capra would once again be dealing with the struggle between fascism (a top-down approach, in which the powerful and deserving got what they wanted) and democracy (in which all men are equal and have the right to pursue their own individual interests). Not only was this struggle playing out in Capra's career as he fought against Cohn and the studio system, but it was also occurring in America, as American citizens were feeling threatened by the spectres of big government and big business. In Capra's fiction films, this battle was fictionalized, and some sort of resolution is reached. In the *Why We Fight* series, however, the fight for freedom could not be resolved as the conflict was ongoing.

Capra stated in his autobiography that in order to make the *Why We Fight* films effective, he would have to center them around a basic, powerful idea. This idea came from a passage in the Bible: "Ye shall know the truth and the truth shall set you free." Capra believed that the fascist Axis powers wanted to take over the free nations by force and that the words and films of the enemies could truthfully prove that fact.[64] This approach is similar to one proposed by Archibald MacLeish, head of the Office of Facts and Figures, who believed propaganda in a democratic society should not tell people what to think, but should be based on a "strategy of truth," which meant citizens should be given honest facts about the struggle in order to create informed opinions.[65] Capra felt that he could convince soldiers to fight by adapting the ideology and dramatic techniques of his past films to the current struggle Europe and the Pacific, using facts and enemy footage as proof of their evil intentions. As a result of this consistent ideology, the *Why We Fight* series would be considered by many to be "the most comprehensive set of war aims released by the U.S. Government in any medium during World War II."[66]

Before further discussions of the relationship between Capra's fiction films and his non-fiction films, a synopsis and background is required for each.

Why We Fight, *Episode 1:* Prelude to War *(1942)*

In Capra's own words, *Prelude to War* was designed to present a general picture of the slave world of the Axis and compare it to the free world of the Allies. It chronicles the rise of the Axis powers from Japan's invasion of Manchuria to Mussolini's conquest of Ethiopia.[67]

Prelude to War, Capra's first propaganda film for the U.S. Army, generated a large amount of praise from top government men when it was shown in the fall of 1942. General Marshall called the film "a most wonderful thing."[68] President Roosevelt applauded it, declaring that "every man, woman, and child in the world should see the film."[69] This comment emboldened Capra, who used his clout with the Academy of Motion Pictures Arts and Sciences to ask the OWI for permission to show the film to a theatrical audience. Lowell Mellett wrote the following reply:

> Appreciate desire of Colonel Capra's Academy friends, but suggest in all sincerity that they refrain from embarrassing him and other able directors who have entered the armed services by confusing their present service as soldiers with their private careers.[70]

Capra believed the OWI placed a ban on *Prelude*'s release because they did not like competition. The real story was much more complicated and political. The OWI stalled the release of *Prelude to War* because they were afraid it would be seen as pro–Roosevelt/Democratic propaganda to Congress, who could pull their funding in retaliation. *Prelude to War* was allowed to be released only after General Marshall assured Oregon Senator Holman that Roosevelt had nothing to do with the making of the film.[71] *Prelude to War* was released in theaters through 20th Century–Fox on May 27, 1943, to generally positive reviews but box-office disappointment. The film was also shown that year in war plants to raise the morale of the workers, but plant managers found it difficult to set aside the 40 minutes needed for his workers to watch the films.[72] It was one of four documentaries to win an Oscar at the March 4, 1943, Academy Awards.

Why We Fight, Episode 2: *The Nazis Strike* (1943)

This film, also directed by Capra, deals mainly with the rise of Hitler and Nazi Germany. It chronicles Hitler's occupation of the Rhineland and Austria, and his subsequent invasion of Czechoslovakia and Poland. It shows that World War II began mainly because of Allied appeasement.

Why We Fight, Episode 3: *Divide and Conquer* (1943)

This film, directed by Capra and released the same year, continues where *The Nazis Strike* leaves off. It describes Hitler's invasion of Denmark and Norway and his clever bypassing of the Maginot line, and ends with the surrender of France.

Know Your Ally: Britain (1943)

This film, the first and only entry in a series that was never completed, chronicles the similarities and differences between the United States and the United Kingdom.[73] (*Know Your Ally: Russia*, written by John Sandford, was never completed, mainly because the U.S. military was unsure about their relationship with the communist country. Ironically, Capra's unit was also asked to prepare a film called *Know Your Enemy: Russia*.) *Know Your Ally: Britain* focuses on the common ideologies of the two countries, and the value they both place on representative government, the freedom of speech, the freedom of the press, and the freedom of religion. The sacrifices of the British, as well as their ability to fight back during the Axis bombings are also highlighted in the film.

Why We Fight, Episode 4: *The Battle of Britain* (1943)

The next three films in the *Why We Fight* series, called the "Battle" films, highlight the achievements of the Allies in the face of Axis aggression. According to Thomas Bohn, in his *Historical and Descriptive Analysis of the Why We Fight Films*, the purpose of the "Battle" films was to describe America's Allies and the common bond that exists, with "the idea of building people up in terms of their courage and fighting ability."[74]

The majority of *The Battle of Britain* deals with the resolute spirit of the English people during the Axis bombings and highlights the accomplishments of the Royal Air Force in fighting back Nazi aggression. *The Battle of Britain*, along with *Prelude to War* and *The Battle of Russia*, was shown to workers in war plants in 1943.

Why We Fight, Episode 5: *The Battle of Russia* (1943)

The Battle of Russia is the longest episode of the *Why We Fight* series (82 minutes), and was released in two parts. The film starts with a history of Russia, describing their people, their size, their resources, and their wars. It chronicles their struggle against the Nazis at Moscow and Leningrad, and their historic stand against Germany at Stalingrad. The footage of *The Battle of Russia* was mostly shot by Soviet cameramen. Stalin himself viewed the film while a translator stood behind him and translated the narration for him. Stalin ordered 500 prints made immediately, and *The Battle of Russia* was ordered to be shown in every Russian theater.

The authorship of *The Battle of Russia* is somewhat questionable, as few people confessed to working on the film later during the Cold War. When asked who was responsible for the film in 1954 by a U.S. Senate Internal Security Subcommittee, Capra testified that when the film was produced, he was in England working on *Tunisian Victory*. In actuality, although it was supervised by Anatole Litvak, the film was mostly completed before Capra left.[75]

Tunisian Victory (1944)

Major General Alexander Surles commissioned Capra to make *Tunisian Victory* after finding out that the British had just completed a new film about the Allied landings in North Africa where, of course, England was given the starring role. The absence of American troops in the film was due to the fact that the footage shot by the Signal Corps, under difficult conditions, was unimpressive compared to the British footage. Capra was ordered to go to London to find out about the possibility of making a joint Anglo-American film about the landing.[76]

What is not mentioned in Capra's autobiography, however, is that before a joint production was decided upon, John Huston, George Stevens and he were assigned to shoot reenacted parts of the campaign. Capra and Huston shot footage in the Mojave Desert, Stevens shot fake footage of tanks in North

Africa, and Huston shot simulated aerial combat in Orlando, Florida. Huston later claimed, when all three filmmakers met in Washington, D.C., to view the footage, that it looked so "false" and so "disgraceful" that they decided to coproduce the film with the British so they could use the superior English footage of the actual event.[77]

The production of *Tunisian Victory* was extremely difficult. Capra arrived in London under the assumption that the film was to be a joint production, but was surprised to discover that the British filmmakers had nearly finished their version and were reluctant to rework it.[78] Capra spent four weeks in England editing his part of the project, and showed the rough cut to several propaganda officials. Angry over the frozen-faced reception of the film, Capra refused all demands for change, claiming that "he would take no orders from the British."[79] American officials fought on Capra's behalf for editorial control of the film, which the British surrendered under protest, and Capra returned to the United States to finish the film.

Tunisian Victory was released in April 1944 and chronicled the invasion of Africa and the subsequent defeat of the Nazis in Tunisia. It documents the preparation and the battles, but also shows British and American troops taking time off to celebrate Christmas during the campaign. Both British and American narrators are used, and the film ends with a plea for Anglo-American cooperation. Upon its release, the British felt the film lacked realism, while many Americans simply believed it was released too late — over a year after victory had been won.[80]

Before Capra left for England to make *Tunisian Victory*, the first five *Why We Fight* films had been completed, with *Know Your Ally: Britain* nearly finished. The last two films of the series, *Battle for China* and *War Comes to America*, were still in production, as was *The Negro Soldier* and the two *Know Your Enemy* films. While Capra was in London, his unit made the transfer to the SCPC in New York, with some staff remaining in Los Angeles with Litvak, to whom Capra turned over command of the 834th in order to become the commanding officer of the Signal Corps Special Coverage Section, Western Division and Assistant Chief of the Army Pictorial Service. Capra still supervised the orientation films, but also had to produce training films, combat reports, and the *Army-Navy Screen Magazine*.

Why We Fight, Episode 6: *The Battle of China* (1944)

The Battle of China documents the total effort of the Japanese to conquer China. It surmises how Japan, if successful in their endeavor, would use

China's manpower and resources to conquer all of Asia. Brigadier General Frederick Osborn, chief of the Morale Branch, described the film as "the least satisfactory of the *Why We Fight* series," because too many sequences were taken from entertainment or other films, rather than from real, historical footage.[81] Capra responded to this criticism by remarking that there was a "heartbreaking dearth of Chinese material" and defended the emotional content of his documentary films, stating that facts need to be presented dramatically in order to stimulate the imagination and impart lasting knowledge.[82] Despite Capra's defense of the film, *The Battle of China* was quickly withdrawn from distribution for "political reasons."[83] In her article "Frank Capra's *Why We Fight* Series and the American Audience," Kathleen German suggests that the film was suppressed by the government because of its drastic stylistic difference from the first five *Why We Fight* films. According to German, unlike the other "Battle" films, *The Battle of China* failed to show the Chinese as individuals, making it difficult for the viewer to identify with them, and its lack of parallel editing "reinforces the passive nature of the Chinese people."[84] As a result, the film was unable to "involve the audience by incorporating its framework of values."[85]

The Negro Soldier (1944)

The Negro Soldier was ordered by the U.S. Army to boost the morale of the African-American troops and to inform white troops of the accomplishments of black soldiers throughout the country's history. At first, Capra did not want to make the film and, by his own admission, tried his best to get out of it. According to Capra, he finally decided to produce the film after Secretary of War Stimson called him into his office and showed him several reports of cases of discrimination against black soldiers that had occurred all over the country. After reading these reports, Capra changed his mind and decided to make the film.[86]

The film follows black troops as they go through basic training and eventually entering the Officer's Candidate School. The entire film is framed around a Sunday service in a predominantly African American church.

In January of 1944, Capra showed the film to 200 African-American publishers, editors, and writers, who reacted positively once they were reassured the film would be seen by white soldiers.[87] Langston Hughes wrote that it was "the most remarkable Negro film ever flashed on the American screen." *Time* magazine reported that black soldiers applauded the film when they previewed it.[88] To modern critics, like Eric Barnouw, *The Negro Soldier* is "condescending" and "unrelenting in its religiosity," never really commenting on the discrimination it was meant to prevent.[89] To audiences of the time it was a breakthrough, significantly contributing to the decision to desegregate the Army in 1948.[90]

Although Capra showed the film in Washington as "his production," his authorship of the film is highly questionable. In a videotaped interview in 1975, the director confessed that he did not want to make *The Negro Soldier* because he had too many other things to do.[91] In reality, he left the African American writer Carlton Moss and the director Stuart Heisler alone to make the film. According to Moss, Capra's first and only discussion with him about it came after the film's release.

Why We Fight, Episode 7: *War Comes to America* (1945)

War Comes to America, the final installment of the *Why We Fight* series was the least shown as it was not released until the last year of the war. Nevertheless, it completes the series by explaining America's involvement in the war. The film deals with how the American public slowly changed their attitude from non-involvement in the war to total commitment. Capra, who is credited as a writer on the archived script, claimed the film was "one of the most graphic visual histories of the United States ever made."[92]

Here Is Germany (1945)

Originally titled *Know Your Enemy: Germany*, *Here Is Germany* took the longest time of any of the orientation films to produce. The first version was directed by the internationally famous director Ernst Lubitsch and then entirely remade by Gottfried Reinhardt. The film primarily uses German footage and newsreels to show the German people's thirst for power throughout their history. In order to prevent another war from occurring, the German belief that they are a superior race must be crushed, and the people must be educated in how to become citizens of the world.

Your Job in Germany (1945)

Your Job in Germany, written by Ted Geisel and Anthony Veiller, and narrated by actor Dana Andrews, was prepared by the War Department for the troops who were to be stationed in Germany after the war. It uses much of the same footage as *Here Is Germany*, reminding soldiers that the German people should still be considered a dangerous enemy as they have been raised throughout their history to crave power. It was also one of the first American films to include footage of the concentration camps. The film asserts that by being cautious with the German people, and not being fooled by their smiles and hospitality, is the only way for American soldiers to prevent another war from occurring. The film was previewed to the Army commanders in Germany, all of whom approved — with the exception of General Patton, who walked out on the film.[93] Despite Patton's objection, prints of the film were shipped to the troops on April 13, 1945.

According to Geisel, Capra was not particularly involved in the making of this film. He was so busy working on other projects that he was only able to direct the narration.[94] In 1945, Warner Bros. redubbed the soundtrack, made a few alterations, and called the new film *Hitler Lives?*, which won the Oscar for Best Documentary Short.

Two Down and One to Go! (1945)

Two Down and One to Go! grew out of a meeting Capra had with General Marshall and other officers. In the special meeting, General Marshall expressed his concern about how the officers were going to deal with the troops in the time between V.E. Day and the surrender of Japan. After sitting in on the meeting for three days, Capra suggested that a film be made to communicate all the military's priorities to the servicemen. His advice was taken, and *Two Down and One to Go!* was put together in 60 days during the summer of 1944. The film, originally produced in Technicolor, mainly describes the defeat of Germany and stressed that there was still an enormous job ahead for the troops in the Pacific. Both Secretary of War Henry Stimson, and General George Marshall are shown in the film, directly addressing the audience.

The most incredible aspect of *Two Down and One to Go!* was its distribution. In preparation for V.E. day, 1,363 technicolor prints were distributed all over the world.[95] On May 10, 1945, the film was shown simultaneously at noon E.S.T. in 700 Army installations as well as civilian theaters in the United States. It was the closest one could get to a worldwide broadcast at that time.[96] (This practice, however was similar to the distribution pattern of Nazi Germany, where Joseph Goebbels decreed that official front newsreels be released on the same day everywhere in the empire.)[97] It was a remarkable achievement nonetheless, especially as the United States had troops positioned all over the world. Within two weeks, 97 percent of the troops overseas had viewed *Two*

Down and One to Go!, and over 800 first-run movie theaters showed the film in the U.S.[98]

Know Your Enemy: Japan (1945)

Know Your Enemy: Japan is considered the most controversial film made by Capra's unit. The film took three years to complete, with Joris Ivens writing the first draft, and the final draft credited to Capra and Geisel.[99] Although released in 1945, three days after the bombing of Hiroshima, it was quickly pulled for political content as General MacArthur felt that such a film was of no value in persuading the Japanese troops of the value of democracy.[100] The film was not aired publicly until 1977.

Know Your Enemy: Japan describes the traditions, history, and customs of the Japanese people, showing they are much to blame for the country's warlike actions. The film attempts, therefore, to place the blame of the war, not on Hirohito, but on the Japanese people themselves. The film also goes into great detail as to how the Japanese have repeatedly cut themselves off from the Western world and explains the slogan *Hakkō ichiu*, an imperialist policy put in place by the Japanese government which announces their intention to place the entire world under one rule. Overall, *Know Your Enemy: Japan* blames the country's problems on the schizophrenic nature of Japan itself, where state of the art production and technology mixes with the oppressive and primitive values of the Middle Ages.

The Stillwell Road (1945)

The Stillwell Road chronicles the Chinese, American, and British attempt to create a new supply road into China after the Japanese took over the important road through Burma. This new road, called the Ledo Road until it was changed to the Stillwell Road in honor of General Joseph Stillwell, was a massive undertaking which required the cooperation and the coordination of several countries to complete. The film details the many difficulties that were encountered during the making of the road and highlights the hard work and sacrifices of the groups and individuals who made the mission a success.

On to Tokyo! (1945)

A difficult film to find, *On to Tokyo!* is mentioned in Capra's autobiography as one of the last war films he produced and released. This short documentary film dealt with the difficulties and challenges America faced as the war in the Pacific was winding down.

Our Job in Japan (unreleased until 1982)

Our Job in Japan was the last film produced by Capra's unit and was finished in March 1946, long after Capra had left the service. Like *Your Job in Germany*, the film was made to train the U.S. occupying forces. It had a much more conciliatory attitude towards the Japanese people than *Know Your Enemy: Japan*, but it, too, was shelved and not shown to the public until 1982.[101]

5

The Capra Formula in His War Documentaries

The construction of Capra's war documentaries is pretty apparent from the start, the aim of each film is told to the viewer by the narrator or written in an opening title. Upon first viewing, one is usually struck by the heavy reliance on facts and figures, the emphasis on contrasts between the two opposing forces, and the large number of filmic effects employed for its time. This heavy reliance on facts and information, of course, is part of the "truth shall set you free" approach that Capra wanted to use for the films in order to make them feel less like propaganda. Much of this information is relayed to the viewer in the form of statistics, direct quotes, and opinion polls. In order to gain authenticity, the films also incorporate as much realistic combat footage as possible that relates directly to the narration.[1] As a result, the films have a straightforward "tell it like it is" approach and feel refreshingly honest, much like the dialogue of Capra's protagonists Smith, Vanderhof, and Deeds.

Like the narrative films of Capra, the construction of the war documentaries is fairly linear and straightforward; there are no hidden surprises or sudden twists. As most of the films were directed at the common soldier, 37 percent of whom did not even have a high school education, their basic arguments and construction made them fairly easy to follow. Such simple construction, however, would lead many, like David Cohn, to dismiss the effectiveness of these films as "too much material was at an elementary school level."[2] Like Capra's narrative films, many of the documentaries begin with a preponderance of exposition and conclude with highly ideological speeches. *Tunisian Victory*, for instance, starts with the planning of the Allied invasion of Africa and ends with a British and an American soldier musing about the uselessness of war and the incomprehensibility of the typical Nazi soldier. Many of the techniques illustrate the theme set forth in first film Capra's unit made, *Prelude to War*, which frames the war as a battle between two opposing forces: the Axis, representing slavery and fascism, and the Allies, representing freedom and democracy.[3] Like in his narrative films, the primary drama of Capra's war documentaries arises from the collision of two opposing sets of

5. The Capra Formula in His War Documentaries

Frank Capra (right) works with two other soldiers on the *Why We Fight* series. (U.S. War Department/Photofest)

ideals. In a 1975 interview, Capra defended the simplistic vision of the opposing forces in World War II in his *Why We Fight* films:

> [The average G.I.] had this free world/slave world as the only way you can reach that guy at that moment. You give him a lot of "but on the other hands" and you confuse him completely. This is it. The chips are down. It is us or them.... Unless you set the idea of survival, you won't understand the war.[4]

According to Erik Barnouw, however, framing the war in this way was extremely beneficial for Capra and his team, as it allowed them to gloss over or ignore some of the more unpleasant and controversial aspects of history, like the division of Poland by the Nazis and the Soviets, and the bombings of enemy civilians by Allied planes.[5]

Also, like Capra's later films, namely *Mr. Smith Goes to Washington* and *Meet John Doe*, Capra stresses the overwhelming power of the "evil" fascist

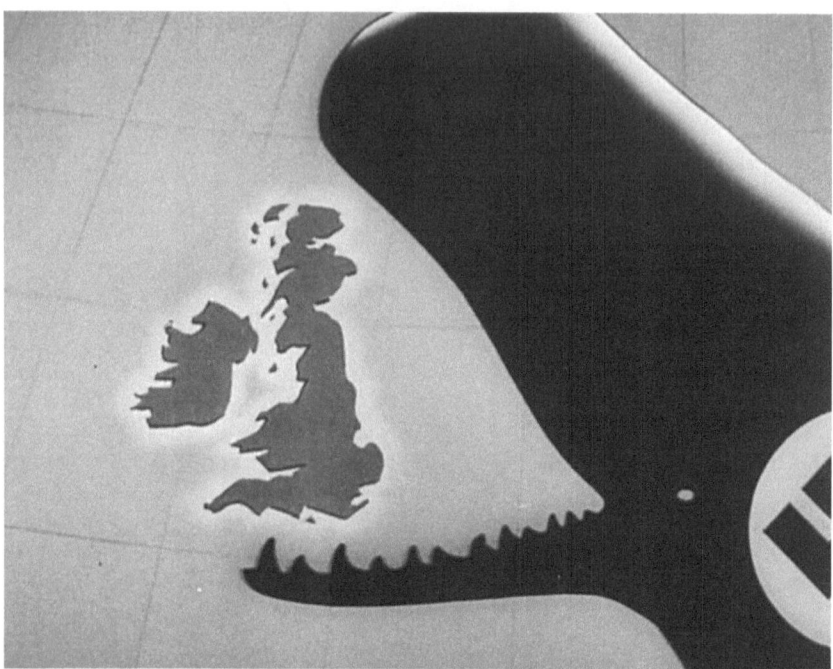

The Battle of Britain **likens the fight between Great Britain and Germany to Jonah and the whale.**

side nearly to the point of hopelessness. *Prelude to War*, *Battle of Britain*, *Divide and Conquer*, and *Tunisian Victory* all use visuals and graphics to illustrate the "overwhelming" air of superiority of the German Luftwaffe. Graphics are used in *Battle of Britain* to liken the conflict between Britain and Germany to the story of Jonah and the whale. *Divide and Conquer* tries to end on an upbeat note praising the leadership of Charles de Gaulle, but cannot overcome the final, overwhelmingly bleak images of the Nazis overtaking France. Like *Meet John Doe* and *Mr. Smith*, *Divide and Conquer*'s attempt at a happy ending does little to comfort the viewer, who is left with a feeling that, despite the heroism of its lead characters, very little will ultimately change. Capra's overplaying of the power of the enemy in all of these films, however, is not meant to leave the viewer with a sense of pessimism, but a sense of dissatisfaction. Ultimately, by leaving the endings inconclusive, Capra hoped to spur his audience to action, as they would realize that the important fight between these two distinct ideals had not yet been won. As the narrator states at the end of *Prelude to War*: "This isn't just a war. This is the common man's life and death struggle against those who would put him back into slavery. We lose it and we lose everything."

5. The Capra Formula in His War Documentaries

Despite its limited budget and inferior film equipment, Capra's unit was able to produce a superior technical product, using a vast array of diverse techniques. According to Thomas Doherty, the films' "orchestration of visual variation and celluloid legerdemain — maps, diagrams, optical printing and double exposures, archival footage both documentary and dramatic, and specially filmed reenactments — was unprecedented." He writes, "Never before had the entire panoply of cinematic devices been put to such concerted and seamless instructional use."[6] Although Capra's narrative films could not employ the vast array of techniques used by these instructional/propaganda films, one can still discern the similarities of Capra's style in both genres. Although the techniques of Capra's films of the 1930s described earlier — the use of close-ups, high and low angles, music, and "singles" to separate individuals from a group — were not particularly original, they nevertheless reflected Capra's overall style. This style is still evident in his documentary films, despite the fact that a large number of the shots used in these films were made by other crews in other countries. More importantly, the visual aspects of his earlier films — the use of shadows and silhouettes to create suspense or heighten mood, the use of silent, staring faces to denote the suffering of the common person — are also employed in these war documentaries.

Like Capra's narrative films, most of the footage used in his war films is shot at eye level. This is, perhaps, done more out of necessity than choice. As mentioned earlier, most of the war footage was shot by a handheld camera, whose operator was out in the field and more interested in documenting events than adding dramatic flair. When looking at Capra's war documentaries, one discovers that most low-angle and high-angle shots are non-battle scenes, which allowed the camera operator more time to set up. Practically every shot of a church, for instance, is shot on a tripod from a low angle, which, increases the importance of the institution. Large interior shots of churches, like the one used in *Know Your Ally: Britain*, on the other hand, are usually shot from a high angle, which like the Senate chamber scene in *Mr. Smith*, emphasizes the grandeur and scale of the location. Thomas Bohn also noticed that high angles are often used in the *Why We Fight* films to show crowds listening to Hitler or Mussolini. This type of shot reduces their power and shows them as a mass rather than as individuals.[7] In *Know Your Enemy: Japan*, several long shots of a crowd worshipping in a religious ceremony are shown with the worshippers' backs to the camera, emphasizing both the conformity and the inaccessibility of the Japanese people. The films also used low-angle shots of the enemy, as enemy cameramen often photographed their own soldiers this way to increase the power of their fighting force in their propaganda films. Footage from *Triumph of the Will* of Hitler making speeches, for instance, was intentionally shot at low angles to emphasize the authority of the dictator. Use of these shots by Capra reinforces the power of the Nazi regime and Hitler's belief that he is above the ordinary man. Strangely enough, Allied leaders like President Roosevelt, Winston Churchill, and Dwight D. Eisenhower are usually shot at eye level, putting them on the same level as the viewer. As a result, American leaders come across as less pretentious and threatening than the leaders of the enemy.

With the possible exception of *Tunisian Victory*, most of Capra's war films employ very few close-ups. Like in Capra's narrative films of the 1930s, Capra and his editors use close shots sparingly. When they are used, Thomas Bohn observes, they are employed only to increase the audience's attention or to show detail.[8] The close-ups in *Tunisian Victory* are examples of this use, as Capra uses close-up details of shells being loaded into cannons during the battle scenes, and shows soldiers' faces the night before a battle and when they look up to view planes. Upon closer examination, however, one can also see examples of close-ups to intensify the feeling of despair, as he did with Ellen in *It Happened One Night*, or as silent witnesses to important events, like Ann during John Willoughby's first radio address, or Conway as he listens to the High Lama. In *Battle of Russia*, for instance, Capra uses shots of dramatically lit Russians as they witness the horrible destruction of the Nazis. *Know Your Ally: Britain* shows a series of three close-ups of British men staring into the camera after Germany violates the Munich agreement. *Prelude to War* ends its description of the slave world with a close-up of a humorless old man as he watches Nazi soldiers marching. The rare close-ups of enemy faces are usually shown in profile, with the subject looking serious or unemotional. Like the shot of Senator Paine in *Mr. Smith Goes to Washington*, this type of shot distances the audience from the subject but more importantly, depicts them as stubbornly adhering to a point of view that is not our own. In *Battle of China*, a Japanese pilot shouts out orders in a close-up profile, and in *Know Your Enemy: Japan*, Capra uses four consecutive profile shots of Japanese soldiers, and primarily employs profile close-ups of Japanese workers, who are shown working in "regimented silence." Nazi soldiers are treated similarly in *Your Job in Germany*, *Here Is Germany*, and *The Battle of Britain*. Allied soldiers, on the other hand, often face the camera, even smile and wave, as British soldiers do in the beginning of *The Battle of Britain*, after their defeat at Dunkirk. In *The Stillwell Road*, General Alexander addresses the camera in medium close-up, and a child sadly looks up at the camera as she walks by with a group of refugees. This difference in reacting to the camera might derive from the differences between the two cultures, but as a result, Allied soldiers are seen as more personable and individualized than their enemy counterparts.[9] The difference in the close-ups between Allied and Axis subjects, of course, reemphasizes the theme of most of the documentaries

5. The Capra Formula in His War Documentaries 143

made by Capra's unit — that there is a fundamental difference between the people who live in a fascist world and those who live in a democratic one.

Capra's use of close-ups in the series also illustrates Capra's fascination with the picturesque faces of common ordinary people. Like his hero, director John Ford, Capra shows a great concern throughout his films for simple human faces and how those faces reflect both their past trials and their current emotional state.[10] The silent faces he chooses to use in his war films, both in close-ups and singles, stay with the viewer long after the films are over, as they reinforce the common humanity of both soldiers and victims. One easily recalls, for instance, the shots of joking G.I.s in *Here Is Germany*,[11] the singles of smiling soldiers representing each Allied country at the end of *Tunisian Victory*, and the triumphant faces of the pilots at the end of *The Battle of Britain*. One also remembers the sweating faces of the British workers in *The Battle of Britain* and the looks of grim determination on the grizzled faces of the Russian soldiers in *The Battle of Russia*. More affecting are the close and solitary shots of women and children weeping in *The Nazis Strike*, and the despairing faces of French men and women as they listen to Nazi orders at the end of *Divide and Conquer*. Much like the picturesque faces of the Great Depression shown in *Mr. Deeds*, *You Can't Take It with You*, and *Meet John Doe*, these "real" faces humanize the ideological content of Capra's films, grounding them in the terrible reality that exists outside the comfort of America.

Enemy soldiers in the *Why We Fight* series are depicted in profile close-ups, which dissociates them from the audience.

Isolated shots are also used in the war documentaries to emphasize the individual from the group. Like Jefferson Smith in the Senate chamber, or Ann, Connell, and the Colonel during John's radio address, Capra's war documentaries often intercut singles of individual characters with group shots to inject the human element into a crowd. This technique is used many times in *Tunisian Victory*: on the deck of the boat where a group shot of men exercising switches to a single of a soldier amongst them, and during the Christmas feast scene, wherein groups of men eating are intercut with singles of

Allied soldiers address the camera after the disastrous Battle of Dunkirk in *The Battle of Britain*.

men consuming their dinner. In a scene when General Patton addresses the troops over a loudspeaker, Capra cuts from a massive group shot to three shots, to two shots, to two single close-ups. *The Battle of Russia* often cuts to the faces of individual soldiers within a massive army. In *The Battle of Britain*, this effect is even used in funeral scenes, with a shot of a mass grave mixed with a shot of a single coffin. The opposite effect is felt in *Know Your Enemy: Japan*, wherein Capra cuts from individual workers to a large group, then to a massive group, which diminishes the individual and emphasizes his need to conform. In sequences in both *The Battle of Russia* and *War Comes to America*, singles are used in rapid succession to represent the ethnic makeup of different parts of the country. This technique is also used at the end of *The Stillwell Road* to show all of the nationalities who worked on the massive project, which (as in the aforementioned films) shows the importance of individuals who represent various ethnic groups as part of a larger diverse whole. It is important to note that this mixing of singles with group shots is hardly ever done with scenes involving Axis soldiers or German or Italian crowds. In *Know Your Enemy: Japan*, Capra employs mostly group shots of Japanese soldiers in training, with the narrator reinforcing the indistinct nature of the

5. The Capra Formula in His War Documentaries   145

troops by comparing the Japanese soldiers to "photographic prints off the same negative." Capra feels no need to show single shots of people in German, Japanese, or Italian crowds, as one person in this crowd is no different than the other brainwashed "slaves." As mentioned earlier, one of the flaws of *The Battle of China* is that Capra treated the Chinese people the same way as he treated the Axis powers, rarely depicting them as individuals in the film even though they were part of the Allied forces.

Single shots are also used in Capra's war documentaries to heighten the importance of certain individuals, much the same way Capra's fictional heroes and villains are separated from groups. Hitler and his leaders, for instance, are often shown in single shots with blank backgrounds behind them. In *Tunisian Victory*, both General Mark Clark and General Eisenhower are presented in single isolated shots, separating them from the rest of the men.

In addition to similarities in the use of close-ups and composition, Capra also employs the same imagery in his war documentaries as in his films of the thirties. Ringing bells are used, as in final scene of *Lost Horizon*, as a sign of conquest and redemption in *Two Down and One to Go!* In addition, the sound of bells is heard in *Know Your Enemy: Japan*, when Christianity brings peace for a short time to the enemy island. In this short war film, bells are shown after the destruction of Germany and are superimposed over shots of Eisenhower, Churchill, and Stalin. The ringing Liberty Bell, also shown in *Mr. Smith*, is a favorite image of Capra, and is shown throughout the *Why We Fight* series in order to equate the Allies with the spreading of liberty and peace.

Like the antagonists Anthony Kirby, Sr., D.B. Norton, James Taylor, and John Cedar in Capra's fictional films, Hitler and the Axis leadership are frequently seen wearing suits and sitting behind desks as they plan out the fate of the world. Hitler is initially introduced in *Prelude to War* as a man tied to wealthy industrialists, shown in a suit with other men in formal attire. In *The Nazis Strike*, German officials are seen working behind desks, meticulously studying the hometowns of America, as are the Japanese in *Know Your Enemy: Japan*. Desks and suit imagery are also associated with the bureaucratic and useless League of Nations in *Prelude to War*, as they do nothing to stop the Italian invasion of Ethiopia. Old French leaders in formal attire surrender to the German army around a table at the end of *Divide and Conquer*, while at the end of *The Nazis Strike* the ineffectual British Prime Minister Neville Chamberlain sits alone behind his desk, visibly disgruntled by Hitler's invasion of Poland. By contrast, the effectual Allied leaders— Winston Churchill, Charles de Gaulle, and Dwight D. Eisenhower are often shown on the move, walking from one place to another, shaking hands, or meeting *outside* with other leaders. It is important to note, however, that one major Allied leader,

President Roosevelt, is conspicuously absent in these films. As early as 1928, writer and public relations guru Edward Bernays, noticed a tendency for American propaganda films to "hero worship" the president, and the absence of him in Capra's films seems to be a conscious choice to prevent such worship.[12] In addition, this choice was also more than likely meant to allay the fears of congressional Republicans that the films were being used to persuade voters to reelect the president. Whenever Allied leaders are shown, however, they are always depicted as men of the people, men who seem active and involved with both civilians and their troops.

In addition, people described as hard working — like the British, the Belgians, the Poles, the Russians, the Chinese, and the Dutch — are usually shown doing some type of manual labor. In *The Battle of Britain*, workers are shown close-up in factories, wiping the sweat off their brow. German workers and Japanese workers, on the other hand, are usually depicted in wide shots, toiling without expression in factories, dwarfed by the machines. For the Poles, Belgians, Russians, and Dutch, hard work is usually associated with farm labor, such as pitching hay, which not only links them with the positive rural work ethic of Capra's populist films, but also hints at their technological inferiority. In *War Comes to America*, the early success of the first American settlers is associated with physical labor, by which men and women worked hard to carve a place for themselves out of the wilderness. *The Battle of China* emphasizes the physical labor involved in the Chinese retreat from Japanese forces and in the building of the Burma road. *The Stillwell Road* illustrates firsthand the backbreaking work of building an airstrip in the middle of a jungle and the intense labor involved in the construction of the Ledo Road. *Prelude to War* depicts shirtless men, happily working outdoors as part of the Federal Work Program. Unlike the German people, who are often portrayed digging ditches for no discernable purpose, or the Japanese, who are shown picking rice, the results of the labor of these Americans — roads, bridges, and dams, are displayed immediately following shots of the men working. Hard physical labor in a democracy (as these sequences seem to illustrate) produces concrete results. As he illustrated earlier with the actions of Longfellow Deeds and Jefferson Smith, Capra once again stresses that important work is physical, draining work.

Bureaucracy in both of these genres is associated with weakness, secrecy, treachery, and ultimately, ineffectualness. The heroes of Capra's narrative films go out into the world to gain inspiration. Jefferson Smith, for instance, is a scout leader who, it is assumed, spent a great deal of time outdoors. The out-of-work John Willoughby is used to sleeping outside. Like Robert Conway, these men are explorers, longing to discover the world that lies outside their door. Longfellow Deeds appears restless in his mansion, more interested

5. The Capra Formula in His War Documentaries

in seeing Grant's Tomb than being pampered at home. Rather than going straight to his office, Jefferson Smith escapes into Washington, D.C., to see the sights. As being out of doors equates to being an active and engaged person in Capra's films, it perhaps comes as no surprise that the Allied leaders in his war documentaries are seen more in outside shots. Winston Churchill is often seen walking outdoors among the people in *The Battle of Britain*. In *Tunisian Victory*, General Eisenhower is always pictured outside, as is President Roosevelt, who sits in an open-roofed car when visiting the troops. In one scene in *Tunisian Victory*, British generals walk over to an outside table to go over their plans. *The Stillwell Road* depicts General Alexander, General Stillwell, and Major General Orde Charles Wingate working outside among their troops, but this may have been out of necessity more than conscious choice. In contrast, the antagonists of his narrative films and the Axis powers of the documentaries perform most of their duties indoors, out of view of the public, in their offices and homes. In *Know Your Enemy: Japan*, for instance, the emperor is often shown inside cars with tinted windows, unseen by spectators.

Throughout these films, Capra equates the indoor world of boardrooms and secrecy with the Axis powers, men who study maps and files, dividing up the world through contracts and meetings. In the beginning of *The Nazis Strike*, Nazi bureaucrats are depicted gathering information in their offices about "your hometown." *Know Your Enemy: Japan* shows innocent-looking Japanese tourists working as spies to collect information. The film also attacks the influence of Bushido, Judo, Kendo, and Sumo wrestling on Japanese culture, claiming that these ancient institutions train the Japanese people to accept treachery and betrayal as necessary strategic tools. In addition, most contractual agreements in these films deal with surrender or futile compromise, as in the surrender of France or the mandates of the League of Nations. In a particularly interesting shot in *Divide and Conquer*, the surrender of Holland is shown through a window, as if done in a secretive manner. Much like he did in *Mr. Deeds* and *Mr. Smith*, Capra used the negative association of contracts to show that bureaucrats, politicians, and lawyers often use bureaucratic systems to work against the wants and needs of the people. French politicians, Nazi leaders, and businessmen (like antagonists John Cedar and James Taylor) work behind the scenes to wrench democracies out of the hands of the people to serve their own selfish ends. In other words, the negation of these secretive and undemocratic contracts proves that, while the leaders of some countries surrendered to the Germans, *their* people did not. Throughout all of Capra's films, then, lies the belief that "democracy's best defense is the common people."[13]

Capra's natural distrust of lawyers and businessmen, as shown in his narrative films, thus served him well in the depiction of the Axis powers, especially with the Nazi leaders, who are called "gangsters," and use clever words and complex treaties to manipulate other countries into giving them what they want. America, on the other hand, is specifically shown honoring its contracts and treaties, reducing our military after World War I (*Prelude to War*) and treating our prisoners with civility (*Tunisian Victory*). The Axis powers, on the other hand, openly defy treaties and contracts. In *The Nazis Strike*, Hitler's non-aggression quote is shown over a destroyed Poland. The same tactic is used throughout *Divide and Conquer*, which contrasts Hitler's pledges not to attack Denmark, Belgium, Norway, and Holland with shots of the destruction of these peaceful nations. Americans, like Jefferson Smith, deal with enemies openly and honestly. The Axis (like James Taylor and D.B. Norton), however, defeat their enemies with the tools of deception and secrecy. A *Prelude to War* montage shows headlines of leaders who did not agree with the policies of their Axis countries murdered in cold blood. Rather than simply invading Norway, Nazis use merchant ships as "Trojan horses" to sneak troops and supplies into their harbors. In a particularly effective animation sequence in *Divide and Conquer*, Nazis, represented as swastikas, eat away at the castle of France like termites, using sabotage, riots, and strikes to cause the French people to "lose faith in their own ideals."

As in Capra's prewar films, the enemies of democracy use the many mass-media outlets to perpetuate their lies. In *Mr. Smith Goes to Washington* and *Meet John Doe*, the antagonists use their control of the newspapers and radio to stifle the voices of the films' heroes. In an animated segment used in both *Prelude to War* and *Divide and Conquer*, radio antennas are shown projecting lies out into the world. In a montage straight out of *Mr. Smith*, wherein men controlled by Taylor are shown disparaging Jefferson Smith on the radio, *Prelude to War* shows puppets of the Axis powers using the radio to "confuse, divide, and soften up their intended victims." A similar montage is used in *Here Is Germany*, which shows men reading fake news. Like Norton and Taylor, the Axis powers used the Allies' free press and free speech against them. It is up to free-thinking Americans, men like Smith and Willoughby, to stand up to them, even if they end up as martyrs to the cause.

The use of shadows and light played just as important a role in Capra's war documentaries as they did in Capra's fictional films. Light, of course, is associated with the good "Free World" in *Why We Fight*, while darkness is associated with the evil "Slave World." In every animated sequence, whether showing battles or conquest, the Axis are shown as black, the Allies as white. *Know Your Enemy: Japan*, for instance, uses animation to equate the island nation to a giant black octopus, and depicts its ancient ancestors as shadowed figures with glowing

An effective use of animation from *Divide and Conquer* illustrates how the Nazis destroyed France from within.

eyes. The film also uses animation to symbolically show that by cutting themselves off from the "light" of the Western world in the 19th century, Japan, surrounded by giant walls, becomes enshrouded in darkness. As a result, the film explains, the Japanese became cut off from the moral and ethical principles of Christian nations like America and Great Britain.

Silhouettes are also used to enhance despair or to increase suspense. In *The Nazis Strike*, for instance, Hitler's face is shown in shadow as he looks out through an airplane window at the destruction of Poland, and the image of a shadowed figure wielding an axe is shown twice in the film as a visual metaphor of Nazi aggression. Although the equation of darkness with evil and goodness with light was not particularly original, having been used in Nazi documentary films as well, it was definitely part of Capra's directing toolkit, a technique to which he often turned to visually depict the two contrasting forces depicted in his films.

Shadows and silhouettes, however, are not always used to depict evil in Capra's war films. Dramatically lit shots, as in Capra's fiction films, are often used to enhance the drama of a scene. In *The Battle of Britain* and *Tunisian Victory*, silhouettes of Allied soldiers and landscapes are used right before

Animated segments throughout Capra's war documentaries depict the spread of Nazism as a thick, black stain.

major battle scenes to create suspense and pique the audience's interest. Capra understood that these picturesque shots were truly unique, and made a special attempt to use them at key moments in the film.

Capra would also keep the audience involved through the use of editing and music. As mentioned earlier, the editing of documentaries is different from the editing of fictional films, as documentaries primarily use found footage. Fictional films require continuity, a semblance that shots in a scene, usually shot out of sequence on the set, logically fit together. This preservation of reality was not as necessary in Capra's war films. Although these films usually present the major events of World War II in chronological order, the filmmaker is free to use a variety of different recorded shots to tell the story. Capra and his editing team, therefore, had the ability to choose the right shot to illustrate particular moments in the soundtrack (most especially the narration), rather than being forced to choose shots automatically linked to a particular soundtrack (as in fictional films, where characters actually speak in shots). According to film critic Andre Bazin, this type of editing was completely new to filmmaking, creating a new genre he named "the edited ideological documentary."[14] He writes:

5. The Capra Formula in His War Documentaries   151

The principle behind this type of documentary essentially consists in giving to the images the logical structure of language, and in giving to the language itself the credibility and proof of photographic images. The viewer has the illusion of watching a visual demonstration, whereas this demonstration is in reality only a succession of equivocal facts held together merely by the cement of the words that accompany them. The essential part of the film is not in its projection but in the soundtrack.[15]

Unlike in his fictional pictures, Capra and his editors had complete control over reality in the documentaries, which was only limited by the footage they received. As a result, they were better able to serve the idealistic vision of their creator, unaffected by the constraints imposed on fiction films, such as continuity, acting, or budget.

As a result, the relationship between the editing of Capra's narrative films and his documentary films is tentative, with similarities only in their pacing and montage sequences. As mentioned previously, the pace of Capra's fictional films was much quicker than the pace of most other films of the time, as Capra cut out entrances and exits and sped up the pace of the scenes when shooting. One can see this preoccupation with speed in Capra's war films, most especially in the *Why We Fight* series, wherein the narrator speaks faster than normal speed, especially during the battle montages. This increase in speed becomes even more apparent when guest army narrators appear. Although these officials lend credibility to the proceedings, they are untrained in the art of voice-over, and often slow down the pace of the film as they lecture about key battles. The quicker the professional narrators speak, the shorter the shots illustrating that narration must pass. As a result, Capra's war documentaries are edited much faster than standard narrative films. According to Thomas Bohn, with the exception of *The Battle of China*, the average length of all the shots in the *Why We Fight* films is an astonishing 3.5 seconds.[16]

As in Capra's fiction films, the fastest paced sequences in Capra's war documentaries are its montages, which are almost exclusively used for battle sequences. Like Vorkapich's montages in *Mr. Smith Goes to Washington* and *Meet John Doe*, the montages in Capra's documentaries are meant to dwarf the human figure and overwhelm the viewer. The battle montages, which occur at regular intervals in the longer historical documentary films like *Tunisian Victory* and the *Why We Fight* films, primarily contain quick shots of guns and explosions. Rarely does the montage slow down to show the human element of battles, usually framing the battles as a duel between machines. Explosions and gunfire dominate the soundtrack, which is usually devoid of narration. The night battle sequence towards the end of *Tunisian Victory* uses such quick and abstract shots and so many sound effects that the viewer has no time to feel or think about what is being shown, left to watch in stunned silence. Although the editing in these montage sequences puts the viewer into the mindset of a soldier pummeled by shells on the front lines, this fast-paced editing technique, which was employed in Nazi campaign films as well, prevents viewers from absorbing the reality of the devastation they are seeing on the screen. Most of the montages follow the pattern of the bombing of Rotterdam sequence in *Divide and Conquer* — quick shots of bombs and explosions, followed by slower paced shots illustrating the human costs of such bombs, usually showing injured or dead women and children. If Allied forces are doing the bombing, as shown in *Tunisian Victory*, sequences showing the suffering of enemy victims are not included. As a result, there is no human element associated with Allied attacks — the montage sequences of these battles are hardly different from fireworks displays.

Capra also uses metric editing techniques, in which a large number of shots of the exact same length are cut together to enhance the monotony of work and/or training, usually of the enemy. These scenes, which are used in the *Why We Fight* films and *Know Your Enemy: Japan*, edits shots of humorless soldiers drilling and marching to a monotonous drumbeat in the background, which emphasizes the soulless conformity of the people depicted.

The use of easily recognizable tunes to identify the "good" institutions or people in World War II is also a technique borrowed from Capra's prewar fiction films. Music, in fact, is used throughout the documentaries. Thomas Bohn discovered in his evaluation of the *Why We Fight* films that music filled 58 of the 63 minutes of *War Comes to America*, and 76 of the 80 minutes in the *Battle of Russia*.[17] This use of wall-to-wall music forces the score of these films into a subordinate position to both the visuals and the narration, usually changing quickly when these two (more important) elements change. Although music is used more frequently in the war documentaries than in Capra's fictional films, the songbook is basically the same, and just as obvious. Easily recognizable tunes like "My Country 'Tis of Thee" and "Yankee Doodle" are used when America is mentioned, while "Jingle Bells," "Roll Out the Barrel," and "Take Me Out to the Ballgame" are used during the Christmastime sequence in *Tunisian Victory*. Music for scenes involving churches alternates between "O Come All Ye Faithful" and "Onward Christian Soldiers." Each Allied culture is associated with a classical or folk song written in that country. Tchaikovsky's "Nutcracker Suite" is used in *The Battle of Russia*, "La Marseillaise" is played behind shots of French troops in *Divide and Conquer*, "Rule Britannia" is played throughout the series when showing England, and a Polish "polonaise" is played during the attack on Warsaw in *The Nazis Strike*. *The Battle of Britain* ends with a large group of soldiers singing a rousing rendition of "There'll Always Be an England." In striking contrast, the music

5. The Capra Formula in His War Documentaries

of the "slave world" of the Axis powers usually involves either constant drumming or a repetitive, three-note tune. Oftentimes, unusual, tuneless ethnic music is used when depicting the Japanese people or exotic Asiatic people, including the Burmese.

Like in Capra's narrative films, "good guys" engage in improvisational music. Allied soldiers are shown in *Battle of Britain* and *Tunisian Victory* loosely playing the piano or fiddling with their guitar in their off time. In *Battle of Russia*, Russian peasants cheerfully play native dance music. In contrast, Germans are shown playing music only in marching bands or in orchestras. *Here Is Germany* uses close-ups of men and women joylessly singing "Deutschland Uber Alles." Members of a slave world, therefore, cannot spontaneously express themselves creatively, nor do they find any joy in such expression; they must be led or organized. Like Anthony Kirby, Sr., who returns to his love of playing the harmonica at the end of *You Can't Take It with You*, they must learn to let loose their creativity and passions in order to be free again.

Free people also seem to have a much greater capacity to play than citizens of the slave world. Capra drew the same distinction between his heroes and his antagonists in his narrative films. In those films, the childlike playfulness of Jefferson Smith, John Willoughby, and Longfellow Deeds sets them apart as unique and individualized. In his war documentaries, the ability to engage in improvisational fun is a characteristic unique to free worlds, where such expression is tolerated and even encouraged. In *Divide and Conquer*, for instance, the editor places a shot of Dutch people riding bicycles when the narrator mentions that they are "free." Bicycling, in fact, is used as a common image in these films to represent freedom. After the German defeat in Leningrad, shots of the newly liberated Russian people are also depicted bicycling. The aptitude for play is also shown in the form of games, usually games associated with the particular culture shown. The British people take time off work to play darts in *The Battle of Britain*, while British soldiers play cricket in *Tunisian Victory*. American soldiers play cards and baseball in their time off in *Tunisian Victory*, which also includes scenes wherein two soldiers fall off a camel, and a group of soldiers play a "staged" practical joke on another soldier. German troops, however, are never shown smiling or engaging in any type of fun. The exclusion of shots of German soldiers at play is intentional on Capra's part, as *Baptism of Fire* and *Victory in the West*, films that Capra continually drew shots from for his documentaries, include long montage scenes of German soldiers relaxing during down time. In one amusing scene in *Victory in the West*, a German soldier pours cold water over a naked comrade. Film scholar Siegfried Kracauer noted that playful scenes are often included in war propaganda films not only because audiences tend to enjoy scenes of everyday life depicted on film, but also because these scenes appeal to instincts common to all people.[18] Capra understood this early in his career, as he often used playful, improvised scenes in his narrative films in order to sell the reality of his characters to the audience. As such, showing soldiers engaging in play makes them seem that much more like real human beings. On the other hand, the absence of similar depictions of the enemy perpetuates the belief that the Americans were completely unlike their enemy, who are consequently represented as soulless automatons.[19] Unique individuals like Longfellow Deeds and John Willoughby, who slide down banisters and play imaginary baseball, could only exist in country like America, which has a tradition of encouraging personal expression and preserving liberty.

As the development of play begins in childhood, we find similar contrasts between the children of Axis powers and the children of the Allies and neutral countries. *Prelude to War* devotes a great deal of time to the depiction of children in both worlds. The kids of the average American (a.k.a. John Q. Public) are shown engaging in all types of activities in a park. These shots are contrasted with group shots of Japanese, Italians, and German children training for war or studying in a regimented atmosphere. In a sequence in *Tunisian Victory*, Allied soldiers imagine what their loved ones are doing in their respective countries. Their children are shown to be engaged in individual, unorganized play, like blowing bubbles and painting. In *The Battle of Russia*, the Soviet government provides its young ones a "Children's Day" (Christmas of 1942), and a statue of children playing is shown in front of the ruins of a destroyed city. In contrast, *Prelude to War* shows that the indoctrination of the young and the hijacking of their freedom to think occurs not only in the Axis schools, but actually starts from birth when children are selectively bred for the state. Another sequence in this film shows shots of German boys of increasing ages participating in Nazi activities, and ends with shots of adult Nazi soldiers. The enemy, therefore, sees children only as future soldiers, and does not make any effort to protect their dreams or to cultivate their individual aspirations. Children of the slave world have no adults like Jefferson Smith watching out for their interests and sheltering them from cynicism and hate, pessimism and hopelessness.

In both his fiction and nonfiction films, therefore, Capra projected a belief that the strength of a country's future lies in the protection of its children, who should represent liberty and innocence. The strength of America's future is shown in the first shot of *War Comes to America*, wherein a group of children recite the Pledge of Allegiance. The destruction of a country, therefore, could best be illustrated by the destruction of its children. As the narrator warns at the end of *Prelude to War*, Axis powers threaten "the hopes we have

5. The Capra Formula in His War Documentaries

Germans in *Here is Germany* (and other films) play music in organized bands only.

for our kids, the kids themselves ... they won't be ours anymore." Throughout the *Why We Fight* series, the most chilling and horrific shots are images of injured and dead children—the direct result of the invasion of Axis forces. *The Nazis Strike* makes sure to include the reactions of Polish children to Nazi attacks. *Divide and Conquer* cuts from the bombing of Belgium to shots of a closed school and crying, injured children in the hospital. Dead children are shown after the Japanese attack on Shanghai in both *Prelude to War* and *The Battle of China*. In a particularly horrifying sequence in *The Battle of Russia*, close shots of dead children alone and in heaps are displayed while the narrator bluntly states, "These are not dolls, these are children." The children who are not killed by the Axis are destined to live a life of want and despair. At the end of *Divide and Conquer*, shots of children crying are used as the narrator describes how they will be left to go hungry.

Like Peter Warne in *It Happened One Night*, who gives his last bit of money to a starving child and his mother, the Allied soldiers and citizens are often seen sacrificing their own needs for the needs of children. As mentioned earlier, the end of *Prelude to War* frames the war as a fight to preserve the liberty and well-being of those without power. Axis soldiers, on the other hand, kill and injure for selfish dreams of conquest. In its Christmas sequence,

Tunisian Victory shows more practical examples of this generosity than do the other films. After showing troops taking a needed break from the war, eating and playing, soldiers are depicted giving candy to the native children. The narrator remarks, "Arab kids are no different than the kids back home when it comes to candy." He adds, "A lot of them looked half-starved, the Germans had picked the land clean." The narrator further explains that, in addition to candy, the soldiers also donated half of their milk rations to the Red Cross to give to the needy native children. Thus, by their actions towards the less-fortunate children, Allied soldiers are portrayed as generous and thoughtful, in contrast to the heartless and selfish Nazis.

In his films of the 1930s, Capra defined heroes not only as those who exercise compassion in the darkest times, but as those who remain faithful to the simple truths of the Bible and the founding fathers. In his war documentaries, Capra extended this definition to the Allied countries, who fight not only on behalf of the oppressed, but also to protect the ideals of religious figures like Jesus and Moses, and historical leaders like Washington, Jefferson, and Lincoln. As in his narrative films, Capra's war documentaries use both historical figures (usually represented by statues) and monuments to represent the traditions of freedom entrenched in the Allied societies. *Prelude to War* even borrows a line from *Meet John Doe*, calling Lincoln and Jefferson "lighthouses lighting up a dark and foggy world." As such, the history of each major ally is discussed in the series using a combination of statuary, monuments, and recreations. As stated in *The Battle of Russia*, "The will for freedom of our allies was born out of their historic traditions." *The Battle of Britain* discusses the freedom-loving nature of the English people and contains shots of Big Ben and Parliament, and *Know Your Ally: Britain* shows the statues of Washington and Lincoln that were erected in London. *Battle of Russia* uses footage from Russian director Sergei Eisenstein's *Alexander Nevsky* to glorify the historic Russian leader, and displays a statue of Lenin when describing the city of Leningrad. *Battle of China* uses ancient statues to represent the great history of China, and *Prelude to War* shows Chaing Kai Shek's army marching along the Great Wall of China. Shots of American landmarks, most especially the Capitol and the Lincoln Memorial, are pictured in *Prelude to War*. The use of monuments and statues in these films reminds the viewer of the permanency of these institutions and the ideals they represent. The history of France is primarily represented in *Divide and Conquer* by one figure, Marechal Ferdinand Foch, commander in chief of all the Allied armies during World War I. The statue of Foch plays a predominant role throughout *Divide and Conquer*, as his motto, "Attack! Always Attack!" was the historic advice the French failed to heed. The film uses the statue of Foch to show that by turning their backs on the historical traditions of their country, which Foch

5. The Capra Formula in His War Documentaries

German children in gas masks in *Prelude to War*.

represents, the French people inevitably lost their country and their freedom to the Nazis. Adhering to these historic ideals means victory over our enemies, who are shown devoid of landmarks and the long tradition of freedom. This absence of landmarks is especially true of Italy, an Axis power whose great history is never recreated and whose numerous statues and monuments are rarely seen in the documentaries.

The loss of freedom is thus represented by the loss of our ideals and the loss of our landmarks. *Prelude to War* asks the audience to imagine Japanese troops marching into Washington, D.C., superimposing a shot of Japanese soldiers marching over the monuments of the nation's capital. Defeat by the Axis, in other words, would mean the destruction of our traditions and freedoms. Our history would be lost. Such destruction is evidenced by the downfall of France in *Divide and Conquer* and *War Comes to America*, whose defeat by the Nazis is represented by images of Nazis in front of landmarks like the Arc de Triomphe and the Eiffel Tower.

As the *Why We Fight* films were shown to soldiers preparing for war, it comes as no surprise, then, that they endorse violence over pacifism. As mentioned earlier, Capra had no problem endorsing aggressive policies as a response to bullies. He, like Longfellow Deeds, believed that sometimes a

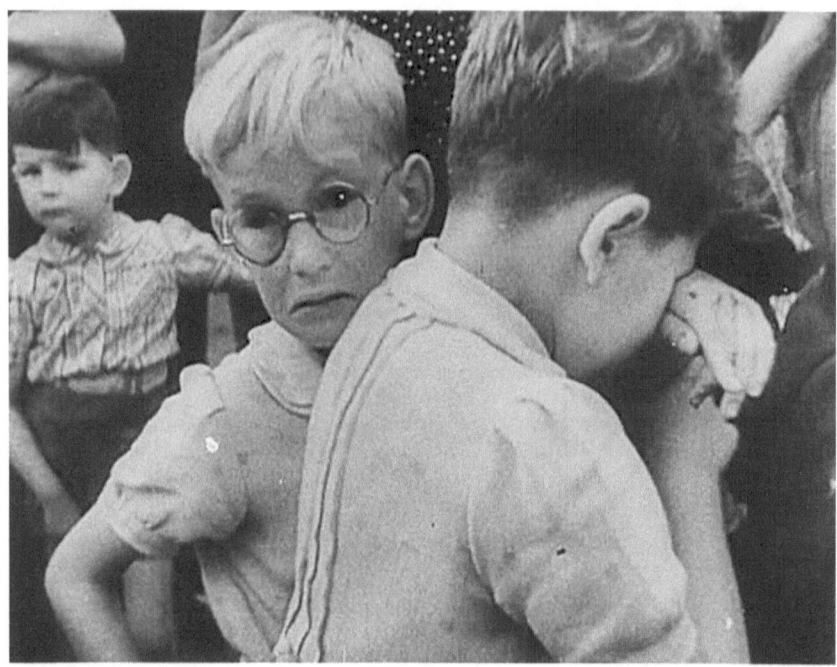

Starving French children worry about their fate during German occupation in *Divide and Conquer*.

"sock in the nose" was the only solution to problems. As such, great respect is shown in the series for men like Foch and Churchill, who chose to act rather than bargain, fight rather than compromise. Allied countries still in the war are shown to have a long tradition of fighting for their ideals. In the beginning of *The Battle of Russia*, for instance, a title shows Secretary of War Stimson, General Marshall, and General MacArthur praising the Russian people for their courage and "fighting spirit." In *War Comes to America*, the narrator states that the idea of democracy grew and took form in the "midst of battle" in the Revolutionary War. It also shows a statue of Patrick Henry, whose motto, "Give me liberty or give me death!" also proposed offensive attack, reminding the American viewer of the importance of fighting for ideals. *Know Your Ally: Britain* equates the Allied country to a lion, one who went from a "drowsy" state dropping leaflets, to a roaring one, dropping bombs.

Advocating action against a corrupt bureaucrat or politician on a safe, level playing field like a courtroom was one thing; encouraging men who had grown up in the isolationist atmosphere of 1930s America to give up their lives for their country was quite another. Capra understood that the war must be framed as a defensive war from the very beginning. Thus, the title of the last film of the series would be changed from *America Goes to War* to *War Comes to America*.[20] After the bombing of Pearl Harbor, it would be easy to sell a war of revenge against the Japanese, but for political reasons, the series primarily focused on justifying the war in Europe instead. In fact, Pearl Harbor is only mentioned twice in the series, once briefly at the beginning of *Prelude to War*, and once at the end of *War Comes to America*. Although public opinion favored making the Pacific war a priority, in the months after Pearl Harbor, American leaders like President Roosevelt believed Hitler was the greater threat, as he would be unbeatable if he defeated the Russians.[21] Capra and his team would thus have the difficult task of encouraging men to fight European countries who had not directly attacked them, while still maintaining that their country wanted peace, not war. Like the antagonists in Capra's narrative films, the Axis powers (more specifically, Germany), push the series' plot forward, with the Allied nations shown responding only to their actions. Thus, the narrator in *War Comes to America* would maintain that the Nazis "declared war on us long before we did anything about it." Footage of the Nazi rally in Madison Square Garden was used in both *War Comes to America* and *Prelude to War*, and Nazi officials would be shown gathering information about "your hometown" and sending German spies disguised as tourists in *The Nazis Strike*. Capra also believed he could advocate the need to fight the same way Churchill and Roosevelt had — as a last-ditch effort to save the world from the fascist powers. In a speech before the House of Commons in 1940, Churchill tried to encourage America to join the war by saying: "If we fail, then the whole world, including the United States, including all that we have known and cared for, will sink into the abyss of a new dark age made more sinister, and perhaps more protracted, by the lights of perverted science."[22]

Roosevelt agreed with Churchill in a speech in Charlottesville, Virginia, adding that the United States could not survive as "a lone island in a world dominated by the philosophy of force."[23] Capra demonstrated his support for this belief in *Prelude to War*, *War Comes to America*, and *Know Your Enemy: Japan* by showing, through animation, how Germany and Japan would use their conquests in Europe and Asia to invade the United States and take over the world.[24]

In reality, no such combined attack on America was planned. After 1941, Germany and Japan undertook no joint diplomatic initiatives, and neither discussed a single combined military or naval operation against the U.S. or any other country.[25] Furthermore, despite the attack on Pearl Harbor, Japan never saw the war as one of total conquest or domination. They never planned to invade the United States, and attacked Pearl Harbor only to gain greater influence in the Far East.²⁶ Although Hitler dabbled with plans for a long-range air arm and an ocean navy, an attack on America never figured in his immediate calculations.²⁷ Even more surprising, Chamberlain's policy of appeasement actually *helped* Britain win the war against Germany. By choosing not to fight when Germany invaded Czechoslovakia, Britain was able to increase their air production and perfect their system of radar just in time to defend the country against the Luftwaffe.²⁸ By justifying the American involvement in the war as an act of defense, however, Capra believed he could encourage soldiers to be like the heroes in his fiction films, who were peaceful only until pushed into aggressive action by powerful bullies. In case this justification did not work, Capra also framed the war as battle of two competing ideologies, hoping to convince soldiers that fighting in the war was a way to protect the ideas of democracy and liberty. In *Know Your Ally: Britain*, for example, the narrator continually states that the Allies are fighting not just for themselves, but for *all* free people.²⁹ Whatever the justification for fighting, Capra made sure the troops watching the film would understand that the time for words had past. A "sock in the nose" was the only way to handle the Axis. (In the years following the war, however, Capra would come to regret his position and become a pacifist.)

As in his narrative films, Capra would have to reconcile the urge to fight with the Christian "Love Thy Neighbor" policy. In films like *Mr. Deeds Goes to Town*, *Meet John Doe*, and *Mr. Smith Goes to Washington*, Capra was able to balance the fighting spirit of his heroes by limiting the amount and scope of their fighting. Jefferson Smith only attacked the reporters who publically embarrassed him; Longfellow Deeds attacked the literati in the restaurant and John Cedar only after they turned on him. In all these instances, Capra's heroes start off as warm, friendly, and respectful to their enemies, and only resort to violence after they are humiliated and betrayed. As discussed earlier, the *Why We Fight* series devotes a great deal of time justifying the need for the United States to enter the war. It would be a much more difficult feat, however, to strike a balance between helping your fellow man and killing your enemy when your main objective was to persuade men to fight. Capra understood that this balance must be found in order to accomplish his goal. The war must be justified morally as well as rationally to be effective. Visually, Capra and his team accomplished this by including very little footage of Allied soldiers actually shooting at the enemy. When enemy soldiers are defeated, they are shown more often as prisoners than corpses. *Prelude to War* and *War Comes to America* also uses narration to persuade its viewers of America's peaceful intentions. The narrator in *War Comes to America* states that Americans hate war and only want peace, while *Prelude to War* argues that peace for Americans means peace for all. *Tunisian Victory* also illustrates

5. The Capra Formula in His War Documentaries 161

This image of a destroyed church is used throughout the *Why We Fight* series to illustrate the antagonism of the Nazis towards Christianity.

this theme by showing shots of Allied soldiers being generous to noncombatants and civilians after battle scenes (e.g., giving candy to children and helping civilians). In *Prelude to War*, fighting is shown as a form of loving one's neighbor, as it repeatedly informs the viewer that isolationist thinking is selfish, as "our individual and national problems were and always will be dependent on the problems of the whole world." Britain, France, and Russia were our neighbors, after all, and we were letting them down by not joining the fight.

Capra further justified the use of force in his documentaries by continually putting Allied countries on the side of Christianity. Unlike the Nazis, who are shown destroying churches and preventing the exercise of religion, the Allied powers revere sacred institutions. (Strangely enough, this tactic was also used in Nazi campaign films, wherein German soldiers are depicted entering and exiting churches and cathedrals.)[30] American soldiers who went to war were not only helping their Allied neighbors, but were also defending Christianity and Christ's commandment to "Love Thy Neighbor." As President Roosevelt stated in his 1939 State of the Union address:

> There comes a time in the affairs of men when they must prepare to defend not their homes alone but the tenets of faith and humanity on which their churches,

their governments and their very civilization are founded. The defense of religion, of democracy, and of good faith among nations is all the same fight. To save one we must now make up our minds to save all.[31]

Capra reinforced the president's message by showing numerous shots of destroyed churches after Nazi attacks. To illustrate that America and its Allies revered Christianity, shots of large churches in low-angle shots were employed throughout the series. In addition, there are numerous shots throughout the series of Americans and their Allies attending church. In *Tunisian Victory* American soldiers are depicted worshipping in an outdoors Christmas service in Africa, thus showing that it is possible to serve one's country and practice one's faith simultaneously. *Know Your Ally: Britain* shows British people attending and leaving church, adding that the two countries are united in their religious freedom. *Prelude to War* uses a quote from Confucius similar to the Golden Rule to prove that America's Chinese Allies, who also never fought a war for conquest, followed the same Christian principles as its Western allies. Even Russian citizens are shown celebrating Christmas with their children in Moscow. By contrast, the religion of Japan is openly mocked in *Know Your Enemy: Japan*. While Germany worships Hitler, the Japanese are described as worshipping ancestors who "float around." In one part of the film, the narrator calls a group of religious Japanese statues "scarecrows." America, on the other hand, was justified in engaging in war because she followed the "Love Thy Neighbor" policy. The violent actions of the U.S. military, then, like the actions of Capra's fictional heroes, are forgiven because at its heart is the protection of the common man. In his war documentaries, Capra was attempting to equate whole nations with the idealistic, fictional characters of his narrative films. As most of his films depict the eventual triumph of the heroes over their enemies by the sheer "rightness" of their character, Capra seemed to be hoping that the same happy ending would be possible for America, as long as they held true to the basic moral truths of Christianity.

The plain-speaking narration in Capra's documentaries is reminiscent of both Capra's autobiography and his fictional heroes. Erik Barnouw called the films' commentary "muscular" and "down to earth," and noted their frequent use of slang and robust metaphors.[32] In *Prelude to War*, the narrator describes Mussolini "beating his chest like Tarzan" and urges the audience to fight because the "chips are down." In *Tunisian Victory*, Capra cleverly uses four narrators—two to provide the viewer with factual information, and two to represent average British and American troops. The American soldier, Joe McAdams from Kansas City, Kansas, speaks almost in complete slang, saying lines like, "There's too darn many ships to see at once" and "We've been hollerin' for action and now we're going to get it." The British soldier, George

5. The Capra Formula in His War Documentaries

Metcalf, does the same for his English brethren, stating at one point that if he's lucky, he'll "scoffer a few Jerries." Like in his prewar films, Capra uses slang and plain language to ingratiate his films with the common man watching them. This plain language also helps to generalize, even gloss over, complex issues and battles. In *Know Your Ally: Britain*, the narrator likens the bombings of England to a boxing match, where the country "took it on the chin" and received "body blow after body blow." In *Divide and Conquer*, the narrator compares de Gaulle's attack on the German supply line to a pin pricking the side of a rhinoceros.

Like the vocal delivery of James Stewart and Gary Cooper in Capra's prewar films, the narrators in Capra's documentaries often speak softly and with emotional honesty, especially after traumatic scenes.[33] In *The Nazis Strike*, for instance, over scenes of Polish suffering, the narrator states forcefully and quietly, "These things the Poles will not forget." Although most of the narration functions as a way to convey facts, Capra understood that difficult scenes must be handled emotionally in order to sell the reality of the moment. Emotional dialogue was also employed in an attempt to explain irrational actions. In a particularly memorable scene in *Tunisian Victory*, ordinary soldiers George Metcalf and Joe McAdams contemplate the actions of their enemy:

GEORGE: What's biting you, Joe?
JOE: I don't know. I can't help thinkin' all the hard work that went into those burnt out tanks and halftracks and aeroplanes. Gone for nothing.
GEORGE: Had to be done.
JOE: Oh, sure it did. But still in all, think of all the trucks and automobiles and things all that junk might have been.
GEORGE: I know. Bloody shame.
JOE: Just because he was told that he was a superman.
GEORGE: Well, he never figured things out for hisself. Never argued the toss same as we do. Too bad he didn't hear some of our arguments at the old Dog and Fox back home.
JOE: You know, I guess that's the real difference between us and them. We argue the toss, as you say, and they don't.
GEORGE: Yeah, if you don't argue the toss anymore, you aren't half a man anymore. You're just a bloomin' tool.

Such heartfelt dialogue not only brings the war home to the audience, but also separates the Allies from their enemies. This sequence from *Tunisian Victory* shows that American soldiers are allowed to speak their minds, while the enemy remains silent and emotionally distant. Throughout the *Why We Fight* series, the dialogue of Hitler and his generals is neither translated nor paraphrased. Often, Hitler's words are written on the screen. Unlike the narration, Hitler's written dialogue is stilted, emotionless, legalese. Like Norton,

Cedar, and Paine, Hitler uses large words and elaborate sentence structure to condescend, lie, and confuse the common man. *Divide and Conquer*, for instance, displays overwritten quotes of Hitler's including, "The Reich has put forth no claim which might in any way be regarded as a threat to Belgium." Such complex wording, when compared to the simple words of the narrator, appears false and emotionless. Simple language, in other words, is evidence of sincerity. A plain talker speaks from the heart, not the mind.

Capra's great distrust of mobs in his narrative films also continued in his war documentaries. As discussed earlier, Capra rarely shows singles of Axis soldiers, preferring instead to represent them as a mindless group. In *The Nazis Strike*, Capra inserts an extended goose-stepping montage, edited to humorous music. In *Know Your Enemy: Japan*, a shot of Japanese children marching is sped up to enhance its ridiculousness. Allied soldiers, however, are depicted as both groups and individuals. Capra illustrates that one need not give up one's individuality to fight for the military. In *Tunisian Victory*, for instance, the men on break all participate in different activities, from writing, to playing music, to playing cards. In one shot in *The Battle of Britain* (obviously recreated for the documentary), a British pilot is shown in profile, flying a plane without goggles and wearing a plaid scarf. Moments before, these pilots are seen scrambling to their planes wearing different types of jackets and different headgear. The same difference between pilots is noticeable in scenes showing the "Flying Tigers" at the beginning of the *The Stillwell Road*.

Capra spends a great deal of time showing the dangers of the Axis civilian "mobs" as well. In *Prelude to War*, the narrator states that the Germans, Italians, and Japanese people gave up their individual rights to become part of a "mass, a human herd." Like the crowd of conventioneers in *Meet John Doe*, these herds are more dangerous than any one individual, because when they get together, they lose the ability for rational thought and are capable of great harm. They also lose the ability to think independently, as illustrated in the many enemy crowd scenes throughout the series where the crowds simply chant one word over and over again. Capra seems to be unsure as to who or what is responsible for this absence of individualism in Axis countries. *Prelude to War* blames the people themselves for their misfortune, arguing that the German people throughout history have exhibited a natural love for discipline and regimentation. Both *Here is Germany* and *Your Job in Germany* show that in the 19th and 20th centuries, the German people lusted for conquest and violence. In *Prelude to War*, the potential harm of a German mob is shown visually by superimposing a club over a shot of a crowd at a Nazi rally.

The ultimate harm or benefit of a crowd, according to Capra (in both his narrative and nonfiction films), however, lies in the morality of its leaders.

5. The Capra Formula in His War Documentaries

When John Willoughby and Ann Mitchell lead the John Does, they are a force of great positive social change. D.B. Norton, however, is able to quickly transform them into a violent mob by distributing newspapers with false information. Americans, who are described as a "joining people" in *War Comes to America*, do not become mobs because they are able to use their power more productively and enact change through their elected officials. Throughout *Why We Fight*, Congress is almost always depicted as answering the will of the people rather than serving private interests.[34] Early in the series, Capra places most of the blame for the Axis atrocities on the leaders of the enemy powers. The citizens of Japan, for instance, were described as "fanatically united" under the emperor. Mussolini is described as an ambitious rabble-rouser in *Prelude to War*, leading the Italian people who mistakenly put their "trust and faith in one man." The first film in the series also includes a shot wherein close-up pictures of the three Axis leaders cuts to a massive group of soldiers. In addition, the actions of the Axis powers are ascribed to their leaders rather than their armies—*Mussolini* took Ethiopia and *Hitler* clubbed Norway into submission. As Thomas Bohn mentions in his book *Historical and Descriptive Analysis of the* Why We Fight *Films*, this tactic is not an uncommon tool in propaganda, as it is easier to focus hate on a specific individual than on an entire people.[35]

As leaders are the controlling force behind mobs, they must contain within themselves all the traits valued by Capra in order to move the mob towards a "Love Thy Neighbor" policy. As in his narrative films, the actions of large groups of people are dependent upon the moral character of the unique men who are placed above them. Men like Jefferson Smith, Robert Conway, Grandpa Vanderhof, John Willoughby, and Longfellow Deeds encourage large groups of people to perform great deeds because they are generous and playful; they work hard, not behind desks, but out in the world. They speak plainly and honestly. Vanderhof, Willoughby, and Deeds engage in spontaneous musical play. These "good" leaders inspire people to engage in positive collective acts. Smith's strong sincerity spurs his boys to print newspapers defending his ideals. Vanderhof's generosity is returned in the courtroom when the people of his neighborhood take up a collection to pay his fine. Willoughby and Deeds turn people towards a policy of "Love Thy Neighbor" through heartfelt speeches, and Conway's leadership role in Shangri-La encourages everyone in his party (except his brother) to use their skills to benefit the community.

The leaders of the Allies in Capra's war documentaries contain similar aspects of the leaders in his fiction films. As explained earlier, the uniqueness of the Allied leaders is perpetuated by the employment of "singles," shots in which they are isolated from others in the frame. In Eisenhower's singles, the general is usually shown as calm and collected, smiling warmly to the camera. *Tunisian Victory* depicts him standing on the side of the road eating his Christmas dinner out of a tin like the others. Winston Churchill is always shown actively engaged in his work, and his direct and emotional speeches are heard on the soundtrack more than any other leader, including Roosevelt. *Battle of Britain* shows him walking among the people, receiving a flower for his lapel from a woman in the crowd. Russia, however, proved to be an admitted "political problem" for Capra, as their current leader, Joseph Stalin, remained a controversial figure in America throughout the war.[36] To account for this problem, Capra modeled the heroism of the Russian people on the historical figures of Alexander Nevsky and Peter the Great. The courage and strength of these men are specifically highlighted in *The Battle of Russia* in order to represent the collective personality of the Russian people; the actions of historic leaders, thus, become the actions of an entire nation.

While Allied leaders are shown as warm, active, and hardworking, Axis leaders are depicted as selfish and manipulative. In *Prelude to War*, the narrator explains that for all Mussolini's promises, he planned to betray the common people for his "own selfish interests." Nazi leaders are described in *The Nazis Strike* as men who do not see the world being made up of "men, women, and children, but of labor and raw materials." In contrast to the warm smile of Eisenhower, the expressions of Axis leaders are usually angry or deadly serious. *The Nazis Strike* describes Hitler, Hess, and Goering as "humorless men." The same can be said about Norton, Taylor, and Cedar in Capra's narrative films. Only Anthony Kirby, Sr., and Senator Paine are able to be converted because they show the capacity for laughter.

The belief that good men are necessary to make positive changes in the world and convert the cynical and the distrustful is similar to Capra's fiction films wherein individual action is necessary before collective action is possible. Capra's films perpetuated his personal belief that individuals, inspired by the ideals of historic leaders of the past, are needed to inspire the collective people, who, in turn, rise up to enact social change. Like Bernays, Capra believed that the group could only make up its mind through the leadership of a trusted leader.[37] This idea, however, sends a contradictory message to the "common man." It grants them power by making them the primary agent of social change, but also requires them to follow the leaders placed above them. Thus, Capra's narrative films, which are supposed to be about the common people, usually place them in the background, focusing instead on the one unique leader who inspires them. This contradiction is also present in Capra's war films, as he attempts to capture both the individuality of soldiers and the power of their collective action. The films stroke the ego of the soldier by telling them they are fighting for individual liberty, while at the same time encouraging them to give up that liberty to follow the commands of chosen leaders. This philosophy of conformity also reflects the ideology of *Arsenic and Old Lace*, which basically encourages turning a blind eye to evil in one's own house, so long as it protects the status quo. Capra, who decided to return to the studio system after the failure of *Meet John Doe*, encourages soldiers to give up their own individuality to privileged leaders (with all their failings) in order to protect the ideals of America and the freedom of all people. Capra, who championed individuality in films like *Broadway Bill, Mr. Deeds Goes to Town, You Can't Take It with You,* and *Mr. Smith Goes to Washington*, seems to be stressing in his war films the need for conformity in times of great danger. As in *Lost Horizon*, wherein Robert Conway learns to enjoy being imprisoned in Shangri-La, Capra, who left a lucrative career to join the army, perpetuates the idea in his war documentaries that giving up one's liberty is necessary as long as you agree with the ideals of its leaders and you are protecting the liberty of your children. By the end of the war, Capra would once again question this belief, forcing him to seek out a new solution for the unending fight for freedom in his narrative films.

The Effect of Capra's War Documentaries

The connection between Capra's popular fiction films and his war documentaries leads to important questions about the relationship between personal beliefs and public responsibility. Although Capra's *Why We Fight* films claimed to be a "factual" account of the events that led up to America's involvement in the war, they also clearly framed the war through the techniques and ideology Capra perfected in his successful "common man" films of the '30s. Capra's reverence for Christian principles and American history, the expression of freedom through play and music, the use of children as a representation of a country's health and well-being, his preference for active, physical labor over intellectual desk work, his fondness for fighting over compromise, and his belief in the importance of plain talking, ideological leaders to spur men to action — all have been proven to play a predominant role in both. The establishment of such a connection leads one to ultimately wonder whether the perpetuation of Capra's ideology in his propaganda films was ultimately helpful or hurtful to America.

The audience of the films was unquestionably massive, playing to every American soldier and citizens around the world. Between 1940 and 1947, more than ten million men had been inducted into the United States armed forces, all being forced to watch the *Why We Fight* films that had been completed.[38] *Prelude to War*, the first film in the series, was shown to over 7,000,000 troops by 1945; as many as 8,000,000 saw *The Battle of Britain*.[39] At the peak of army enrollment, these films had a nightly audience of over 1,900,000 men, and over 10,500,000 hours of soldier time was used each month in watching them.[40] As a result, more people saw educational and informative films during World War II than any time before or since.[41] And yet, the mandatory showings of these propaganda films to millions of Americans caused few protests at the time. Erik Barnouw speculated this was a result of the large amount of respect the people had for General Marshall and because the films maintained a fairly mainstream view of the war.[42] The *Why We Fight* films were also translated into Spanish, Portuguese, and French, and distributed throughout Europe, South America, and Canada.[43] The entire series played in theaters in Great Britain, and American embassies played the films during the months of occupation, charging ten-cents admission.[44] *The Battle of Russia* was translated into a number of Russian dialects and shown throughout the U.S.S.R.

The effect of these films is hard to measure, as the soldiers who watched them came from a variety of different backgrounds and possessed different degrees of education. The experimental section of the Research Branch in the War Department's Information and Education Division did, however, conduct a series of studies of the first four films of the *Why We Fight* series. The survey showed that troops definitely preferred the films to the lectures. A majority of the men who saw the films liked them, and, perhaps more importantly, remembered much of the information from the films a week later.[45] Criticisms of the film usually revolved around the use of "faked" or "staged" material, and the repetitions of certain shots in different films. While the films were praised as a teaching tool, the survey concluded that they were not very persuasive. The *Why We Fight* films, apparently, explained the causes of the war well, but did not change soldiers' opinions about the war itself, create new opinions, or affect the motivation of soldiers.[46] Barnouw, however, noted that there was a sharp reduction of anti–British sentiment after the viewing of *The Battle of Britain*, that stayed with troops weeks afterward.[47] McBride mentions that soldiers had a greater estimation of the enemy's strength after watching *Prelude to War*, which may have actually *decreased* their motivation.[48] Thomas Bohn also acknowledges that, while the films may not have changed opinions, they may have been effective at reinforcing and strengthening opinions concurrent with those in the films.[49]

This lack of ideological interest among the soldiers of World War II has been documented in several interviews, surveys, and journals of the time. Bill Mauldin, Ernie Pyle, and John Hersey all noted in their dealings with troops on the front line that most U.S. soldiers were more interested in the simple life back home than in the causes and politics of war.[50] Michael Adams wrote in *Best War Ever* that World War II soldiers were possibly the *least* ide-

5. The Capra Formula in His War Documentaries 169

ologically motivated American force. In a study of enlisted men, only 5 percent stated that they fought for idealistic reasons, compared to 14.5 percent during the Vietnam war.[51] Adams writes that "there was a sense among the troops that the war was simply a job to be done. Most soldiers wanted to do their part and go home. Very few felt they should serve until the war was won."[52] Thus, the ideologically minded Capra was out of touch with the practical, realistic soldier from the very start.

This data, however, does not necessarily conclude that Capra's war documentaries were ineffective. The purpose of this work is to determine the connection between Capra's war documentaries and narrative films, hoping that connection will lead to a greater understanding of Capra's approach and the relationship between fiction and propaganda films. While there is no real conclusive evidence that the latter influenced the opinions of soldiers going to war, there can be no doubt that Capra's beliefs, as presented in his documentaries, played an influential part in how the war was perceived by both soldiers and citizens. In addition, these films perpetuated certain ideas about the war that America still holds to this day. Throughout the films, for instance, Capra shows a distaste for appeasement, even though it has been proven that appeasement gave both Russia and Britain valuable time to build up their military to stop future Nazi attacks. This anti-appeasement policy influenced the federal government's foreign policy in the decades following the war.[53]

In addition, Capra seems to elevate America over the other Allied nations throughout the series. Both *The Battle of China* and *The Battle of Britain* show that these countries needed America in order to defeat the Axis powers. As mentioned earlier, *Know Your Ally: Britain* shows statues of Washington and Lincoln in London. In one particularly disturbing image in *Prelude to War*, the world is shown with American flags on every continent. Such imperialist imagery, of course, elevates American culture as superior to all other cultures. In *Know Your Ally: Britain*, the narrator explains that the British consider talking about themselves bad form, while Americans call it "damn silly," adding that there is nothing about John Britain that America could not cure with a "correspondence course in showmanship." This negation of other cultures in order to elevate America would occur throughout the postwar era. There is no doubt that after the war, the United States was the most powerful, prosperous democracy in the world. After all, the war never destroyed any of its property or infrastructure. As a result of this newfound power and the belief that "they" won the war, America increasingly felt compelled to impose its view on other countries of the world. As John F. Kennedy explained in 1963, his generation of Americans, the World War II veterans, were "watchmen on the walls of freedom." Such beliefs could be said to have directly led to the involvement in Vietnam.[54]

The assumption of the guilt and corroboration of citizens during the war in films like *Know Your Enemy: Japan, Your Job in Germany*, and *Here Is Germany* was also perpetuated by Capra and played an increasing role in American policy during the last two years of the war. Even in the *Why We Fight* series, the German and Japanese people are shown as slaves, blindly obedient automatons who follow the commands of their godlike leader. This assumption of civilian guilt, however, would directly lead to decisions to bomb Axis towns and cities in order to discourage the enemy. Before the war, Capra did not seem to have many qualms about killing enemy civilians. In 1918, Arthur Noyes, chairman of the National Research Council, visited Throop Polytechnic and asked the young Capra his feelings about *Schrecklichkeit* — the willingness to kill noncombatants to achieve a military objective. Capra replied, "Theirs or ours? If you mean theirs, it's all right with me."[55] In World War II, at least 635,000 civilian men, women, and children in Germany died from American and British air attacks, including 25,000 during a single day of bombing Berlin, and 35,000 died during the firebombing of Dresden ten days later.[56] The reinforcement of such anti-civilian propaganda may have also been the reason very few officials questioned the dropping of atomic bombs on Nagasaki and Hiroshima. President Harry S Truman, for instance, later wrote that he "regarded the bomb as a military weapon and never had any doubt that it should be used."[57] Churchill added that "the decision whether or not to use the atomic bomb on Japan was never an issue. There was unanimous, automatic, unquestioned agreement around our table; nor did I hear the slightest suggestion that we should do otherwise."[58] Although Capra ultimately broke with this idea after witnessing the bombings in London, he did help in perpetuating the notion that enemy civilians were just as indoctrinated and irredeemable as the enemy soldiers.

Throughout the documentaries, Capra repeatedly shows the results of war through citizens or Allied soldiers, but does not include many shots of dead American soldiers. In *Tunisian Victory*, one dead American soldier is shown in a ditch, but the camera pans over to a living soldier shortly thereafter. Casualties are mentioned but never shown. It is not unusual for propaganda designed to encourage men to fight not to show graphic depictions of death and dismemberment. Such propaganda, however, paints an unrealistic portrait of the true nature of war. Battle scenes in Capra's films are more exciting than realistic, mainly showing the back-and-forth interplay of opposing cannon fire. Battles are loud in the films, but not brutal. As shown earlier in the narration of *Tunisian Victory*, Joe mourns the loss of equipment and raw materials rather than the loss of his fallen brothers. This was not always the case with war documentaries directed by other men. John Huston's critically praised film, *The Battle of San Pietro*, for instance, ends with showing

5. The Capra Formula in His War Documentaries

Americans burying their fellow soldiers and reminds the viewer that some of the living men pictured have since died. John Ford ends the *Battle of Midway*, too, with a burial sequence. Of course, unlike Frank Capra, these men had actually seen the destructive nature of war first hand. After witnessing such horrific events, they surely must have felt compelled to pay their respects to those who had fallen.

This lack of realism in showing war scenes, while understandable, also contributed to a glorification of war, especially among American civilians, who, like Capra, never witnessed the horrors of combat firsthand. As a result, there was less criticism of defense spending before and after the war.[59] Even more importantly, because civilians were spared scenes of dead American soldiers, most mainstream magazine editors believed that there would be very little adjustment time needed for returning veterans to recover from the trauma of war. *Good Housekeeping*, for instance, told wives that their returning husbands should be able to stop "oppressive remembering" in just two to three weeks.[60] Such glorification of war also prevents leaders from delivering more acceptable solutions to conflicts, mistakenly believing that war will bring prosperity and patriotism to their country. As Michael Adams wrote in *Best War Ever*:

> When nostalgia drives us to depict war as a golden age in our cultural development, a time of cheerful production, team spirit, prosperity, and patriotism, we trivialize the event by slighting the real suffering that took place; we make it a carnival. And we lose sight of the fact that war is inherently destructive — wasteful of human and natural resources, disruptive of normal social development. We risk initiating human catastrophes in the questionable belief that history shows us that wars will cure our social problems and make us feel strong again.[61]

When Capra decided to make his *Why We Fight* films and frame the war around his own perspective and beliefs, he perhaps unknowingly participated in the perpetuation of war. By explaining to soldiers why they were fighting, Capra may have also provided justification to continue fighting long after the war was won. Perhaps it was this realization that led him to become a professed pacifist in his later years. Although Capra's extremely productive war films may have given him the creative boost he needed after the failure of *Meet John Doe*, they also clearly affected the films he made after the war, especially *It's a Wonderful Life* and *State of the Union*, which continued to deal with the conflict between one's individuality and the powers of authority. With these films, Capra would be forced to update his idealistic and nostalgic view of life for the modern world, a world still reeling from the horrors of World War II.

6
It's a Wonderful Life *and Beyond*

Capra emerged from the war a different man, filled more with questions than answers. One thing he did not doubt, however, was that his service to the country made him any less relevant than he was before the war. In his autobiography, he claimed that he had been chosen to be the "first Voice of America" when he was asked to make his orientation films, and when he left the army, newly decorated with the Distinguished Service Medal, he felt a renewed sense of confidence about his role in reshaping postwar America.[1] The following passage in *The Name Above the Title* effectively describes Capra's feelings after the war, illustrating not only Capra's renewed belief in his talents but also revealing the lingering questions he still had about the horrific consequences of war:

> The cataclysmic aftermaths of war — hunger, disease, despair — would breed gnawing doubts in man. Why? Why? Why did my wife and children have to be blown to bits? Where is God now?... "Because," the minions of Big Brother were beginning to say in films and books," because, little man, of yourself you can do nothing to protect yourself from the fat exploiters. Wise up. You've been had. There is no God, no freedom, no democracy. Lies they are. Lies that cause wars. To hell with God and mother and your neighbors.... No, my films will explore the heart not with logic, but with compassion.... I will deal with the little man's doubts, his curses, his loss of faith in himself, in his neighbor, in his God. And I will show the overcoming of doubts, the courageous renewal of faith, and the final conviction that of himself he can and *must* survive and remain free.... And I will remind the little man that his mission on earth is to advance spirituality, that to surrender his free spirit to Big Brother's concentration camp is a step backward to the jungle.... And finally, my films must let every man, woman, and child know that God loves them, and that I love them, and that peace and salvation will become a reality only when they all learn to love one another.[2]

By the end of the war, Capra had come to see himself as a powerful force in the fight for the soul of the postwar survivor, a champion of the "little man" who demanded his films show people the correct way to live. But first, he would have to come to terms with his own feelings about his place in a

6. It's a Wonderful Life *and Beyond* 173

Capra uses the character of George Bailey (James Stewart, seated) to reflect the depression and anxiety both he and a number of Americans felt after the war. (RKO Radio Pictures/Photofest)

world that could be as horrific as it was beautiful. Capra's service to the country had also left him with questions about where one's individuality fits into society as a whole. Could one's individual actions truly change the world, or must one sacrifice his/her individual dreams for the sake of the community? In a system of pure liberty, where everyone acted the way he/she wanted to, would people ever be able to rise up as a collective to defeat the forces of corruption and deceit? How important are one's past achievements in a world where the rules have been forever changed? Capra's attempt to answer these questions, as well as his renewed confidence in his abilities as a filmmaker, would lead him to make his most important film to date, a film that after a long and winding path to success, would become one of the most beloved motion pictures of all time.

Postwar Capra and It's a Wonderful Life

World War II aroused contradictory feelings in Capra, as it must have done in any leader who encouraged American men to give up their lives to fight. Although Capra, like most Americans, believed the cause was right, the incredible atrocities brought about in the conflict gave him pause. The United States, the "good guys," won the war, but they also firebombed Dresden and dropped two atomic bombs on Japan. Millions of innocent civilians on both sides were killed, and a war with the Soviet Union seemed inevitable. What had really been accomplished? Had fascism been destroyed, or would it reemerge again? Could what happened in Germany and Japan occur in the United States, a country that had risen from the ashes as the world's foremost economic and military superpower?

These questions seemed to plague Capra, who wrote in his diaries during the war that he was personally appalled by the civilian casualties the Allies inflicted during the bombing raids.[3] He spoke of these feelings in a later interview:

> I didn't want to see anything more of war — the brutality of it upset me and so filled me with a feeling of the incompetence of the human race. If the best way they can think of settling an argument is dropping bombs.... There's nothing accomplished by that. Nobody's licked, because you can't lick the people.[4]

Although Capra only witnessed the carnage of the front lines from the safety of an editing booth, it is apparent that he was also profoundly affected by the bombings he witnessed in London. In an interview 30 years later, the memories of the event still haunted him: "Just to see those trembling people in London during the Blitz, poor, sick old ladies crying in terror.... Right then and there I felt that war, which had been pretty glamorous to me before — seemed pretty unglamorous, and rotten."[5]

Capra had become a believer in the idealized picture of the war he had created in his documentaries and found it difficult to understand the world of grey that emerged once it was finished. In an interview in 1972 for *Film Comment* he confessed that he did not understand how the government could send thousands of young men off to fight Germany and Japan, only to become their ally years later.[6]

Capra's mixed feelings about the war led to some substantial changes in his approach, not only to filmmaking, but to life itself. First of all, the brutality of the war made Capra wonder whether making films and taking an active part in the Hollywood scene were frivolous undertakings in serious times.[7] After some serious soul searching, however, Capra returned to filmmaking with a renewed dedication to the people. Having claimed never to have lost faith in the people during the war, Capra blamed most of the horrors of war on the leaders of the countries involved.[8] The war taught him that in a democracy, one could not stir people to action through regimentation and force. Furthermore, in the disillusioned postwar environment, he believed only entertainers could convey messages effectively. In addition, Capra felt that attacking the problems created by the war would be too transparent to American audiences. As a result, he decided not to make any films specifically about the war. Films like *The Best Years of Our Lives* no longer held interest for him. Like many "populists" after the war, Capra chose to retreat into the world of fantasy rather than harsh realism.[9] Finally, the sheer brutality of the war caused a personal change in Capra. Once leaving the service, he became a confirmed pacifist. As a result, none of the heroes in Capra's postwar films would ever resort to aggressive physical action to solve conflicts (although George does punch Bert the cop in order to escape in the nightmare sequence of *It's a Wonderful Life*).

When Capra decided to start making narrative films again, he found Hollywood a changed town. In his autobiography, Capra stated that during the war, the studios had switched from making quality pictures to "quantity" pictures. Capra saw this new preference for cheaper, faster pictures and mediocre talent as a death knell for the "one man, one film" idea.[10] As a result, Capra believed that the only way to preserve his independence and make good quality films was to once again break out on his own. This time, rather than creating another company with writer Robert Riskin, Capra partnered with producer Sam Briskin, director George Stevens, and director William Wyler to form Liberty Pictures. The company, incorporated in April 1945, reached a production agreement with RKO to make nine films, three from each of the company's famous directors. Briskin was placed as the business head and the company moved into a private bungalow in the center court of RKO studios. With Stevens still serving in the army and Wyler finishing *The Best Years of Our Lives* for Samuel Goldwyn, Capra would be the first to make a film for the fledgling independent company.

Capra considered many different projects before finally deciding to make a film based on a short story sent out as a Christmas card by Phillip Van

Doren Stern. In this story, titled "The Greatest Gift," a depressed banker named George Pratt is shown what the world would have been like had he never been born. Capra saw promise in the story as it contained many of the elements of his earlier films—a disillusioned, small-town hero, a message of hope amidst great despair, and the importance of family and generosity. Capra immediately secured James Stewart for the leading role, (renamed George Bailey), and hired Albert Hackett and Frances Goodrich to adapt the story, as Robert Riskin and Sidney Buchman were busy working on other films. After adding a few key scenes of his own to Hackett and Goodrich's script, Capra rounded out the cast with veteran actors Lionel Barrymore and Thomas Mitchell and newcomers Donna Reed and Gloria Grahame. On April 8, 1945, production began on *It's a Wonderful Life*, a film that would not only epitomize everything Capra had been trying to say as a filmmaker, but would also cause his imminent decline as America's top director.

It's a Wonderful Life
Based on the short story "The Greatest Gift"
by Phillip Van Doren Stern
(Released December 1946)

The plot of *It's a Wonderful Life* is fairly well known. As such, it is not necessary to go into a detailed summary of the film, but rather explain the differences between the short story and the completed script. Capra wanted his film to be a "celebration of the lives and dreams of America's ordinary citizens," who conduct their lives on a regular basis with warmth, honesty, and integrity.[11] As such, where the story focuses on the magical night when George discovers what the world would be like had he not been born, the majority of the film deals with the background of George's life, and the sacrifices he continually makes for his family and the community. In addition, because Stern chose to reveal the effects George had on the community to the reader only by having George react to their absence on Christmas Eve, the reader is passively engaged in the story—limited only to viewing the changes through George's point of view. Because Capra spends a great deal of screen time chronicling the positive contributions of George's life before the film enters the nightmarish world of Pottersville, the audience is more actively engaged; they are rooting for George to recognize what, to them, has been obvious all along—that George's life *is* important. Because the film focuses so much on the central character, Capra elevates George's status and importance in the community. In Stern's short story, George is an everyman with two children and a job at the First National Bank. In the film, however, George

6. It's a Wonderful Life *and Beyond*

is an icon in the community and runs the Building and Loan company, which not only allows the people of Bedford Falls to own their own homes, but is the only business in town that has not sold out to Mr. Potter (Lionel Barrymore). George in Capra's film is more than an everyman — his "specialness," his generosity, integrity, and passion makes him the only true defense against the evils of fascism. This may also be why Capra chose to kill off George's father, Peter Bailey, in the film (in the story his father is still alive). Capra understood that the removal of George's father early in the film would not only cause the audience to empathize with the young hero, but would allow George to quickly come into his own as an important, self-sufficient man in the community, albeit one with a profound link to the ideals of the past. George's "specialness" also allows Capra to exaggerate the effects of Pottersville, which has degraded into a den of corruption without George's leadership. While the changes in "The Greatest Gift" are more personal in nature, George's absence in Bedford Falls has left a large hole in the community, as no one has stepped forward to fill the vacuum left by him. Even Mary (Donna Reed), who is married with kids in the short story, has not been able to find a man equivalent to George in the parallel world of Capra's film, choosing to be an old maid rather than settling for someone less "special." Capra's film also includes historical details about what American life was like during the Great Depression and World War II, evoking a sense of nostalgia in the audience that is not necessary in the short story. As will be noted later, the addition of the war to Capra's story, most specifically that his brother Harry was a war hero, leads to greater insight about Capra's own feelings about the war and its place in American culture. Finally, it is Capra's addition of the villainous Potter that so drastically changes the nature of the story as originally written by Stern. In Stern's book there is no external conflict, only a vague internal one. The only Potter mentioned is a photographer who once took a picture of George and his brother, and George is not driven to suicide by an inciting event, but simply because he is feeling depressed. Capra needs an external adversary for George, not only because he is comfortable framing the story around the usual fight against fascism, but because adding Potter to the story makes it more understandable why George would be driven to suicide. In fact, in Capra's film, George starts out his Christmas Eve day in a wonderful mood. It is the careless actions of his Uncle Billy (Thomas Mitchell) and the unethical actions of Mr. Potter that drives him to the brink. The inclusion of Potter also shows that Capra believed that the fight against fascism had not ended with the defeat of Hitler, as the sometimes unequal capitalist system of the United States could still create oppressive regimes.

The technical aspects in the flashback sequences of the film are very similar to Capra's other films. The film is shot primarily from a slightly lower than eye-level point of view, and most of the scenes are either covered in medium shots or long shots. The silent reactive close-up is employed sparingly throughout the film — when Mr. Gower tastes the poison; when Mary first sees George at the dance; when George finds out the board will vote with Potter after his father's death; and when George is pushed away from his mother in the nightmare sequence. The editing of the film feels quicker than the editing of Capra's earlier films, and Capra quickly advances through the main chapters of George's life without the use of titles and establishing shots. Like most of Capra's villains, Mr. Potter wears a suit and tie and sits behind a desk, while George is rarely shown in his office and most of the time appears fairly disheveled. Capra continues his use of the bell, not only to mark the beginning and end of the picture, but also in the film's final act when he is reminded that "every time a bell rings, an angel gets his wings." George is shot in singles throughout the film as Capra most certainly wanted the audience to sense the isolation he feels throughout the picture. In a scene in Potter's office, for instance, when Potter asks George if he wants to work for him, Capra places an assistant behind Potter, but leaves the wall behind George empty. In addition, like Capra's other films, there is very little orchestral music in the film (save for the Pottersville sequence), and Capra once again uses traditional music in the opening and closing credits. Many times in the film, characters bond over a shared improvisational song. George and Mary sing "Buffalo Bill" and the entire town of Bedford Falls sings "Hark! the Herald Angels Sing!" and "Auld Lang Syne" in George's living room at the end of the film.

Capra also borrows some of the plot devices and thematic techniques from his earlier films. He invokes the policy of "Love Thy Neighbor" throughout *It's a Wonderful Life*, but does not include the use of churches as locations or ministers as characters. The film, however, is the most religious work of Capra's career, not just because it employs an angel as one of the characters (in Stern's story, it is never mentioned that the little man who helps George actually is an angel), but because God is so often invoked throughout the film. In an interview with Frank Capra in the *Los Angeles Times* right before the film went into production, Capra stated that one of the most important agendas for *It's a Wonderful Life* was "to combat a modern trend towards atheism which [was] very much present in the world."[12]

Like Jefferson Smith, George Bailey inherits the ideals of his father and suffers for it at the hands of greedy, powerful men. The main climax of the film, as in most of Capra's films, revolves around the increased suffering of the main character at the hands of his enemy. This suffering, which leads to his near suicide, forces the people who know and respect him to come to his aid in his darkest hour. As in *Meet John Doe* and *Mr. Smith Goes to Washington*, however, the triumph of the common people changes very little of the prevailing social structure of the town. Although thwarted in his most recent effort to suppress the hero, Potter (like Taylor and Norton) still retains most of his power at the end of the film. In fact, as Leland Poague points out, Potter's power actually grows stronger throughout the film.[13] Finally, as in many of Capra's films, *It's a Wonderful Life* shows that groups of ordinary people can be capable of extreme generosity and extreme anger, although the people who make a run on the Building and Loan in this film are much more cordial and inviting than the typical Capra mob. Perhaps Capra's service in the military and his witnessing of the suffering of ordinary people during the war softened his beliefs in the danger of mobs, as in the films after *Wonderful Life*, the mob mentality of ordinary people is all but obsolete. The descent of many of the Bedford Falls citizens and the subsequent change in their personalities with the absence of George Bailey also reinforces Capra's belief that ordinary people must be led by righteous individuals in order to be happy and successful.

For all the attributes that *It's a Wonderful Life* shares with Capra's prewar films, it possesses some marked differences from his earlier works. A substantial number of these differences derive from the changes in both Capra's personality and his filmmaking style that took place during the making of the war documentaries. First of all, despite the "magical" qualities of *It's a Wonderful Life* (and possibly because of them), there seems to be a greater sense of reality present in this film as opposed to his earlier films. The set design is more complex and detailed in both the flashback sequences and the later Pottersville scenes. There are more exterior scenes, and as a result, Bedford Falls appears bigger and more substantial than either Washington, D.C., in *Mr. Smith* or New York City in *Mr. Deeds*. In addition, Capra juggles more recurring characters in *It's a Wonderful Life*, which helps to sell the realism of the film's location. As Capra was better able to sell the reality of Bedford Falls and Pottersville through the use of detailed sets and recurring characters, he leaves out the use of silent, picturesque faces he so frequently employed to recreate reality in his early films. Capra's newfound commitment to reality may have originated from his continued exposure to the inherent reality contained in the documentary footage used in the war documentaries. During the war, Capra attempted to seamlessly integrate "manufactured" footage with real footage. As the producer of the war films, Capra must have developed a skill to detect the potential "phoniness" of these recreated shots in order to preserve the reality. This skill certainly could have leaked over into the production itself. The realism of the film, in fact, leaks over to into the acting as well. Never before had Jimmy Stewart appeared so vulnerable and real as he does playing George Bailey. Capra allowed the actor to dig deep into his dark side, which may have come easier for Stewart after his service in the war. After his dark turn in *It's a Wonderful Life*, more complex roles were offered to him, resulting in a vibrant second career after the war, working with great directors like Anthony Mann, Alfred Hitchcock, and John Ford. Even though Capra had not directed an actor for more than four years, his directorial skills in *It's a Wonderful Life* are top-notch. All the actors in the film feel like they actually live in Bedford Falls, and there is not one poor performance in the bunch. Capra even manages to get decent performances out of the child actors in the opening scenes of the film.

In addition to the lack of violence in the film, Capra's first postwar film has a gentleness about it that is equaled only by *Lost Horizon*. That gentle spirit is perhaps due to the lack of any particular deadline until the final half hour of the film. As in most Capra films, the director spends a great deal of time allowing us to get to know and love the major players so we can empathize with them in the film's final moments. The rare use of flashbacks allows Capra to create expectations and suspense for the viewer (who knows that George is about to kill himself) without burdening the main characters with that knowledge. As such, we often get to see George in moments of real happiness because he is, at that moment, completely unburdened. We witness the joy on George's face as he interacts with his father at the dinner table, the excitement he feels waiting for his brother to return from college, and the impatience and nervousness on the day of his marriage. As on Christmas Eve, however, all these great days end up dramatically different than how they started. What makes *It's a Wonderful Life* so fresh (even after multiple viewings), is that the tragedies in the film always seem to catch us unexpectedly, as they occur right on the heels of the film's most enjoyable moments.

The gentleness of the film also comes from the amount of genuine caring moments we witness between the characters. Unlike Capra's previous heroes (John Willoughby, Longfellow Deeds, and Jefferson Smith) who are taken to foreign environments where they have no real allies or friends, George (like Apple Annie) has a great number of people who truly care about him and share in both his dreams and his misfortunes. Mr. Gower gives George a suitcase for his trip overseas, Bert and Ernie assist Mary in renovating the house on 320 Sycamore, Mr. Martini shows genuine concern for George in his bar on Christmas Eve, and of course, they all pitch in to help George replace the missing funds to keep him from going to jail. This sense of community is hinted at in other Capra films, like *You Can't Take It with You* and *Lady for a Day*, but the communal scenes in these films are few and far between. The sense of community pervades *It's a Wonderful Life*, and it is my assertion that this feeling is derived from Capra's wartime service, where he and his community of workers and filmmakers bonded closely together, working long hours under impossible deadlines with substandard equipment to meet the needs of a country in crisis. Although Capra left the service disillusioned by the brutality of war, he also forged intense friendships that would last for decades. This communal spirit benefitted the story of *It's a Wonderful Life* because the film is essentially a love story between a man and his home town. George Bailey's main flaw is his continued underestimation of the love and support of his family and friends. Instead of embracing this love, George continually fights against it, wishing to leave Bedford Falls for destinations unknown. His lack of awareness nearly causes him to forfeit his own life.

George Bailey is also a much different character than Capra's previous heroes. For one, George is a married man and, as such, has devoted ally in his wife, Mary. George is also a father and, as such, cannot employ the risk taking measures of single men like John Willoughby and Jefferson Smith. George's commitment to his family adds to the despair of his situation on Christmas Eve, which is poignantly illustrated in the scene wherein George returns home after learning that Uncle Billy has lost the money. In this scene, which Sam Girgus claims is "one of the most moving and powerful in American film history," Capra cleverly intercuts single shots of George tearing up the living room with groups shots of Mary and the children.[14] Such composition and editing enhances the pain and isolation George feels, and helps the audience understand why George crawls to Potter for help, an act no other Capra hero would ever do.

In addition to George's status as a family man, he stands out amongst Capra's other heroes because of his active voice. Unlike Deeds, Smith, and Willoughby, who must learn to speak for themselves, George has no difficulty speaking his mind as a child, or later to Potter. No learning curve is needed. George's moving words not only convince the board of directors not to sell the Building and Loan to Potter, but also prevent a run on the bank. George's only real difficulty with Potter is the old man's persistence. Had Uncle Billy not misplaced the deposit money, Potter would never have gained the upper hand.

Unlike Mr. Deeds and Mr. Smith, George Bailey rarely engages in playful activity, with the exception of the memorable scene with Mary following the dance. Unlike Capra's other heroes, George is burdened with responsibility for both the Building and Loan and his family. As a result, George is much more experienced, less imaginative, and more intellectual than his predecessors. As he is less childlike, George is also less naïve, seeing through Potter's attempt to hire him as a way for the old man to take control of the town. George is also more conflicted, torn between his responsibilities to the community and his longing to escape Bedford Falls. The unresolved conflict causes him to lash out in anger and sometimes fall into depression. The tension

George feels between these two contrasting goals also allows him to be easier prey for Potter, who frequently exploits the young man's inner turmoil to his own advantage. As pointed out by Charles Maland, while George's external conflict is very close to other Capra heroes, it is his internal conflict that makes him unique.[15] He is more complex and definitely not "too good to be true." Capra's disillusionment with the war may have led to a realization that an idealized character might do more harm than good. He also may have been responding to the needs of a postwar audience who, having seen the inhumanity of the war, had come to accept that the human perfection of Jefferson Smith and Longfellow Deeds was impossible. As such, both *It's a Wonderful Life* and its follow-up, *State of the Union*, contain flawed but idealistic protagonists. George's conflict, the juggling of moral responsibility and personal ambition greatly resembles the conflict of Frank Capra at the time he signed up for the service. He admits in his autobiography that he made *Arsenic and Old Lace* entirely for the money. He had sacrificed his independence and failed the "little man" who had challenged him to only make films that said something. He, no doubt, felt that his service in the army compensated for this misstep, but his devotion to his patriotic duty ended up hurting his lucrative film career. Like George Bailey, Capra had chosen responsibility over personal ambition, but still mourned the loss of what might have been.

Furthermore, George's conflict between morality and ambition, responsibility and power, had also been felt by President Lincoln, who was constantly torn between the right thing to do and the selfish, convenient choice. While George does not directly mention Lincoln or other historical figures, as do Capra's previous heroes, Capra does feature Lincoln in one of the film's most stirring scenes. As George rips up his living room in front of his wife and children out of frustration over the missing money, a picture of the 16th president can be seen in the background. As in *Meet John Doe*, the placement of this picture behind the hero is no accident. It is meant to equate George with President Lincoln, a smart everyman who was also torn apart by his morality, his personal ambition, and his sense of duty.

Upon viewing *It's a Wonderful Life* most recently, however, I was taken aback by two aspects of the film I had previously overlooked — its self-reflexivity and its assimilation of the major issues of World War II. Unlike the previous films of Capra, which, except for the montages, refrained from using techniques that would call attention to the filmic aspects of the medium, *It's a Wonderful Life* is filled with innovation and self-conscious techniques. The opening sequence, for instance, uses animation to depict the angels as blinking stars. Images are blurred and pulled into focus for Clarence (and, thus, the audience) to view George's past, and in the first scene with Jimmy Stewart, the frame stops and holds on him. Dissolves and wipes are used throughout,

6. It's a Wonderful Life *and Beyond* 183

A painting of Abraham Lincoln is placed in the background behind George Bailey (James Stewart) when he tears up his office in one of *It's a Wonderful Life*'s most powerful scenes.

and voice-over commentary of the angels and Clarence are employed during the film's flashback scenes. Such techniques would have been unheard of in Capra's prewar films. After using these techniques so effectively in his war documentaries, Capra must have felt confident in employing them in a narrative film. As in the war documentaries, these tricks may have been intentional, in order to distract the audience from the inherent ideological contradictions in the material.[16] Such techniques, along with the "magical" quality of the story, make this Capra film especially unique.

In addition to breaking from his normal style with the use of self-conscious techniques, Capra also drastically changes the entire look and feel of the film during the nightmarish "Pottersville" sequence. In this engrossing part of the film, Capra uses low-key, dramatic lighting, wide-angle close-ups, and a noticeable musical score to drastically set this version of Bedford Falls apart from the Bedford Falls to which we have grown accustomed. The traditional hymns and standards of Bedford Falls have given way to the jazz and dance music of Pottersville. Much like the *Why We Fight* series, Capra is not only showing us two contrasting worlds, dark and light, but also suggesting that both of these worlds are equally plausible in the United States. In addition, Capra proved with this sequence that he could make moody film noir stories as well as any postwar director of the time. The abandonment of this dark style at the very end of the film also proved that, although Capra could shoot films in that stylized manner, he preferred not to. In the noir world of Pottersville, Capra's old style, like George Bailey, is completely unrecognizable. There is a hint of this film noir style at the end of *Meet John Doe*, but the abruptness of the change in *It's a Wonderful Life* calls attention to the filmmaking process itself. (Much like the scene where Marty McFly arrives in Hill Valley in the 1950s in *Back to the Future*, viewers of Capra's films are rewarded by noticing the many subtle differences between the two worlds.) Subtleties in set design and costuming lead to enjoyable, multiple viewings, and encourages deconstruction. Like God, Capra proves to the audience that he has the power to change the scenery and the style of the filmmaking at any time, and this abrupt change in style adds some much-needed dramatic weight to the story.

These self-conscious techniques remind viewers that they are watching a film, and adds to the self-reflexive nature of the plot itself. From the very beginning, we are told by the angels that we are watching George's past life from the view of the present—the same approach used in the *Why We Fight* films. As in a film, all the action has already happened—we, like Clarence, are simply reviewing the main points and scanning for important details. We are placed in the position of observers, with George and the cast set up as the major players. George's primary problem is that he does not realize that he is a character in a film. He is always surprised by fate, unaware that the script has already been written and his character arc has been worked out. Like Truman Burbank in the *Truman Show*, George keeps trying to leave his home town in order to break out of the current narrative, even though the audience knows he will never make it out of Bedford Falls. Only a few people seem to understand that George is the main character of the film. Mr. Potter recognizes George's importance in the boardroom after Peter Bailey's death, and immediately becomes a catalyst for change, trying to transform the traditional Capra idealistic narrative (which he finds boring and naïve) into a story fueled by man's baser instincts (as in the nightmarish Pottersville sequence).

Both George's wife and mother, however, understand that the film is about George's relationships with those around him, and manipulate him into following the intended narrative. From the moment George and Mary throw rocks at the old house on Sycamore, the audience understands that Mary is in charge of the narrative proper. While George tells the viewer his wish out loud, Mary does not have to reveal her wish at all. We, like Mary, know from the beginning of the dance scene that George and Mary's relationship is inevitable—it does not have to be said out loud. Only George is ignorant to this playing-out of fate. In a later scene, George's mother encourages him to visit Mary the day Harry comes back from college, as if knowing that Mary is necessary for George to move on to the next chapter. George goes one way, but ends up at Mary's house as if magically teleported there. Mary, aware that their relationship has a deeper meaning, places reminders of the earlier scene (the "George Lassos the Moon" drawing and the "Buffalo Bill" song) in an attempt to convince George that two scenes are connected as part of a larger narrative. The whole film feels as if Mary were watching George with one eye and the script with the other. In a later scene, it is she, not George, who offers up the couple's money for their honeymoon to prevent the bank run — another surefire way to keep George in Bedford Falls. Mary, who saw the importance of the house on Sycamore the minute she stood in front of it with George, arranges to spend their wedding night in the old house in order to give their future home added significance. The feeling of inevitability is furthered in the way the flashbacks are broken up, as each scene ends with George making the decision towards family or towards staying at the Building and Loan and Bedford Falls. In each case, Mary attempts to make that decision easier for George, greasing the wheels for the narrative to move smoothly from one point to the next. George's reward for making the right decision is the ability to move forward in the narrative. When Uncle Billy loses the money, George once again doubts his place in the story. As illustrated in the film's final scene, had he simply told Mary his problems at that point, the happy ending would have taken place then. Instead, George again feels the need to break away from the intended narrative, this time wishing to be removed from the story completely. Clarence obliges, and proves to George (and the audience) that a film without an idealistic, optimistic hero is nothing more than melodramatic trash. George's wish to become part of the story again, and his subsequent return to the house, proves that he has regained confidence in the narrative Mary has created for him. In fact, everything Mary has done throughout the film adds up to the final scene in their living room — her marriage, her children, the renovation of the old house, the people who arrive to give George the money, even the Christmas tree in the background — are all there due to her actions. She even tells George to stand in front of the tree to produce the maximum effect, as all the supporting characters line up for what amounts to a curtain call. In the end, George finally follows Mary's commands (going along with the story) and receives his happy ending.

The evocation of World War II in *It's a Wonderful Life* is particularly interesting, especially as the film was made immediately after Capra completed his war documentaries for the United States government. Analyzing the role the war plays in the film leads to interesting insights into how Capra viewed his service in the war and what he felt America should be after its victory. Like Capra, George Bailey does not directly fight in the war, but participates in the fight by working tirelessly on the home front. His brother Harry, who actually served in the war receives all the honor and attention. Capra, however, hints at George's superiority to Harry throughout the film. Without his older brother's sacrifice, for instance, Harry would not have been able to go to college and meet his future wife. In fact, without George, Harry would not exist at all. Furthermore, by saving Harry's life in one of the opening scenes of the film, George's ear becomes damaged, which in turn makes him ineligible for the war. Had it not been for Harry, George would have been able to serve his country overseas. Had it not been for George, Harry would never have served at all. As Clarence points out in the Pottersville cemetery, had George not saved Harry, all the men Harry saved on the transport would have died. Through this clever twist, Capra seems to be saying that the values, sacrifice, and devotion of men like George, although usually unrecognized, is actually what caused America to achieve victory the war. George's superiority is further confirmed by Harry himself at the end of the film. Harry—the man the whole town has been talking about, the man who made the front page of the newspaper—toasts George, the one who stayed behind, as the "richest man in town." Harry's admission of George's superiority is Capra's way of congratulating himself for his work during the war. Without Capra's films, the American soldier might not have been inspired to fight, as without George's sacrifice, Harry would not have been able to save the men on the transport.

Harry's deference to George also serves another purpose, as it reflects Capra's desire to redirect America back to traditional values after the war. When Harry holds up his glass to George, Capra is illustrating that America's military achievements (as represented by Harry) are *not* what makes this country great. What sets America apart from all other countries is its preservation of liberty and the hard work and dedication of its chosen leaders (as represented by George). While Harry fought against fascism overseas, George had been fighting against fascism and the rights of the common man his whole life. Without George's continued devotion to the common man, there would be no Bedford Falls at all, just the police state of Pottersville. The real fight against fascism is where Capra has shown it to be all along in his narrative films—on the home front. Thus, in *It's a Wonderful Life*, Capra is trying to redirect the public's attention away from America's victory in the war and back to its cities and towns, where the Potters of the world still exist. In fact, too much attention to America's military achievements could make us overconfident and distract us from the more important battles at home. Capra's warning to America not to let down its guard is best illustrated in the fateful scene when Uncle Billy loses the money. Billy, beaming over Harry's war hon-

6. It's a Wonderful Life *and Beyond*

ors in the paper, loses the money to Potter when he tries to rub Potter's nose in Harry's success. His overconfidence, inspired by Harry's victory, nearly leads to the destruction of the Building and Loan, the only business in town that protects Bedford Falls from Potter's greed and machinations. If we lose ourselves in these critical times, Capra seems to be saying, we could lose everything for which we fought. Thus, Harry toasts George (a representation of both American traditions and, in a way, Capra himself) because George has fought through both the disillusionment and heady optimism of postwar America to continue the fight against Potter. Harry has become irrelevant — America needs new leaders like George Bailey to remind the common people of the values of their ancestors, inspiring them to continue the fight for freedom, this time on American soil.

Much has been made about the ending of *It's a Wonderful Life*. Film scholar Robin Wood, for instance, believes the genius of the film lies in its complex ending. Although it seems to end on a happy note, the audience is all too aware of the "extreme precariousness of its basis." Good men like George Bailey can be pushed to suicide; Bedford Falls can easily turn into Pottersville.[17] Furthermore, the absence of Mr. Potter in the final scene means that the old man never gets his comeuppance. He remains unpunished and unrepentant to the end. According to Sam Girgus, Capra's ending offers a way out for those disillusioned by the war. When George Bailey is faced with a major crisis in his life, he, like many war veterans of the time, becomes cognizant of his insignificance and the fragility of civilization. The ending reveals, to those affected by war, that the material possessions promised by the American Dream cannot heal the enormous psychic break caused by war. As in the *Why We Fight* series, the ending illustrates that a community, strengthened by the ideals of leaders and knit together by compassion and charity, is what is truly necessary to keep the American Dream alive. On a more somber note, the ending of *It's a Wonderful Life* also repeats the theme of *Arsenic and Old Lace*, that a certain amount of conformity is necessary in order to appreciate life. As Girgus points out, George Bailey's return home to face the consequences of the missing money signifies that one must not only be willing to give up one's freedom and independence in order to move on after difficult times, but one must also learn to accept that "death, aggression, and unhappiness" are a part of everyday life.[18] Throughout his journey, George has been unwilling to accept these truths of the modern world, driving himself to the point of hysteria by taking on all the problems single-handedly. He does not understand until the end of the film that a certain amount of acceptance of the world's sinful nature is necessary in order to better recognize and appreciate the good. The Pottersville sequence forces George to witness the darker sides of the people he loves, and by choosing to "live again" (in spite of this knowledge) shows that George has learned to accept both the good and the evil in the world. Potter's comeuppance is not necessary because he has become irrelevant. Ultimately, *It's a Wonderful Life* is not about the fight against evil and fascism as these battles will continue to rage until the end of time. George's final decision reminds us that it is the decision to live in spite all of these problems that makes humankind truly exceptional.

It's a Wonderful Life demonstrates a vast amount of personal introspection on Capra's part which, I believe, ultimately grew out of his service to his country. He entered the service in order to bring about a change in the world, but found that once the war was over, the world had stayed relatively the same. Those who had once been our enemies were now our allies, and big businesses in America had only grown larger. The studio system was still in place and still stifled the creativity of the individual. In *It's a Wonderful Life*, Capra shows the understanding that fascism will always exist because the desire for power and fame is within each of us. In order to effectively rise up against the Potters of the world, we must learn to accept that there is a little bit of Potter in each of us. Because every individual is capable of selfishness and inhumanity, the battle will never end.

Whereas many creative people would use this realization as an excuse to write stories teeming with despair and cynicism, Capra left the war with a renewed sense of purpose, hoping that he could finally solve the problem that had troubled him for the past decade. The eternal struggle in America, as Capra saw it, was between the individual and those who wanted to stifle his/her unique voice. As long as the conflict was external and the heroes were pure, as in *Mr. Deeds*, *Mr. Smith*, and *You Can't Take It with You*, the problem was fairly easy to solve. As mentioned earlier, the goodness of the individual would either defeat the villains or convert them. As war in Europe became inevitable, Capra seemed to understand that the force behind the fascist power was growing stronger, and in *Meet John Doe* he was unable to realistically find a way to defeat those powers. Not only were the men in power untouchable, but the internal conflict of John Willoughby between his own selfish aspirations (wanting to be a pitcher) and the need to help the ordinary, everyday people made it all the easier for men like Norton to turn the people against him. In *Arsenic and Old Lace*, Capra seemed to suggest that rampant individualism may, in fact, be a bad thing for society, and one must learn to find peace with America's unending struggle between forced conformity and individualism. One can achieve this peace by focusing on one's own immediate family and by not reflecting too much on the bodies buried in the cellar. America of the present (as symbolized by Mortimer Brewster) could only move forward by embracing its valued traditions (represented by Elaine) and putting its knotty past (the Brewster House and family) in proper perspective.

6. It's a Wonderful Life *and Beyond*

In the *Why We Fight* series, Capra proposed that the valued traditions and ideals of America would ultimately mean victory over fascism. This victory would allow America to be born anew — its internal struggles would give rise to a new belief in individual freedom in the United States, its values and traditions vindicated by the defeat of the Axis. Capra anticipated this "purity" of America by idealizing its values and history. If soldiers were to fight for their country, they would have to be convinced of the goodness of its past, present, and future motives. Thus, with the *Why We Fight* films, Capra ignored the internal conflicts of both our country and ourselves and focused once again on the external struggle for freedom.

Capra's subsequent disillusionment of the war, brought about by the bombings he witnessed in London and the civilian bombings of Japan and Germany by the Allies, caused him to once again doubt the "purity" of the United States. Making America "too good to be true" as he did with his heroes of the '30s, may have helped to win the war (as it helped America get through the Great Depression), but may have damaged the country in the postwar world by creating a sense of overconfidence and superiority. These attitudes could cause the common people to revere those in power, who would, in turn, use that power for their own greedy ends. During this time, Capra was also struggling with his own decision to conform in times of risk. He had abandoned his independent company to make *Arsenic* for Warner Bros. and signed up for the U.S. Army. Now that the war was over, however, Capra's choice to start his own company meant that he would once again make films warning individuals of the dangers of mass conformity — only this time, his hero would have to win the fight for freedom without being too good to be true. Capra would have to come up with a permanent solution to the problem of *Meet John Doe*.

It is my opinion that *It's a Wonderful Life*'s solved the difficult dilemma posed by Capra in *Meet John Doe* — how an internally divided individual can fight against a powerful elite, single-minded in their selfishness. Capra understood that after the war, few would accept a character who completely embodied purity and goodness, so, as mentioned above, he made sure that George Bailey would be constantly torn between his own selfish desires and his responsibility to the community. Unlike John Willoughby, who is undeservedly placed on a pedestal from the very beginning, however, George Bailey *earns* his leadership role by personally making connections with the people in his community. While John Doe is distant, confused, and scared by the people who follow him, George lives with them, loves them, and cares about them. This change in the Capra hero may have grown out of Capra's own reignited feelings of unity with the common people — feelings that came about through his empathy with the victims of the bombings in London and through the inspiring teamwork of his *Why We Fight* productions. In *Meet John Doe*, the ending feels forced because the "John Does" who show up to save Willoughby from jumping, like the audience, do not really know *who* Willoughby is. Thus, we do not understand why they would want to join John in the fight. In *It's a Wonderful Life*, Capra includes many instances of George unselfishly helping the people of Bedford Falls, and we understand why they would help him in his time of need. George's past failures are outweighed by his continued generosity. Although flawed and conflicted, he is still able to momentarily triumph over the forces of fascism by inspiring others to join him in his cause by living a life of continued service and generosity.

The ending of *It's a Wonderful Life* also helped Capra with his own internal conflicts. Like George Bailey, Capra realized that, with a little help from God, he would be able to view his life and career with greater perspective. George Bailey's happy ending illustrates that, while we all have selfish dreams and a desire for power, if we can look back on our lives and see that overall we had a positive impact on the world, then we can be proud what we have accomplished. *It's a Wonderful Life* proves that Capra had finally come to terms with the guilt he had carried over his own success, a problem that had plagued him since *It Happened One Night*. Yes, he had made a great deal of money by making films about the "little guy," but his films also gave hope to millions of Americans when they needed it most. *It's a Wonderful Life* showed that Capra no longer viewed the American public as an unknown mass of people waiting to judge him, but as a group of human beings who would support his efforts, despite his flaws, as long as he continued to champion their causes. Because it seems to solve all of the issues addressed in both Capra's '30s films and his service in the war, *It's a Wonderful Life* has become his most important film. As such, the films he made afterwards feel little more than a prolonged epilogue.

Although both Frank Capra and Jimmy Stewart considered *It's a Wonderful Life* their favorite film, when it was released in December of 1946, the public largely stayed away.[19] The film grossed only $3.3 million in its initial release, $480,000 less than the cost of making the film.[20] At the time, *New York Times* critic Bosley Crowther believed the film's ending embraced illusions rather than true realities, and felt that Lionel Barrymore's Mr. Potter was no more than a "caricature of Ebenezer Scrooge."[21] Critic Roger Ebert partly blames the film's failure on its trailer, which played up the love angle of the film and played down its message and its gloom.[22] The film's failure was disheartening for Capra, who blamed its disappointing reception on the economy; as the war industries had closed down, civilians and servicemen were too busy scrambling for jobs to go to the movies.[23] Although it was nominated for Best Picture, Best Actor, and Best Director, William Wyler's *The Best Years of Our Lives* beat *It's a Wonderful Life* in all three categories (including Best Actor, even though Stewart was rumored to be the favorite).

Like *Citizen Kane*, *It's a Wonderful Life* was not appreciated in its own time, but would grow in status in the decades after its release. Despite the *New York Times*'s negative initial reaction to the film, it was still included in the publication's *Guide to the Best 1,000 Films Ever Made*. Roger Ebert ranked it alongside *Casablanca* and *The Third Man* as one of those timeless films that can be viewed on numerous occasions without losing its appeal. "Like great music," he writes, *It's a Wonderful Life* actually "improve[s] with familiarity."[24] In 1990, Capra's first postwar film was selected for preservation by the National Film Registry and was ranked number 11 on the "100 Years, 100 Movies List" issued by the American Film Institute in 1998—higher than both *Mr. Smith Goes to Washington* (29th) and *It Happened One Night* (35th). The eventual embrace of the film by the American public also encouraged Capra to go on lecture tours during the last decades of his life, where he would encourage students and film aficionados to fight for their visions of the world. These tours, along with his bestselling autobiography, would ultimately secure his place in the Hollywood pantheon.

Capra's Final Films

Capra's film output severely diminished after *It's a Wonderful Life*. Between 1948 and 1961, he would direct only five feature films, two of which would be remakes of earlier films. These five films, while retaining some elements of the films he made in the most successful period of his career (*American Madness* to *It's a Wonderful Life*) do not come close to the level of quality of his greatest work. Of these later films, only *State of the Union*, which Capra himself described as the "last Frank Capra film" and his science shorts deserve genuine praise.[25] The others—*Riding High*, *Here Comes the Groom*, *A Hole in the Head*, and *Pocketful of Miracles*, while entertaining, contain very little of the strong thematic material so prevalent in his earlier films. In his autobiography, Capra blames the poor quality of these pictures on "Balaban's Law," a law set up by the president of Paramount Pictures, Barney Balaban, that no film made by the studio should exceed $1.5 million. Having sold the independent Liberty Films to Paramount after *State of the Union*, Capra could no longer make the films he wanted to make. Because of Balaban's Law, he could not make the two films he really wanted to make at the time—*Friendly Persuasion* and *Roman Holiday*, two stories to which he owned the rights. He would eventually give these great stories to his Liberty partner William Wyler, who would turn them into huge, award-winning hits. As Wyler, Hitchcock, and Ford's careers would soar in this difficult time, Capra, his wings clipped by the cost-cutting studio system, would never return to greatness.

State of the Union
(Based on the Play by Howard Lindsay and Russel Crouse)
(Released April 1948)

In an interview in the late '70s, Capra called *State of the Union* his "most perfect film in handling people and ideas."[26] While the actors in the film are admittedly first-rate, the film itself is unable to capture the true ideological spirit of Capra's earlier films. Many of the elements are still there, but the film lacks the fire and passion of films like *Mr. Smith Goes to Washington*. For the first time in his career, Capra is "playing house" with sophisticated adults, and while the film makes many important points, its seriousness and compromised ending takes out much of the joy.

Based on a popular and timely play of the same name by Howard Lindsay and Russel Crouse, *State of the Union* concerns wealthy businessman Grant Matthews (Spencer Tracy) and his attempted run at the presidency. During his run, Matthews is handled by his mistress, editor Kay Thorndyke (Angela Lansbury), career politician Jim Conover (Adolphe Menjou) and writer Spike McManus (Van Johnson). The three believe that Matthews is under their control as he starts his campaign, but when Matthews goes on tour with his estranged wife, Mary (Katharine Hepburn), she reminds him of his past ideals and persuades him to be his own man. The story climaxes with a staged television broadcast in the Matthews home, where Grant, seeing his wife pulled apart by his past infidelity with Kay and realizing he has let down the common men who supported him, decides to abandon his run for the presidency. Capra, hoping to add greater depth to Matthews and his relationships, supplements the original play with some great scenes, including one in which Mary and Grant spend their first night back together, and one in which Grant discusses history with an old man in front of the White House. Capra also makes Grant a more spontaneous and exciting character. He does this by including a scene wherein Grant performs aerial tricks in his plane, then jumps out of it wearing a parachute. Capra and his writing team of Myles Connolly and Anthony Veiller increase the drama in the film's final scene by changing the forum from a dinner party to a live television broadcast. Such scenes slightly open up the film, but in the end, Capra cannot overcome the inherent "talkiness" of the play. Many scenes in the film go on entirely too long and, by doing so, grind the forward momentum of the story to a halt.

In addition, while Capra gets fine performances out of both Tracy and Hepburn in the film's stirring final scene, the ending is ultimately anticlimactic. While Capra added some much needed emotional weight to the cynical play in the film's final minutes, the simple fact that Grant decides to give up his bid for the presidency does not live up to the idealism of the earlier scenes and is ultimately unsatisfying for the viewer.

And yet, the film contains many of the Capra elements described in this book. There are some terrific silent close-up reactions of Mary, especially in the scene when Mary listens to Grant on their first night back together, where he wonders aloud what it would be like to run for the presidency. In the film's final scene, as Grant starts to question his television speech, a common-faced man looks at him condescendingly. In addition, the villains of the film, Kay and Conover, do most of their scheming behind desks and show a disdain for ordinary people. Following the rules established by Capra's earlier films, Spike is the only one who ends up converted to Grant's cause because he is the only one of the three that speaks frankly, using slang and colorful metaphors. The film also starts with the death of a prominent man (Kay's father) a plot device used in *Mr. Deeds* and *Mr. Smith*. At the end of the film, Grant forgets his anniversary, as Tom Dickson did in *American Madness*, much to his wife's dismay. Like *Mr. Deeds*, *Mr. Smith*, and *Meet John Doe*, the love of the female character in the film inspires the male lead to speak honestly and from the heart. Grant's speech at the end of the film, given without notes, mimics many of the themes Capra covered in his earlier films. In one part, for instance, he warns people not to surrender their freedom in times of crisis by stating: "When people are cold and hungry and scared they gather together in panicky herds, ready to be led by communists and fascists, who promise them bread for freedom, and deliver neither." The speech is a highlight of the film, but unfortunately, when it is all said and done, the end of *State of the Union* is basically an admission that one cannot affect change in a system from within. By refusing to run, Grant regains his freedom (and his wife's love), but loses his influence. As his fame grows, Grant realizes that his personal flaws will only magnify if he continues down the path to the presidency. Consequently, the only way to save his idealism is to give up his power.

Grant Matthews, in fact, contains many of the attributes of Capra's most influential heroes: he speaks openly and honestly, he reveres his country and its history, he solves complex problems with down-to-earth sensibility, and he has a playful, vibrant spirit. He is also, however, cheating on his wife. This particular subplot is meant to make Grant Matthews a flawed hero, like George Bailey, but Capra ultimately shows no real interest in selling the relationship between Kay and Grant. As would be expected, Angela Lansbury shares none of the chemistry with Tracy as does Hepburn, and the critical scenes between the two fall flat. Furthermore, while many viewers today can identify with George's dreams to travel the world, far fewer can forgive infidelity. This flaw in Grant proves that he is more selfish than George Bailey, which forces the viewer to identify primarily with Mary, who ultimately becomes the martyr in the film. In the end, the film is worth watching for the fine performances of Hepburn and Tracy, the noticeable Capra moments, and the interesting thematic points, but one cannot help but wonder what Capra could have done with the material ten years earlier.

Riding High
(Based on Frank Capra's 1934 film *Broadway Bill*)
(Released April 1950)

In the age of mail order rentals and streaming video, one wonders why anyone would choose to watch *Riding High* over *Broadway Bill*. This Bing Crosby vehicle, which is basically a scene-for-scene remake of Capra's earlier, better film (even including footage from the original film), stinks of unoriginality and artistic desperation, especially if one watches the original film first. Raymond Walburn, Douglass Dumbrille, Clarence Muse, and Margaret Hamilton all reprise their earlier roles without adding any further depth to their characters, and the replacements of Myrna Loy, Walter Connolly, and Warner Baxter in no way live up to these original performances. The relatively unknown Colleen Gray has nowhere near the gravity or screen presence as Myrna Loy, and the film suffers for it. In addition, Bing Crosby, while extremely likeable in the film, is too smooth and too casual to bring any real emotional weight to the proceedings. According to Charles Maland, this "softening" of the narrative edge, takes away much of the film's appeal.[27] In addition, although Capra claimed that he recorded the songs in the film live on the set, Crosby's amazing vocal talents render these scenes less spontaneous and improvisational than they should be.

Riding High also seems to sacrifice much of the emotional weight of the original film with subtle changes to the narrative. Rather than having Dan already married to Alice's older sister, he is merely engaged in *Riding High*. This reduction in the relationship causes Dan's breakaway from the Higgins family to be less dramatic and renders his relationship with Alice less dangerous and more acceptable. The film is also less critical of the world of millionaire J.L. Higgins, which softens the underlying class conflict felt throughout *Broadway Bill*. In another unusual decision, Capra removes the picturesque everyman face from Bill's funeral and cuts the scene from the ten minutes of the original film to just three. According to Capra, this scene was hurriedly shot due to inclement weather, but along with the removal of Dan's irredeemable close-up, one gets the sense that he was simply trying to lessen the oppressive unhappiness which weighed down the original film. After watching *Riding High*, however, one wishes Capra had left *Broadway Bill* well enough alone.

Here Comes the Groom
(Released September 1951)

Here Comes the Groom, Capra's last picture for Paramount, was another star vehicle for Bing Crosby. It begins with a promising premise for a romantic comedy: Peter Garvey (Crosby) an American journalist stationed in Paris, adopts two war orphans to whom he has grown increasingly attached. In order to keep the children, however, he must marry quickly. He immediately thinks of Emmadelle Jones (Jane Wyman) his love back home, and promises to marry her. Unfortunately, the adoption process in Europe takes entirely too long, and by the time Peter arrives to marry Emmadelle, he finds she has already become engaged to another man, the wealthy and attractive Wilbur Stanley (Franchot Tone). Needing to marry Emmadelle in order to keep the children, Peter connives to break up the wedding, even moving into Stanley's guest house during the week of the wedding in order to win Emmadelle back. The most surprising aspect of *Here Comes the Groom* is that Wilbur goes along with the plan, and shows nothing but respect for Peter's situation. He even offers to adopt the children in order to keep them in the country. According to Charles Maland, the positive portrayal of Wilbur Stanley drains the film of all drama and conflict.[28] Seemingly afraid to portray a successful man as a villain so he would not be labeled a communist, Capra makes a film that is enjoyable but ultimately uninvolving. As a result, it was only a moderate hit, earning $2.5 million and finishing 19th in the box-office overall.[29] The only really important aspect of the film was that it featured the Oscar-winning Hoagy Carmichael and Johnny Mercer song, "In the Cool, Cool, Cool of the Evening."

In some ways, Peter Garvey seems like a typical Capra hero. He is loved by kids, embraces spontaneity, talks openly and honestly in the modern vernacular, and employs music to bring people together. Unfortunately, as in *Riding High*, Crosby's casual approach to the character lessens the emotional resonance of the story and decreases its suspense. Like Capra's other heroes, Peter is not portrayed as a sexual being (he plans to take the children on their honeymoon), but unfortunately, unlike his other films, *Here Comes the Groom* is primarily a romantic comedy, and as such, needs to have some kind of sexual attraction between the two lead characters in order for the plot to work. Capra attempts to forge a bond between these characters by having them engage in a playful duet of "In the Cool, Cool, Cool of the Evening," but unlike his earlier films, which feature improvisational play, this scene comes across as too polished and too rehearsed to be effective. This goes for most of the musical numbers, including "Christopher Columbo," a completely useless scene wherein Crosby and several prominent Paramount players (including Dorothy Lamour and Louis Armstrong) sing and play on the plane back to the States. The ending, in which Emmadelle, a fisherman's daughter, ends up with the journalist Peter instead of the wealthy Wilbur, ultimately upholds the class system in the United States, especially since Wilbur ends up with his rich fourth cousin Winifred. As a result, *Here Comes the Groom*, although light and fast paced, is too conventional, too casual, and too conservative to make any lasting impact.

The Bell System Science Films

Here Comes the Groom marked the end of Capra's contractual obligation to Paramount Pictures. At the end of 1951, he found himself under suspicion by the United States Government for communist activities, and vehemently defended himself with papers denouncing the charges, including character references from John Ford and longtime friend Myles Connolly. The charges were quickly cleared, and Capra subsequently proved his loyalty to the government by attending the Indian International Film Festival in order to prevent the showing of communist-leaning films. Shortly after returning from India, Capra was asked by Cleo Craig, president of AT&T, if he would be interested in making a series of science programs for television, which would be sponsored by Bell Telephone. Capra, who believed film was a great tool for communicating and sharing ideas, agreed to work for Craig, and between the years of 1952 to 1956 produced four science shorts—*Our Mr. Sun, Hemo the Magnificent, The Strange Case of Cosmic Rays,* and *Unchained Goddess.* Capra enjoyed working on the films, which, because of the small crew (he claimed he never had more than four people working on the film), allowed him to regain the directorial authority he needed to pursue his personal vision. Capra described his enthusiasm for the project in his autobiography:

> The years of 1952–1956 were as productive and as packed with achievement as the war years of 1941–1945. But this time I was not revealing the ugly facts of war

but the awe and wonder and fascination of nature to youngsters from eight to eighty.[30]

As in the creation of the war documentaries, Capra dove into the work and rediscovered his passion for the filmmaking process. Like his work on the war films, he employed found footage and animation to verify, illustrate and document what was being said in the voice-over narration. Only this time, the completion of these films would leave him with no moral or ethical dilemmas. As a result, these films are a delightful addition to Capra's postwar career, and prove his expertise in communicating important and difficult material in a simple and entertaining way.

At first glance, the most noticeable aspect of the films is that they were filmed in color, as would all of Capra's films after this point. Although he once claimed that "color was too novel and distracting for films,"[31] he handles the new medium well, even though the films were broadcast on television in black and white. Another aspect that is striking about the films is their self-reflexivity. In the film's opening the two main characters— Dr. Research (Dr. Frank Baxter), and Mr. Fiction Writer (Eddie Albert in *Our Mr. Sun*; Richard Carlson in the remaining three)—discuss how they are going to write the special. Mr. Fiction Writer then brings in the "magic screen," where the two live action characters discuss their topic with animated characters and puppets. The conversations between the two men and the magic screen characters lead to the sharing of information and deeper insights. Unlike the war films, which featured faceless "ghost" narrators, the science films were able to humanize the information being relayed to the audience. The question-and-answer format also imbues the film with an improvisational atmosphere that renders the educational aspects of the piece more palatable. Furthermore, by having the live-action characters communicate directly with the puppets and animated drawings on the magic screen, Capra sells the realism of both the "magic" device and the unusual-looking characters depicted on it.

The character of Mr. Fiction Writer is also interesting because he possesses so many of the characteristics of the heroes of Capra's earlier films. He is casually dressed, without a jacket and wears a loose tie, and frequently places his hands in his pockets. The attacks of the animated screen characters in the films force him on the defensive, where he emotionally and optimistically fights on the side of science, using slang and colorful phrases. In *Our Mr. Sun*, for instance, he tells Dr. Research to "give 'em the whopper," and in *The Strange Case of Cosmic Rays*, he shows the magic screen characters a "honey of a device." Mr. Writer also acts like the audiences surrogate, often expressing a healthy skepticism or disbelief about the facts Dr. Research presents, asking questions to the scientist, and translating his technical verbiage into the language of the common people.

Like Capra's other films, his science films also illustrate Capra's disdain for intellectuals. In *Our Mr. Sun*, for instance, the sun character shows contempt for the philosopher Anaxagoras, who started the process of demythologizing the sun and taking away its power. The film also describes thinking as "spreading like the measles" and mourns the fact that intellectuals tend to reduce the power of nature by breaking it down into charts and numbers. According to the sun, modern man "thinks he's got all the answers." Dr. Research sets himself apart from the despised intellectuals by still retaining a sense of humility. He accepts the fact that he does not know all the answers and shows a healthy deference to nature and to God. At the end of *Hemo the Magnificent*, he lists a number of questions scientists have about the human body and answers them all with a steady stream of "we don't know's." Dr. Research also presents many examples throughout the series of "real" scientists actively engaged in physical labor, whether they are carrying crates containing scientific devices through forests or measuring particles in different parts of the world.

Finally, there is a sense of idealism and optimism about the capabilities of man in all the films, especially in their final moments. *Our Mr. Sun* ends with a montage of all the progress man has made, and Mr. Writer, in *Hemo the Magnificent*, states that while all of life's unanswered questions "are riddles that challenge the spirit of man ... the men of science will solve them. " Such optimism in the capability of man, however, is always metered by the religious aspects of the films. Ironically, the science films of Capra's are also his most religious. *Our Mr. Sun* and *Hemo the Magnificent* both begin with Biblical quotes and end with prayers or religious writings. At the end of *The Strange Case of Cosmic Rays* Dr. Research claims that the more we discover in science, the closer we "get to the Creator." Thus, in these films, Capra tries to create a common ground between science and religion — both are ways for the optimistic and the curious to think about our world and our place in it. With the Bell Telephone science films, Capra attempts to prove that science is not an academic exercise for the purpose of winning prizes and accolades, but a collective, continuing journey filled with humility, discovery, inspiration, and most of all, faith.

A Hole in the Head
(Based on a play by Arnold Schulman)
(Released July 1959)

Newly invigorated by his experience with the success of the science series, Capra decided to return to the world of Hollywood at the age of sixty. He describes both his enthusiasm and trepidation in his autobiography:

For eleven of the last fifteen years I had been out of circulation in Hollywood — five years in Army information films, and now I had wound up six years of making educational films. Wonderful years they were, meeting fresh, vigorous minds — exploring minds that charged me up with new enthusiasms, new ambitions. Now I was itching to come out of hiding and do my thing; make the best films of my life.[32]

Capra had come out of his experience of making nonfiction films ready to make another masterpiece, as he believed he had made with *It's A Wonderful Life*. What he needed was a star — and thankfully, one approached him at just the right time.

Apparently, Frank Sinatra had been wanting to work with Capra on a film for quite some time, and after he bought the rights to *A Hole in the Head*, he saw that opportunity. Capra, understanding that the new Hollywood was "not a director's business, but an actor's business," quickly signed on, only to find out that he would have to wait nearly 15 months before Sinatra's schedule would open up.[33] In the meantime, Capra decided to take on one more film for Harry Cohn and Columbia, a Biblical adaptation entitled *Joseph and His Brethren*. Inspired about the prospect of finally making a religious picture, Capra drove to his favorite writing spot in La Quinta and quickly hammered out a treatment. The film, however, was not destined to be, as Cohn's sudden death put the New York executives in charge of the studio. As with *Soviet*, nearly twenty-five years earlier, Capra saw his dreams to make a big picture go up in smoke. *Joseph and His Brethren*, Capra bluntly wrote, was "canceled before Cohn's body was cold."[34] Whether he liked it or not, his next film would be *A Hole in the Head*.

Arnold Schulman had written *A Hole in the Head* as a television comedy special, but upon a suggestion by Garson Kanin, the story was expanded into a Broadway play. The comedy-drama, about a Jewish widower who runs a hotel in Miami while juggling his son and his dreams of making it big, played for nearly five months on Broadway and was a moderate hit. Despite Arnold Schulman's insistence that his play not be rewritten, Capra convinced him to change the Jews in the script to Italians and give the hero a happy ending. Capra and Schulman also added the most memorable sequence in the film to the play, when Tony (Frank Sinatra), at the end of his rope, tries to convince his rich friend Jerry Marks (Keenan Wynn) to finance his dream to open up an amusement park in Florida.

The film, Capra's first feature in both widescreen and color, mainly revolves around Tony's attempt to pursue his individual dreams while raising his son, Allie (Eddie Hodges). When the bank threatens the foreclosure of his hotel, the Garden of Eden, Tony calls his successful brother, Mario (Edward G. Robinson), for financial assistance. Mario and his wife, Sophie

(Thelma Ritter), concerned about the welfare of Allie, impulsively fly to Miami to confront Tony and offer him an ultimatum: settle down and give up your wild dreams or hand over custody of Allie. While in Miami, they set Tony up on a date with Eloise Rogers (Eleanor Parker) in order to convince him of the virtues of settling down. While the match is encouraged by Allie, Tony, while attracted to Eloise, tells her on their date that the only reason he agreed to go out with her was to convince his brother to loan him money. In a last-ditch effort to preserve his individuality, Tony tries to convince his old friend Jerry to lend him money to open an amusement park in Florida. In order to do so, he puts on the false front that he is successful, selling his car and placing exorbitant bets at the racetrack with Jerry. When he loses all the money by "letting it ride," Tony's desperation shows through and Jerry nixes the deal, confessing that he was never really interested in Tony's proposition. The only reason he had kept Tony around that night was because he wanted to spend time with an old friend. Tony, who told Allie that he had raised the money, is subsequently forced to crawl back to the hotel and admit defeat to his brother, whom he allows to take Allie. The next day, however, on the way to the airport, Allie runs away from Mario and Sophie and joins his father and Eloise (who happens to stop by) on the beach. Mario and Sophie, inspired by the love between Allie and Tony, join them on the beach as the film happily ends.

At first, the production of *A Hole in the Head* was not an easy one. Capra, having won the battle with Schulman, also had to balance the egos of its two stars, Frank Sinatra and Edward G. Robinson. While Sinatra grew impatient with the slow methodical process of film production, Robinson preferred long rehearsals on the set. Capra, needing to keep Sinatra fresh and involved for the crucial first takes of the scene, asked Robinson to rehearse with a stand-in rather than Sinatra himself. Robinson, insulted, stormed off the set, but after an emotional conversation with the director, agreed with Capra's decision. Thus, Capra's talent for managing difficult personalities allowed him to regain control of the set, a difficult feat in a time when directors were steadily losing control of their films to their actors/financiers. Capra's authority impressed Sinatra, who was pleased with the final film and immediately tried to put together another film with the director.

A Hole in the Head was a success for Capra, doubling its production budget of nearly $2 million.[35] The film's upbeat message and hit song "High Hopes" resonated with audiences and seemed to signal Capra's triumphant return to narrative filmmaking. *New York Times* critic Bosley Crowther called the film a "thrill" for fans of Capra and wrote that the character of Tony could stand "along with Mr. Deeds and Mr. Smith," as one of the great guys that Mr. Capra has escorted to the American screen.[36]

The character of Tony Manetta is important because he adds a wrinkle to Capra's earlier theme of man's continued fight for freedom. Despite Crowther's observation, Tony shares more in common with George Bailey than either Longfellow Deeds or Jefferson Smith. Like George, Tony must learn to balance his selfish dreams with his responsibility to his family. He may be a flawed hero, but he *is* a hero for whom the audience wishes great success. Like George, after an unsettling humiliation at the hands of a powerful authority figure, however, Tony learns the valuable lesson that human relationships are more important than material success. Thus, the film effectively illustrates both the positive and the negative effects of pursuing one's selfish dreams. Like Deeds and Smith, Tony is playful, childlike, and imaginative, but the addition of Allie in the picture also paints him as irresponsible, delusional, and selfish. Tony's desire to be free, represented by his relationship with the free-spirited Shirl (Carolyn Jones), ultimately hurts his relationship with his son. Unfortunately, Sinatra's performance, although better than Crosby in absorbing the dark, emotional content of a Capra film, cannot compare to the realistic and convincing portrayals of actors like Gary Cooper and Jimmy Stewart. Although Sinatra was praised for his performance, a less restrained actor could have better illustrated Tony's internal conflict in a way that would have increased the film's core emotional conflict.

Wisely, *A Hole in the Head*'s ending does not entirely endorse the values of conformity and conservatism. The film effectively shows that the formally dressed Mario, the symbol of these values, has his flaws as well. Mario's adherence to traditional values and hard work also renders him grumpy and unimaginative. He admits at the end of the film that his relationship with his son is nothing like the one between Allie and Tony, and his devotion to his work has made him sick with ulcers and prevented him from taking a vacation and enjoying time with his wife. In addition, Allie's choice of his irresponsible father at the end of the film clearly shows that, between the two men, Capra prefers the values of the newly humbled Tony to his conservative brother. Allie, in fact, ends up as the true role model of the film, sharing the best traits of both the brothers. Like his father, Allie is imaginative, playful, friendly, and a believer in the importance of dreaming, but he is also studious, responsible, and traditional like his uncle. Through Allie, Capra shows that there is hope for the future so long as the positive attributes of conformity and individualism are effectively balanced.

With *A Hole in the Head*, like *Riding High* and *Here Comes the Groom*, Capra also attempts to soften the external struggles of its hero by lessening the role of the villain. Jerry Marks, although sharing a similar purpose in the climax of the film with Mr. Potter, is nowhere near as unlikeable or as unfriendly as that crippled old man. Although Jerry is harsh to Tony at the racetrack, we understand his point of view and identify with his need to connect with an old friend. With *A Hole in the Head*, Capra continued his postwar theme that, after the defeat of Hitler and the Axis powers, the real fight for freedom no longer took place in other countries but occurs within each of us. Like America, we must learn to understand both the benefits and the dangers of individuality if we are to be prosperous.

Pocketful of Miracles
(Based on the film *Lady for a Day*)
(Released December 1961)

After the success of *A Hole in the Head*, Capra had several opportunities to make another film. When his attempt to make *The Jimmy Durante Story* (with Frank Sinatra, Bing Crosby, and Dean Martin) fell through, Capra set his sights on three different possibilities: an adaptation of Gore Vidal's political play *Best Man*, a film about the true story of "Lord Haw-Haw," the controversial Irish defector who broadcasted anti–British propaganda during World War II, and *Pocketful of Miracles*, a remake of *Lady for a Day*. Capra, concerned about the growing inclusion of sex, violence, and lewdness in American films, decided to buck the system and make the most sentimental and old-fashioned of the three: *Pocketful of Miracles*. The choice is disappointing and regrettable, as it marks a retreat for Capra into safety and security, a tactic that earlier resulted in the production of films like *Riding High* and *Here Comes the Groom*. After seeing *Pocketful of Miracles*, one wonders what Capra's legacy would have been had he decided to make the other, riskier, political films, or the film he really wanted to make — the story of the conversion of St. Paul starring Frank Sinatra in the leading role. These films would all have continued to develop the theme behind Capra's most passionate and creative films: the struggle for individuality in a world which seems to thrive on massism, conformity, and witch hunts. Instead, Capra scholars are left with an overly long, widescreen, color remake of one of Capra's most saccharin, least complex films.

Not that *Pocketful of Miracles* is a terrible film. Capra's final film is both enjoyable and competently made. Its main drawback is that it is terribly old-fashioned, and adds nothing to the Capra legacy. In addition, as in *A Hole in the Head*, the widescreen process prevents Capra from employing much of his trademark style, including silent, dramatic close-ups and fast-paced editing. Except for the quickly moving beginning, the pace is dramatically slower than the earlier version, which ran for only 88 minutes, compared to the 136 minutes of the update. The film plays out primarily in brightly lit wide shots.

Although most of Capra's films from the '30s were shot this way, there are no scenes of dramatic contrast to break up the "sameness" of the story, or add some much-needed visual interest, as can be found in *Mr. Deeds, You Can't Take It with You, Meet John Doe*, and *It's a Wonderful Life*.

Pocketful of Miracles attempts to correct some of the earlier difficulties of *Lady for a Day*—with mixed results. Dave the Dude plays a much more prominent role as the star power of Glenn Ford commands. Ford, who was named the top box-office star of 1958, [37] gives Dave the Dude a screen presence equal to Bette Davis, who plays Apple Annie, but cannot give the role any more than the meager amount of emotion it requires. The story, too, still suffers from the lack of a main character. While Dave the Dude's role is increased in *Pocketful of Miracles*, the story is really Apple Annie's, who is once again forgotten in the middle of the film. The addition of Joy Boy (Peter Falk, who was nominated for a Supporting Actor Oscar for his performance), a role similar to Happy Maguire in the original film, gives the film a much-needed jolt of honesty, slapstick, and farcical energy. Edward Everett Horton, in the role of the butler, also inspires a great deal of laughs. But, while the addition of Hope Lange in the role of Dave the Dude's girlfriend, Queenie, gives the film some added emotional weight, her scenes slow down the urgency of the Apple Annie storyline. Other scenes add more signature Capra elements to the film, including an improvisational singing of "Polly Wolly Doodle" between a cab driver and Annie's beggar friends and a subplot involving Queenie's inability to cry. As if to illustrate Capra's increasing interest in religion, *Pocketful of Miracles* also adds a scene wherein Annie prays and receives communion in a Catholic church.

The box-office failure of *Pocketful of Miracles* effectively ended Capra's career as a director. While in his autobiography, he lists a number of reviews that were generally positive about the film, Capra himself admitted that he has not pleased with the final result, writing:

> *Pocketful of Miracles* was not the film I set out to make; it was the picture I chose to make for fear of losing a few bucks. And by that choice I sold out the artistic integrity that had been my trademark for forty years.... I lost that precious quality that endows dreams with purport and purpose. I had lost my courage.[38]

Instead of leveraging the success of *A Hole in the Head* to make a more personal film, Capra, tempted by the promise of a second life, chose safety over risk, and it cost him his career. In *The Name Above the Title*, a glowing testament of the importance of the "one man, one film" approach to pictures, Capra blamed the failure on his inability to live up to that ideal. According to Capra, from the beginning of the film's production, Glenn Ford, who was getting paid $35,000 a week to make the film compared to Capra's $1,500, wrestled control over the picture out of Capra's hands, a feat neither Harry Cohn nor Jack Warner had been able to accomplish. Throughout the production, Ford called the shots, making casting decisions and taking creative decisions out of Capra's hands. Capra personally believed that his searing migraine headaches during the production of the film were his body's response to this conflict. He felt that holding in the anger over the loss of control of the picture had caused some "bung to blow."[39] In addition, he remarks in his book that Sam Briskin believed the movie failed because United Artists distributed the film badly. Bolstered by the great reviews and eager for nominations, United Artists decided to open the film in many theaters at once, instead of the customary way of gradually rolling out the picture in one or two well-known theaters first.

While Capra seems to admit that the failure of *Pocketful of Miracles* was a result of his inability to control every aspect of the production, he also saw the inability of the American public to embrace the film as a symbol of their decadence. Even though many of the most popular films of the '60s—*The Guns of Navarone*, *West Side Story*, *The Longest Day*, *Mary Poppins*, *The Sound of Music*—perpetuated traditional old-fashioned values, Capra believed that the '60s were a lost decade, taken over by the "Marquis De Sade."[40] He likens his failure with the failure of other studio-era directors who saw their careers ending around the same time as Capra; men like John Ford, Alfred Hitchcock, Billy Wilder, William Wyler, and Howard Hawks, who fought for films to be made on their own terms. In the same breath, however, he shows serious doubts that the young directors of the time—Sidney Lumet, Arthur Penn, Mike Nichols, Arthur Hiller, and Stanley Kubrick—were capable or greatness, especially if they degraded the values of love and glorified its dementia.[41]

In the concluding pages of his book, Capra alternately blames the failure of American cinema on the lack of strong directorial voices *and* its immoral content, which glorifies "minus" people and makes apologies for brutish behavior.[42] Such arguments, however, do not make logical sense. Men like Stanley Kubrick, Mike Nichols, Sidney Lumet, and Arthur Penn all possessed unique styles and actually helped reestablished the importance of the directorial control over the filmmaking process. Furthermore, Hollywood studio films were hardly tributes to decency and morality, as famous directors like Alfred Hitchcock, Billy Wilder, Otto Preminger, and John Huston made careers out of directing films with questionable moral content and anti-heroes. At the end of his career, Capra revealed that he was once again torn between the need for control and the importance of the individual. He wanted young directors to fight for control over their films, but also wanted them to make films like the ones he had made: promoting love and the power of morality. In 1987 with Gene Siskel, director Stanley Kubrick openly disagreed with Capra's opinion of what movies should be, saying:

> Capra presents a view of life as we all wish it really were. But I think you can still present a darker picture of life without disliking the human race. And I think Frank Capra movies are wonderful. And I wish life were like most any one of them. And I wish everybody were like Jimmy Stewart. But they're not.[43]

To Capra, filmed images should be molded and manipulated into uplifting, meaningful stories that are greater than mere reality. Holding film up as a reflection of the real world seemed absurd to a man who worked the greater part of his career on soundstages and back lots. Even more absurdly, while Capra blamed the poor reception of *Pocketful of Miracles* and the fall of his career on his lack of risk taking, he also condemned the Hollywood system for committing the same sin. Frank Capra, for all his intellect and understanding, simply failed to see the key reasons why he no longer sparked the imagination of the American people.

In actuality, Capra's films had changed, not the American public. I have witnessed first-hand the enthusiastic reception of *It Happened One Night, Mr. Smith Goes to Washington*, and *It's a Wonderful Life* in both my classroom and in my home. My students have admired the clarity and methods of the *Why We Fight* series, many confessing that their parents have copies of the series in their homes. I have had long conversations with relatives and friends about *Mr. Deeds Goes to Town* and *American Madness*. The ultimate failure of Capra's postwar career is not the result of the times changing or even Capra's lack of control. His earlier films were simply better films, and good films are good films, regardless of when they were made. Capra traded the sincerity of actors like Gary Cooper and Jimmy Stewart for Hollywood stars like Bing Crosby, Frank Sinatra, and Glenn Ford, who were not willing to compromise their images for emotional truth. With the exception of *It's a Wonderful Life, State of the Union*, and perhaps *A Hole in the Head*, Capra had simply run out of things to say. Reluctant to take on the important issues of the day out of fear of being targeted by the HUAC, Capra simply stopped making films that mattered. Although we can admire the clarity and technical mastery of his science films, they do not match the passion and artistry of the *Why We Fight* films. One gets the sense with Capra's films (after *State of the Union*) that he was running away from the fight. By making films without clear and passionate messages, without villains and righteous heroes, without an underlying sense of anger and indignation about the evils of the world, Capra simply strived for competently directed, inoffensive entertainment films. From 1932 to 1948, Capra produced films that illustrated his unwavering belief in the importance of personal liberty in a world threatened by the power of the fascist governments and the wealthy upper class. As a result, he was extremely passionate about how these films were made, and he fought for control over them. The audience felt this passion, and as a result, Capra helped the American people through times of severe crisis. After all, there is nothing more inspiring than a speaker who ardently believes in his own message. When Capra stopped believing in the importance of his ideas, when he stopped believing in the power of films, he ceased to become a relevant force in American cinema.

7
Capra's Legacy

Many Capra scholars devote whole chapters analyzing Capra's rapid loss of popularity after the war. In a sense, this is unfair to Capra, who, while not enjoying the rare long-term popularity of directors like John Ford and Alfred Hitchcock, still had an impressive 16-year run between 1932 and 1948. Capra's ultimate failure was that he continued to make films after *State of the Union*. While the creative and innovative science films (and possibly *A Hole in the Head*) remain the only bright spots in the last 13 years of Capra's career, one can only imagine what would have happened if Capra had been allowed to make the films he was truly passionate about: *Joseph and His Brethren* and a film about the life of St. Paul. The Biblical source for these films would have allowed Capra to continue his theme about the importance of the individual and the need to take a stand against the establishment without him being branded a communist. Perhaps Capra would have had the career of William Wyler in the '50s had he been allowed to direct *Roman Holiday* and *Friendly Persuasion*, two Oscar-nominated films once owned by Capra but directed by Wyler.

The later choices in Capra's career are regrettable, but these lesser films should not be unfairly held against him. After all, like Capra, both Billy Wilder and Alfred Hitchcock saved their worst films for the end of their careers. Rarely do directors hold up after they produce their most important works. Capra's talent reached his zenith with *It's a Wonderful Life*, a film which became the culmination of everything Capra's previous films had been about. It is only natural that all the films afterwards would feel anti-climactic in comparison. In fact, one can trace the decline of most American filmmakers after their greatest achievements, many of whom had shorter careers than Capra. Did Francis Ford Coppola's career improve after *Apocalypse Now*? How about Billy Wilder's after *The Apartment*? Steven Spielberg's after *Schindler's List*? Robert Zemeckis's after *Forrest Gump*? Directorial comebacks like Robert Altman's *The Player* are few and far between in Hollywood. Once directors produce what they consider to be their greatest work, a natural decline is inevitable, as they no longer feel the need to prove themselves to the world.

While to many, Capra's adherence to morality and idealism feels out of date in today's cynical and relativistic world, one certainly cannot negate Capra's importance to film history. Not only was Capra able to make the films he wanted to make when the studio system was at its most powerful, he also played a substantial role in helping our country through its most difficult years. Capra also played a significant role in establishing Columbia as a major studio. As Neal Gabler pointed out in *An Empire of Their Own*, "No other studio was as dependent on a single artist as Columbia [was] on Capra."[1] In addition, with the exception of his films of the 1950s, Capra was ahead of the curve on his treatment of women in his films. According to Elizabeth Kendall, in *The Runaway Bride*, Capra was not afraid to imagine "what it might feel like to be a woman" and treated the female characters in his films as real companions for his heroes, not just as "icons of femininity."[2] Furthermore, Capra's decision to create an independent studio at the height of his popularity has been imitated by some of Hollywood's most successful directors, including Coppola, Spielberg, and Lucas, who created their own companies because they wanted to tell the stories they wanted to tell without the approval of the major studios.

In addition, Capra's influence can be traced throughout modern film history, as many of his signature techniques and ideas have shown up in America's most popular films for nearly 35 years. Although the anti-hero became popular from the mid–'60s to the mid–'70s, the blockbuster era led to a new generation of "too good to be true" mainstream heroes. The major films of this era—*Superman, Star Wars,* and *Close Encounters of the Third Kind*—all feature idealistic heroes who, like Jefferson Smith and Longfellow Deeds, fight for their values against the forces of fascism and bureaucracy. Luke Skywalker and Superman also adhere to the values of an older generation, which, in turn, converts skeptics to their righteous cause. Even Indiana Jones, Steven Spielberg's most iconic character of the 1980s, works tirelessly to prevent fascist and bureaucratic forces from hijacking history for their own selfish purposes. Like Jefferson Smith, John Willoughby, and Mr. Deeds, Indiana Jones is constantly placed on the defensive by the actions of the villains, which forces him to engage in spontaneous activity. In addition, a great number of recent blockbusters feature childlike innocents forced to defend themselves from oppressive forces which prevent them from achieving their simple goals. The innocent and unjustly persecuted heroes in critically acclaimed films like *The Lord of the Rings* trilogy, the *Harry Potter* films, *Slumdog Millionaire, WALL-E, The Shawshank Redemption, Dead Poet's Society,* and *Field of Dreams* also convert others to their cause as a result of their courage and inherent goodness. Penny Marshall's *Big*, which actually puts a boy's brain inside a man's body, illustrates the power of optimism and the importance of

7. Capra's Legacy

Peter Appleton (Jim Carrey) testifies before a HUAC committee in *The Majestic*, Frank Darabont's tribute to the films of Frank Capra. (Warner Bros. Pictures/Photofest)

play to reform the adult business world. In addition, *Big* and the aforementioned films all imitate Capra's best work because they all incorporate optimistic and hopeful themes openly and honestly, without the veil of irony and cynicism.

In some cases, entire plots are lifted from Capra's films. *Billy Jack Goes to Washington*, produced by Frank Capra, Jr., updated the story of *Mr. Smith* and incorporated the popular '70s movie hero Billy Jack (Tom Laughlin) into the story. The animated film *Shrek Forever After* borrows the story of *It's a Wonderful Life*, as the popular titular character experiences firsthand what life would be like had he never existed. In an opposite version of *It's a Wonderful Life*, Brett Ratner's *The Family Man*, Jack Campbell (Nicolas Cage) wakes up in a world that shows him what life would have been like had he married the girl he loved (Téa Leoni). The plot of the hit movie *Crocodile Dundee* is extremely similar to the first half of *Mr. Deeds*, as Mick Dundee travels from a place where he is revered to New York City, where he is misunderstood and mistreated. The film even features a scene in which Mick knocks out a man who makes fun of him at a dinner table. Comedian Adam Sandler also remade *Mr. Deeds Goes to Town* as *Mr. Deeds* in 2002. Such a move is not surprising, as Sandler has made a whole career out of playing childlike, belligerent characters who, although loved by the common people, fight against the vain, the selfish, and the supercilious.

Two-time Academy award winner Clint Eastwood has also acknowledged that many of his films dealt with Capraesque themes. A big fan of both *Mr. Deeds Goes to Town* and *Mr. Smith Goes to Washington*, Eastwood admits that he has been especially drawn to Capra's point that just "because a person is different doesn't mean he is necessarily wrong."[3] Eastwood's *Bronco Billy*, in fact, owes a great debt to Capra's films, most especially *It Happened One Night*, as it concerns a runaway socialite and her on-the-road relationship with a rugged, down-to-earth cowboy. Like many Capra heroes, Eastwood's Billy is admired for his straight talk, his stubborn adherence to the forgotten values of the past, and his generosity to those less fortunate. Furthermore, he is loved by children, quick to use his fists, and has a soft spot for the world's misfits. Unfortunately, Sandra Locke is no Claudette Colbert, and Eastwood has neither the comic timing nor the light touch of Gable. In addition, unlike the non-sexual relationship between Ellie and Peter, Eastwood's film solves the conflict between the two main characters with Billy's sexual conquest of Antoinette. As a result, Antoinette is the one who is tamed, reduced to talking less and following Billy around like a lovesick puppy in the film's final act.

Even Oliver Stone, director of such realistic films as *Platoon* and *Born on the Fourth of July*, claims to have been influenced by the films of Frank Capra. In an interview in 1992, Stone admitted that he made Jim Garrison a Capraesque hero in his film *JFK* because, like Mr. Deeds and Jefferson Smith, Garrison was struggling for truth in the face of overwhelming odds. *JFK*, like *Mr. Deeds Goes to Town* and *Mr. Smith Goes to Washington*, also ends with a rousing speech meant to stir the audience to action. In the interview, Stone stated that he believed "Capra was very aware of fascism," and that his films were much "darker than the rather sentimental image that Americans have of them."[4] Like Capra, filmmakers like Stone perpetuate the theme of the common man against the system because he, like many others, believes the theme is still relevant in America and throughout the world. As America continues to balance the two worlds of fascism and individualism, Capra's thematic films will always inspire others to join the cause.

The use of spontaneous play, used so effectively in films like *It's a Wonderful Life*, *Mr. Deeds Goes to Town*, and *You Can't Take It with You* as a means of bringing two characters closer together, is also employed in many recent, popular films. Frank Oz's *Housesitter*, starring Steve Martin and Goldie Hawn, features a couple who bond by continually lying and spontaneously making up stories. In one of *Big*'s most memorable moments, Josh Baskin (Tom Hanks) and his boss (Robert Loggia) play songs on a giant keyboard at F.A.O. Schwartz. In such diverse films as *The King's Speech* and *The Fisher King*, two completely different people become good friends after engaging in several rounds of creative, spontaneous play. Impromptu music plays an important part in the bonding process in *A League of Their Own* and *Dead Poets Society*. In *Tootsie*, Michael Dorsey (Dustin Hoffman) bonds with Julie (Jessica Lange) and her father (Charles Durning) by playing old-fashioned songs on the piano. In one of the most touching moments in *Harry Potter and the Deathly Hallows, Part I*, Harry Potter (Daniel Radcliffe) and Hermione Granger (Emma Watson) take time out of their fight against Voldemort to dance with one another and just "be." Once attuned to its characteristics, the spirit of Capra seems to pop up everywhere, proving that his films and ideas are still relevant and influential.

In the last 20 years, there have been a few films that directly address the meaning of Capra and his work with mixed success. These films, *The Hudsucker Proxy, Dave, Hero,* and *The Majestic*, all made by competent, well known directors, are attempts to understand the power of Capra's legacy in the modern world. *The Hudsucker Proxy*, made by the Coen Brothers in 1994, although not filmed in the Capra style, nonetheless borrows a great number of elements from Capra films. Like *It's a Wonderful Life*, it begins with a voice-over and the attempted suicide of its hero—this time on New Year's Eve, and utilizes a flashback to illustrate how a good man could be brought to such a desperate state. Like *Mr. Smith Goes to Washington, State of the Union,* and *Mr. Deeds Goes to Town*, the journey of the hero begins with the death of a powerful figure. Just as the small-town hero Norville Barnes (Tim Robbins) enters Hudsucker Industries, Waring Hudsucker (Charles Durning) commits suicide at the height of the company's success by jumping out a window— in the middle of a board of directors meeting. Rather than mourning the death of his boss, Sidney J. Mussburger (gamely played by Paul Newman) sees Hudsucker's death as an opportunity to take control of the highly-successful company. Under Mussberger's guidance, the board of directors decide to appoint a "patsy" in Hudsucker's place, in order to drive the stock down so low that it can be snatched up by Mussburger and his cronies for "pennies on the dollar." Mussburger chooses Norville Barnes for the job, hoping that the innocent, wide-eyed boy from the mailroom will drive down the company's fortunes. As in *Meet John Doe*, Barnes has no idea he is being used as a pawn for the ambitions of powerful men. Like *Mr. Deeds*, Norville is set apart from the selfish and greedy denizens of the city from the beginning of the film. In a company full of vertical and horizontal lines, Norville's dream, as written on a wrinkled and battered piece of paper, is a simple circle. In a plot element borrowed directly from *Mr. Deeds Goes to Town*, journalist Amy Archer (Jennifer Jason Leigh) pretends to be a hungry small-town girl in order to get closer to Norville so she can find out the real scoop on Hudsucker's new president. Norville hires her as his secretary, and like Saunders and Jefferson Smith in *Mr. Smith*, they work together to implement the hero's plan — which, in Norville's case, becomes the Hula Hoop. The simple toy becomes a sensation, and much to Mussburger's dismay, Hudsucker's stock is higher than ever. Unlike Jefferson Smith and Longfellow Deeds, however, the success of the company corrupts Norville Barnes, much to the dismay of Amy, who has fallen in love with him. She quits her job as secretary, and without her guidance, Norville unjustly fires an idealistic elevator boy, who later claims that Norville stole the Hula Hoop idea from him. The ending of the film combines elements of both *Mr. Deeds* and *Meet John Doe*, as Mussburger reveals Amy's real identity to Barnes and Barnes is unjustly branded as a liar and a fake. On New Year's Eve, Norville gets drunk and decides to kill himself by throwing himself off the top of Hudsucker Industries. Just as he changes his mind, however, he slips and falls just at the stroke of midnight, only to find himself fantastically saved by the stopping of the clock. With the intervention of the spirit of Waring Hudsucker himself, Norville survives the fall and lives to regain control of the company.

While the plot structure and brisk pace of *The Hudsucker Proxy* is undoubtedly meant to resemble Capra's films, the film's overstylized acting drains the film of the sincerity that made Capra's films so inspiring. While Tim Robbins adds a needed touch of emotional honesty to the cartoony and exaggerated enterprise, Jennifer Jason Leigh's performance as Amy is devoid of any depth or emotional resonance. With *The Hudsucker Proxy*, the Coen Brothers evoke the feeling of Capra's films by incorporating several of its themes and plot elements, but fall short of making a great movie by continually choosing irony and exaggeration over sincerity and emotional honesty.

The same criticism could be made of Stephen Frears's *Hero*, a film that also incorporates many Capraesque elements, only to end in compromise and cynicism. In *Hero*, Bernie Laplante (Dustin Hoffman), a divorced and embittered felon, risks his life to save people from a plane that crashes right in front of his car. One of the people he saves is Gale Gayley (Geena Davis), an award-winning news reporter who is having doubts about her career. Bernie loses a shoe as he saves the victims of the plane crash, and, unable to drive his now-totaled car, gets a ride from a homeless man named John Bubber (Andy Garcia). In the hospital, Gale is told the story of her unknown rescuer, and seeing the possibility of finally reporting on an inspiring story, persuades her boss (Chevy Chase, in an uncredited role) to offer up a $1 million reward to anyone who fits the missing shoe found on the scene. Busted for trying to sell Gale's credit cards (he stole her purse while saving her), Bernie is unable to come forward to claim the prize. John Bubber, however, who gained possession of the shoe when he gave Bernie a ride, steps forward and claims that he was the man who saved all the people. Dubbed "Mr. Cinderella" (shades of *Mr. Deeds*), John, a war veteran, inspires the nation with his generosity and humility. As Bernie, now bonded out of jail, futilely attempts to brand Bubber a fake, John goes through his own crisis of conscience. Like John Willoughby, he is torn between the inspiration he gives to people and the knowledge that he is not the person he claims to be. Gale, who is starting to fall for John, slowly begins to doubt her hero's story, especially after the police return her stolen credit cards. At the film's climax, when Bernie steps out on a ledge to talk John out of committing suicide, her doubts are confirmed — Bernie was the man who saved her life. The film ends with Bernie and John reaching a compromise: John will pay Bernie some of the money and help get him out of jail as long as John continues to play the role of hero for the American public. Gale, now knowing the truth behind Bernie's heroism, still decides to go along with the fake story, as she realizes it is better to inspire the public than to tell the truth.

To all outward appearances, John Bubber is the typical Capra hero. He is a man with no past, a soft-spoken, humble man who is good with kids and generous to others. He is also a liar. Unlike John Wiloughby, who claimed to write a letter only to get his arm fixed, John Bubber claims to have saved people from a burning plane for one million dollars. As a result, the audience does not quite know how to feel about Bubber, which is exactly what Frears wants. With *Hero*, Frears questions the foundations of Capra's idealistic notion that good men are necessary to inspire the world. To Frears, it is the "idea" of the good man that inspires us, not the reality. When Gale interviews the victims of the plane crash, they alter their stories to make their hero more inspirational. According to Frears, we are all liars because we continually choose myth over reality. By upping the fakery of John Bubber and by clueing the audience in early about Bernie's heroism, Frears forces us to witness how readily we allow ourselves be deceived by "Cinderella" stories. In the end, only the manufacturers of the stories (represented by Gale) and the actual participants know the truth. The rest of us live unaware of the deception, believers in "false gods" and "manufactured" stories. As such, *Hero* is a hard film to watch because it condescends to the audience, shouting at them to "wake up" when they really prefer to dream. While Capra's films are inspirational, there is little doubt that they are fantasies of good will, myths that help us cope with the day-to-day hardships of life. With *Hero*, Frears wants it both ways: he tells us that films are lies, and then wants us to listen to him. All in all, though, *Hero* is an important film because it does make some valid points, points especially relevant when discussing news and Capra's war documentaries, which often idealized real people and real events. Frears tells us with *Hero* that if we continue to demand perfection from our heroes, not only will we have to become accustomed to being lied to, but we will also miss the "ordinary" men and women who perform heroic acts every day.

These are all important points, but in the end, Bernie never really receives credit for his heroic act, and the truth is never really revealed. As a result, the end is thought provoking, but not necessarily rewarding entertainment.

Ivan Reitman's *Dave* is the only film of the four to truly capture the comedic spirit of Frank Capra's best films. In *Dave*, Dave Kovic (Kevin Kline), temp-agency owner and presidential impersonator, is requested by the White House to briefly stand in for Bill Mitchell (also Kevin Kline), the current president. Unfortunately, the plan goes awry when President Mitchell suffers a severe stroke and slips into a coma in the middle of sexual relations with an office aide. Chief of Staff Bob Alexander (Frank Langella) views Mitchell's coma as an opportunity to grab power and encourages Dave to keep pretending to be the president. The chief of staff's plan — to create a scandal that would cause the vice president (Ben Kingsley) to resign, and have Dave (as President Mitchell) nominate him for the vice presidency. Eventually, Dave would step down, thus handing the presidency over to Alexander, without the need for an election. Alexander and his assistant Alan Reed (Kevin Dunn) convince Dave to go along with the ruse in order to protect the country from the mentally unstable vice president. As Dave plays the president, however, he becomes less and less under the control of Alexander, as Dave's kind spirit and gentle heart inspires the press and the American people during public appearances. In one instance, Dave, feeling empowered by the positive press, elicits the help of his friend Murray (Charles Grodin) to save a homeless shelter. The move infuriates Alexander, but impresses the first lady (Sigourney Weaver), who supported the shelter. As Dave becomes more confident in his role, his warm personality earns the friendship, not only of the first lady, but also Alan Reed and Duane (Ving Rhames), a secret service agent. With his new allies, Dave fires the demanding Alexander and joins forces with the first lady to make changes in how the government is run. Alexander, however, with one last trick up his sleeve, releases paperwork leveling corruption charges against the president. In order to get himself out of the mess created by Alexander, in an address to Congress, Dave takes the blame for the corruption, clears the vice president's name, then promptly fakes a stroke. His body is replaced with Mitchell's and Dave returns to obscurity. The film ends with the first lady arriving at Dave's temp agency, now a campaign office for Dave running for a city position. They kiss in Dave's office just as Duane steps in front of the door and blocks our view.

Dave has a great number of genuine Capra moments because Dave Kovic is such a terrific Capraesque character. A good-natured, common-sense, unironic American, Dave, endearingly played by Kline, is both believable and inspirational. It is no wonder that he shares much in common with Longfellow Deeds, John Willoughby, and Jefferson Smith. Like Deeds, Dave is well respected and loved in his small circle, is intimidated by women, does not like people waiting on him, enjoys singing, and, most importantly, using his power to help people. Like Smith, he is smart but naïve about politics, learns to speak from his heart about issues that matter to him, and knows how to relate to kids. Like Willoughby, he starts off as the pawn of a selfish man in power and continually wrestles with the inner knowledge that he is a fake. Dave also works for the people rather than for big businesses, and prevents Bob Alexander from subverting democracy for his own selfish ends.

Dave, like the best Capra films, truly benefits with the addition of a strong female character and a villain. Weaver's Ellen Mitchell, like Capra's most memorable female leads, is both ambitious and intelligent, but her personality softens throughout the film, as she becomes more drawn to the idealistic and caring leading man. Unlike Saunders, Ann, and Babe, however, Ellen does not withhold important information from the leading man. Instead, she is the one who is deceived. Like the heroines of Capra's films, Ellen does not reveal her love for the main character until the film's final scene, but she learns to feel comfortable with Dave in a round of improvisational play. In a particularly memorable scene, Ellen and Dave are pulled over by a police officer in a public area for a moving violation. When the police officer sees what appears to be the president and the first lady getting out of the car, Dave de-escalates the situation by convincing him that they are just imitators of the famous people. To sell the story, Dave begins an impromptu duet of "Tomorrow," which Ellen awkwardly joins. The police officer, convinced, lets Dave off with a warning, but candidly advises him that the first lady imitator "needs work."

Additionally, Frank Langella adds to the film's success with his portrayal of the villain, making the well-dressed Alexander sharp, intense, and intimidating. The inclusion of a villain, as in Capra films, not only allows the contrast of two competing ideals to play out but also increases the stakes for the hero. My only complaint about the film is that the stakes are not ramped up enough. Because Dave is playing a part, he is never really personally affected by his actions as president. Unlike Capra's heroes, who are pushed to the brink of desperation, Dave rarely breaks a sweat. The decision not to push the conflict further gives the film a gentle and affable spirit, but does not emotionally involve the audience. Unlike Capra, who was willing to push his comedies into heavy drama, Reitman prefers to safely remain within the comedy genre. Furthermore, *Dave*'s complete and easy resolution to the hero's problems in the film does not challenge the audience to continue his fight. As such, the film's message, which, like *Mr. Smith*, extols the virtues of democracy and reinforces the importance of a government working for the people, gets lost in a sea of amiability and good-natured humor.

In *The Majestic*, director Frank Darabont comes very close to incorporating the best dramatic elements of Capra's films into a cohesive and emotional narrative. The story, set in the early 1950s, begins with Peter Appleton (Jim Carrey), an up-and-coming Hollywood screenwriter, being targeted by the HUAC for his past communist activities (he attended a meeting in college with a girl he liked). He is laid off from his work, and after wallowing in self-pity and getting thoroughly drunk (shades of *It's a Wonderful Life*), drives his car off a bridge in the middle of a violent storm. He washes up on the shore of a small California town called Lawson, a congenial but depressed town that lost 62 of its young men in the war. Peter, who lost his memory in the accident, bears a striking resemblance to one of those men, Luke Trimble, the son of Majestic theater owner Harry Trimble (Martin Landau). Harry believes Peter to be his son returned from the war, and as Peter has no memory of his former life, moves in with the old man into the closed-down theater Harry and Luke used to run. Luke's supposed return from the war adds excitement to the town, and although Peter has doubts whether he really is Luke, he goes along with their fantasy. While in Lawson, Peter strikes up a relationship with Adele (Laurie Holden), Luke's old girlfriend, and helps Harry reopen the theater. He also inspires the town to finally publicly display the memorial statue honoring the boys who gave their lives for their country. Despite all this excitement, dark clouds loom on the horizon. The FBI have found Peter's car and are investigating the accident, which brings them closer to Lawson. Peter regains his memory when the film he wrote plays at the theater, but before he can tell Harry, the old man has a heart attack. On Harry's death bed, Peter finds that he cannot reveal the truth to his "father." On the day of Harry's funeral, Peter reveals to Adele that he is not Luke, and as she runs off, federal officers show up to expose Peter as a liar in front of the entire town. Before heading back to Hollywood, where he plans to read a prepared statement accepting his guilt and naming names, Peter meets up with Adele at Luke's grave. Peter confesses to Adele that he was glad he did not go overseas to fight, because in the real world, when you fight for a cause "you get mowed down." At the train station, Adele's father (David Ogden Stiers) hands Peter a small package from his daughter — a book of the Constitution of the United States, with a letter inside. In the letter, written by Luke to Adele during the war, Luke asks Adele not to mourn his passing and to live her life honoring the cause he is fighting to achieve. "When bullies rise up," he writes, "the rest of us have to beat them down whatever the cost." The day Peter testifies in front of the HUAC, the whole town of Lawson listens on the radio as Peter stands up to read his prepared statement. Rather than going through with the plan, however, he begins to have second thoughts. His voice quavering like Jefferson Smith, Peter speaks from the heart, imagining what a courageous man like Luke would have said in front of the committee. As he gains confidence, Peter reads from the Constitution book and challenges the committee to live up to the ideals for which the country's veterans fought in the war. The citizens of Lawson are touched by Peter's inspiring speech, which truly honors the sacrifice of their sons. Peter walks away from the committee, to thunderous applause. At the end of the film, Peter is absolved of his crimes by the government, and instead of pursuing his Hollywood dreams, he returns to the people of Lawson and the theater he helped restore.

Like the films of Frank Capra, *The Majestic* upholds the value of small-town idealism, the importance of the individual to inspire people to stand up against the powerful, and the need to live one's life with courage, integrity, and conviction. Unlike *Hero*, which cautioned against idealism, *The Majestic* shows us that idealist thinking encourages us to fight battles which, at first, seem impossible to win. Both films, however, provide the audience with the "reality" of the idealized situation. The audience knows, for instance, that John Bubber did not actually save the passengers, just as they know that Peter Appleton could not possibly be Luke Trimble. But while *Hero* seems to condemn the common people for embracing fiction over fact, *The Majestic* attempts to understand the reasons human beings embrace fantasy. The people of Lawson have had their fill of reality, and Luke's appearance encourages them to dream again. This action is symbolized by the restoration of the movie theater, a place of dreams, where the people of Lawson can witness the "good guys" winning again, even if they know deep down it is just a movie. This is why both Adele and Emmett (Gerry Black), the theater's usher, go along with the delusion even though all along they had doubts that Peter was actually Luke. In true Capra spirit, Darabont uses *The Majestic* to illustrate that idealism is sometimes necessary before collective action is possible. The town of Lawson never would have helped restore the Majestic or erected the war memorial had they not been inspired by Luke's return. This projection of "goodness" of the town on Peter also helps to alleviate the "too good to be true" characters in Capra's films. Peter's amnesia, although not particularly believable, makes him the necessary blank slate upon which the people of Lawson can project their idealism, but also allows the audience to buy into Peter's exceptional generosity and goodness. In addition, the fact that Peter becomes a good man only when he forgets his ambitious past, illustrates that all men are capable of greatness if they are freed from the need to fulfill their selfish desires. In that sense, *The Majestic* plays out like the opposite of *It's a Wonderful Life*. While George Bailey sees how Bedford Falls would have changed without his existence, Peter catches a glimpse about how much better his life would have been had he lived his life as a person of self-sacrifice and conviction. While George Bailey attempts throughout *It's a Wonderful Life* to break free from the role in which life has cast him, Peter embraces the role of Luke, and subsequently provides the town with the clichés and the symbolic moments they require to move on from tragedy. Like Capra's heroes, this newfound idealism manifests itself in generous actions, spontaneous music, and physical labor. Becoming Luke changes Peter, just as an actor becomes affected by the role he is playing. In the end, Peter, like the people of Lawson, turns to an idealistic conception of Luke in order to provide him with the confidence he needs to stand up to the HUAC committee. Although the ending of the film is pure Capra, idealistic and moving, *The Majestic* falls just short of greatness because we see most of the plot coming. Darabont revels in clichés, but unfortunately, such devotion to formula makes the film somewhat predictable. A faster pace may have overcome this problem. Unlike Capra's films, *The Majestic* also drags out its ending and relies too much on its musical score to instill emotion. In addition, the film could also have used more comedy bits in order to lighten up its message. Even though it runs about 30 minutes too long, *The Majestic* is a fitting tribute to the films of Frank Capra, as it deftly mixes inspiring messages with heartfelt performances.

The Hudsucker Proxy, *The Majestic*, *Hero*, and *Dave* all ask us to ponder the effects of the Capra ideology in the modern era. Whether the heroes of these films are too good to be true, like Dave Kovic, or flawed individuals like Bernie Laplante, the directors of these films understood that filmmakers must continually attempt to understand the forces that shaped and continue to shape America. The best Capra films challenged American audiences to live up to the ideals upon which their country was founded and to recognize the dangers of fascism in both ourselves and in our own backyards. That Capra, a man who continually fought for freedom in both his films and his career, sometimes succumbed to those powers for profit and safety, makes studying his life and career all the more provocative. America, like its citizens, like Capra himself, is fascinating in its contradictions. As long as filmmakers like Frank Capra continue to push audiences to examine these contradictions and reestablish its priorities, the democratic aspects of this country will continue to flourish. Yes, Capra produced propaganda, but unlike Riefenstahl, who used the power of film to overwhelm audiences and compel them to submit, Capra's war films asked soldiers to examine what made their country different from the fascist powers they would face on the battlefields of the world. His narrative films, on the other hand, ask us to consider how dangerously close we are to them as well. Capra, along with Longfellow Deeds, Jefferson Smith, and George Bailey could have just as easily used their power to gain control over those who entrusted them for their own selfish means. Capra arrived on the scene at a time when film was becoming the most powerful tool for manipulation on the planet, and luckily for us, he decided to use the medium to encourage individuals to fight against those who would take away their uniqueness and their freedoms.

This decision to use the medium to promote individuality during our country's most difficult times must have truly confounded the fascist regimes that offered the opposite solution. Like America, however, Capra's films are both complex and contradictory, and could be easily misunderstood. While his unique heroes profess that they fight for the rights of the "little guy," Capra's films also illustrate how "special" individuals could be used to encourage the underprivileged masses to rise up against the wealthy and the powerful. On an interesting note, when the Russian troops broke into Hitler's bunker at Berchtesgaden, they found only three American films. One was the Fred Astaire/Ginger Rogers musical *Top Hat*. The other two were Capra films: *It Happened One Night* and *Mr. Deeds Goes to Town*. One cannot help but wonder: When watching *Mr. Deeds*, did Hitler cheer for Longfellow Deeds or John Cedar?

In conclusion, as it has become clear that Capra's war documentaries played an important role, not only in Capra's film career but also in American history, it is hoped that the study of these films will continue to be included in the Capra scholarship. There are still many topics regarding the connection of Capra's narrative films and war documentaries which are beyond the scope of this book that would lead to a greater understanding of Capra's life and work. The treatment of women as both victims and saviors, in both his documentaries and his narratives, would be extremely enlightening, as would Capra's treatment of minorities in both genres. An investigation into Capra's relationship with the Russians during the '30s and '40s, as well as his subsequent investigation by HUAC, may also yield interesting results. More than any other filmmaker (with the possible exception of John Ford), Frank Capra influenced the way Americans felt about their country and themselves during times of extreme crisis. Any investigation into his life and work, consequently, would surely be worthwhile to scholars of both history and film studies. Furthermore, it is hoped by this author that modern filmmakers continue to develop the ideas proposed by Capra in his films so many decades ago, as they are still relevant to Americans today. As the incredible recent success of the *Harry Potter* films, the *Lord of the Rings* trilogy, and *Avatar* have shown, the world continues to desire films that explore the concepts of fascism and individuality with honest emotion and true conviction rather than irony and cynicism. These successful films not only continue the Capra legacy into the 21st century, but also render his work all the more revelatory.

Chapter Notes

Preface

1. Frank Capra, *The Name Above the Title* (New York: Macmillan, 1971), 314.
2. Joseph McBride, *Frank Capra: The Catastrophe of Success* (New York: Simon & Schuster, 1992), 449.
3. During World War I, George Creel, head of the Committee on Public Information, enlisted the help of director D.W. Griffith and producer Carl Laemmle to his cause. Griffith made the film *Hearts of the World*, which was built around incidents between German troops and French civilians. Michael J. Sproule, *Propaganda and Democracy: The American Experience of Media and Mass Persuasion* (New York: Cambridge University Press, 1997), 11.
4. Brian Winston, "Documentary: I Think We Are in Trouble," in *New Challenges for Documentary*, edited by Alan Rosenthal (Los Angeles: University of California Press, 1998), 22–23.
5. Leland Poague, ed., *Frank Capra Interviews* (Jackson: University Press of Mississippi, 2004), 79.
6. Charles Maland, *Frank Capra* (New York: Twayne, 1995), 128.
7. Poague, *Frank Capra Interviews*, 81.
8. *Ibid.*, 59.
9. *Ibid.*, 61.
10. *Ibid.*, 58.
11. Thomas Schatz, *The Genius of the System: Hollywood Filmmaking in the Studio Era* (New York: Pantheon Books, 1988), 243.
12. Eric Smoodin, *Regarding Frank Capra: Audience, Celebrity, and American Film Studies* (Durham: Duke University Press, 2004), 2.
13. Edward Bernays, *Propaganda* (New York: Ig, 2005), 166.

Chapter 1

1. McBride, *Catastrophe of Success*, 449.
2. Bernays, *Propaganda*, 37.
3. McBride, *Catastrophe of Success*, 131.
4. General Marshall would often refer to Capra as "that fellow Capra." "That fellow" was a term Marshall reserved only for people he admired. *Ibid.*, 456.
5. Erik Barnouw, *Documentary: A History of the Non-Fiction Film* (New York: Oxford University Press, 1993), 157.
6. McBride, *Catastrophe of Success*, 100.
7. *Ibid.*, 717.
8. Poague, *Frank Capra Interviews*, 47–48.
9. Bernays, *Propaganda*, 72.
10. Neal Gabler, *An Empire of Their Own: How the Jews Invented Hollywood* (New York: Anchor, 1989), 164.
11. Richard Schickel, *The Men Who Made the Movies* (Chicago: Ivan R. Dee, 1975), 61.
12. Capra, *The Name Above the Title*, 223.

13. Poague, *Frank Capra Interviews*, 39.
14. Gabler, *An Empire of Their Own*, 166.
15. Maland, *Frank Capra*, 66.
16. *Ibid.*, 67.
17. Capra, *The Name Above the Title*, 131.
18. *Ibid.*, 134.
19. Maland, *Frank Capra*, 58.
20. Poague, *Frank Capra Interviews*, 14.
21. Capra, *The Name Above the Title*, 144.
22. Maland, *Frank Capra*, 79.
23. Leland Poague, *Another Frank Capra* (New York: Cambridge University Press, 1994), 38.
24. Schickel, *The Men Who Made the Movies*, 72.
25. Maland, *Frank Capra*, 84.
26. Schickel, *The Men Who Made the Movies*, 73.
27. In 2005 dollars, the film would have made nearly $124 million. Alex Block and Lucy Autrey Wilson, eds. *George Lucas's Blockbusting* (New York: HarperCollins, 2010), 180.
28. Capra, *Name Above the Title*, 172.
29. *Ibid.*, 176.
30. McBride, *Catastrophe of Success*, 318.
31. *Ibid.*, 319.
32. Capra, *Name Above the Title*, 185.
33. William M. Drew, "A Lighthouse in a Foggy World" in *Frank Capra Interviews*, ed. Leland Poague (Jackson: University Press of Mississippi, 2001), 180.
34. Poague, ed. *Frank Capra Interviews*, 54.
35. *Ibid.*, 246.
36. Nichols, Peter, ed. *The New York Times Guide to the Best 1000 Movies Ever Made*, 651.
37. Block and Wilson, *Blockbusting*, 196.
38. Ray Carney, *American Vision: The Films of Frank Capra* (Hanover, NH: Wesleyan University Press, 1996), 268.
39. Poague, *Another Frank Capra*, 96.
40. *Ibid.*, 94.
41. Capra, *Name Above the Title*, 186.
42. *Ibid.*, 196.
43. *Ibid.*, 197.
44. McBride, *Catastrophe of Success*, 357.
45. According to McBride, the film's final budget (including the cost of prints and advertising), came to $2,626, 620. *Ibid.*, 351.
46. *Ibid.*, 353.
47. *Ibid.*, 355.
48. *Ibid.*, 354.
49. *Ibid.*, 353; Block and Wilson, *Blockbusting*, 196.
50. Maland, *Frank Capra*, 101.
51. Pogue, *Frank Capra Interviews*, 55.
52. Capra, *Name Above the Title*, 203–204.
53. Poague, *Another Frank Capra*, 152.
54. Peter Nichols, ed. *The New York Times Guide to the Best 1000 Films Ever Made* (New York: St. Martin's, 2004), 583.
55. Capra, *The Name Above the Title*, 202.
56. *Ibid.*, 201.
57. Victor Scherle, and William Turner Levy, *The Complete Films of Frank Capra* (New York: Citadel, 1992), 19.
58. Poague, *Another Frank Capra*, 128–129.
59. Capra, *The Name Above the Title*, 201.
60. Poague, *Another Frank Capra*, 49.
61. Frank Doherty, "He Has the Common Touch," in Poague, 20.

Notes—Chapter 1

62. *Variety*, September 7, 1938, p.12
63. Maland, *Frank Capra*, 104.
64. Poague, *Another Frank Capra*, 21.
65. McBride, *Catastrophe of Success*, 402–403.
66. Poague, *Frank Capra Interviews*, 83.
67. Gerald Gardner, *The Censorship Papers: Movie Censorship Letters from the Hayes Office, 1934–1968*. (New York: Dodd, Mead, 1987), 101.
68. *Ibid.*, 103.
69. McBride, *Catastrophe of Success*, 416.
70. Sam Girgus, *Hollywood Renaissance: The Cinema of Democracy in the Era of Ford, Capra, and Kazan* (New York: Cambridge University Press, 1998), 81–82.
71. Block and Wilson, *Blockbusting*, 218.
72. Nichols, ed. *The New York Times Guide to the Best 1000 Films Ever Made*, 654.
73. *Ibid.*, 1148.
74. Scherle and Levy, *The Complete Films of Frank Capra*, 168.
75. Girgus, *Hollywood Renaissance*, 77.
76. Capra, *The Name Above the Title*, 297.
77. Capra was the cover story for the August 1938 issue of *Time*.
78. Schickel, *The Men Who Made the Movies*, 80.
79. Poague, *Frank Capra Interviews*, 87.
80. McBride, *Catastrophe of Success*, 435–436.
81. *Ibid.*, 435.
82. Glenn Phelps, "Frank Capra and the Political Hero: A New Reading of *Meet John Doe*," *Film Criticism* 5, no. 2 (Winter 1981), 56.
83. Schickel, *The Men Who Made the Movies*, 78.
84. Poague, *Another Frank Capra*, 4.
85. McBride, *Catastrophe of Success*, 437.
86. Maland, *Frank Capra*, 111.
87. Capra, *The Name Above the Title*, 309.
88. Maland, *Frank Capra*, 119.
89. Capra, *The Name Above the Title*, 311.
90. Figures for *It Happened One Night*, on which Capra had a 10 percent share, are not available. McBride details the amounts Capra received as follows: $299, 406 for *Mr. Deeds Goes to Town*; $262,084 for *Lost Horizon*; $212, 043 for *You Can't Take it With You*; and $42, 125 for *Mr. Smith Goes to Washington*. McBride, *Catastrophe of Success*, 331.
91. Maland, *Frank Capra*, 40.
92. Schickel, *The Men Who Made the Movies*, 66.
93. Schatz, *Genius of the System*, 272.
94. Poague, *Frank Capra Interviews*, 89.
95. *Ibid.*, 109–110.
96. *Ibid.*
97. *Ibid.*, 81.
98. Capra, *The Name Above the Title*, 186.
99. In Capra's autobiography, the director claims that the first film in which his name was placed above the title was *Mr. Deeds Goes to Town*. According to McBride, this is inaccurate. On *Deeds*, the words, "A Frank Capra Production" appeared on the title card of the film, but *below* the names of the stars. McBride, *Catastrophe of Success*, 330.
100. Poague, *Frank Capra Interviews*, 43.
101. McBride, *Catastrophe of Success*, 259.
102. *The Dick Cavett Show*, which originally aired January 21, 1972.
103. Scherle and Levy, *The Complete Films of Frank Capra*, 13.
104. Maland, *Frank Capra*, 19.
105. McBride, *Catastrophe of Success*, 272.
106. *Ibid.*, 296.
107. *Ibid.*

108. *Ibid.*
109. Maland, *Frank Capra*, 65.
110. Capra, *The Name Above the Title*, 148; Poague, *Frank Capra Interviews*, 50.
111. McBride, *Catastrophe of Success*, 291.
112. *Ibid.*, 591.
113. *Ibid.*, 599.
114. Schickel, *The Men Who Made the Movies*, 72.
115. Scherle and Levy, *The Complete Films of Frank Capra*, 123.
116. Poague, *Frank Capra Interviews*, 52.
117. *Ibid.*, 84–85.
118. *Ibid.*, 50.
119. Capra, *The Name Above the Title*, 244.
120. McBride, *Catastrophe of Success*, 293.

Chapter 2

1. Poague, *Frank Capra Interviews*, 5.
2. Fred Hift, "Capra of Deeds and Smith Sagas Sees Hollywood Now Over-Intellectual," in Poague, 71.
3. Capra, *Another Frank Capra*, 40–47.
4. Maland, *Frank Capra*, 23.
5. Carney, *American Vision*, 228.
6. Poague, *Frank Capra Interviews*, 85.
7. Harry Hargrave, "Interview with Frank Capra," *Literature Film Quarterly* 9, no. 3 (1981): 198.
8. Carney, *American Vision*, 341.
9. Poague, *Frank Capra Interviews*, 25.
10. Hargrave, "Interview with Frank Capra," 201.
11. Maland, *Frank Capra*, 27.
12. Poague, *Frank Capra Interviews*, 111.
13. Carney, *American Vision*, 227.
14. Hargrave, "Interview with Frank Capra," 198.
15. Carney, *American Vision*, 37.
16. Poague, *Frank Capra Interviews*, 178.
17. Capra, *The Name Above the Title*, 139–140.
18. Schickel, *The Men Who Made the Movies*, 69.
19. Maland, *Frank Capra*, 108.
20. Poague, *Another Frank Capra*, 102.
21. John Mariani, "Frank Capra," in Poague, 139.
22. Carney, *American Vision*, 305.
23. *Ibid.*, 305.
24. Neil Hurley, "Capra; the Voice Behind the Name Behind the Title," in Poague, 196.
25. Maland, *Frank Capra*, 20.
26. *Ibid.*, 90.
27. Bernays, *Propaganda*, 121.
28. Schickel, *The Men Who Made the Movies*, 74.
29. Mariani, 138.
30. Ted Sennett, *Laughing in the Dark: Movie Comedy from Groucho to Woody* (New York: St. Martin's, 1992), 90.
31. Capra, *The Name Above the Title*, 67.
32. *Ibid.*, 443.
33. *Ibid.*, 130.
34. Poague, *Frank Capra Interviews*, 196.
35. Capra, *The Name Above the Title*, 241.

36. Bryan Sterling, *The Best of Will Rogers: A Collection of Rogers' Wit and Wisdom, Astonishingly Relevant for Today's World* (New York: M. Evans, 2000), 193.
37. Maria Elena de las Carreras Kuntz, "The Catholic Vision in Hollywood: Ford, Capra, Borzage, and Hitchcock," *Film History* 14 (2002): 123.
38. Kuntz, "The Catholic Vision," 126.
39. Maland, *Frank Capra*, 92.
40. *Ibid.*, 87.
41. Kuntz, "The Catholic Vision," 128.
42. Maland, *Frank Capra*, 86.
43. *Ibid.*, 82.
44. McBride, *Catastrophe of Success*, 47.
45. Poague, *Another Frank Capra*, 162.
46. *Ibid.*, 51.
47. Capra, *The Name Above the Title*, 256.
48. *Ibid.*, 260.
49. Carney, *American Vision*, 52.
50. Poague, *Frank Capra Interviews*, 18.
51. Patrick Gerster, "The Ideological Project of *Mr. Deeds Goes to Town*," *Film Criticism* 5, no. 2 (Winter 1981): 36.
52. Michael Rogin and Kathleen Moran, "Mr. Capra Goes to Washington," *Representations* 84 (Autumn 2003): 226.
53. James Childs, "Capra Today," in Poague, 95.
54. Carney, *American Vision*, 308.
55. Poague, *Another Frank Capra*, 55.
56. Poague, *Frank Capra Interviews*, 117.
57. Carney, *American Vision*, 333.
58. *Ibid.*, 337–341.
59. Girgus, *Hollywood Renaissance*, 63.
60. Maland, *Frank Capra*, 65.
61. Carney, *American Vision*, 233–234.
62. David Kennedy, *Freedom from Fear: The American People in Depression and War, 1929–1945* (New York: Oxford University Press, 1999) Kindle Edition, loc.4238–48.
63. Poague, *Another Frank Capra*, 157.
64. Capra, *The Name Above the Title*, 243.
65. Carney, *American Vision*, 323–324.
66. John O'Leary and Rick Worland, "Against the Organization Man," in *The Sitcom Reader*, ed. Mary M. Dalton and Laura R. Linder (Albany: State University of New York Press, 2005), 81–82.
67. Schickel, *The Men Who Made the Movies*, 62.
68. Poague, *Frank Capra Interviews*, 95.
69. Mariani, 143.
70. Capra, *The Name Above the Title*, 6.
71. Jon Savage, *Teenage: The Creation of Youth Culture* (New York: Viking Penguin, 2007), 291.
72. Poague, *Another Frank Capra*, 38.
73. Carney, *American Vision*, 314.
74. McBride, *Catastrophe of Success*, 58.
75. Wes D. Gehring, *Populism and the Capra Legacy* (Westport, CT: Greenwood, 1995), 6.
76. Poague, *Frank Capra Interviews*, 182.
77. Sterling, *The Best of Will Rogers*, 1; Richard Gertner, ed. *Motion Picture Almanac of 1983* (New York: Quigley, 1983), 40a.
78. Childs, 93–94.
79. McBride, *Catastrophe of Success*, 256.
80. *Ibid.*, 242.

Chapter 3

1. Schatz, *The Genius of the System*, 312.
2. Capra, *The Name Above the Title*, 314.
3. *Ibid.*, 314.
4. McBride, *Catastrophe of Success*, 312.
5. Capra, *The Name Above the Title*, 315.
6. *Ibid.*, 315.
7. *Ibid.*, 9.
8. *Ibid.*, 299.
9. McBride, *Catastrophe of Success*, 409, 411.
10. *Ibid.*, 389–392, 398.
11. Capra, *The Name Above the Title*, 287.
12. *Ibid.*, 289.
13. *Ibid.*, 288.
14. Gardner, *The Censorship Papers*, 100.
15. McBride, *Catastrophe of Success*, 450.
16. *Ibid.*, 89.
17. *Ibid.*, 438.
18. *Ibid.*, 451.
19. John Huston, *An Open Book* (New York: Alfred A. Knopf, 1980), 88.
20. McBride, *Catastrophe of Success*, 486.
21. *Ibid.*, 486.
22. Richard MacCann, "World War II: Armed Forces Documentary" in *The Documentary Tradition, Second Edition*, ed. Lewis Jacobs (New York: W.W. Norton, 1979), 213.
23. Capra, *The Name Above the Title*, 318.
24. *Ibid.*, 328.
25. McBride, *Catastrophe of Success*, 133.
26. Capra, *The Name Above the Title*, 327.
27. Thomas Bohn, *An Historical and Descriptive Analysis of the* Why We Fight *Series* (New York: Arno Press, 1977), 38.
28. *Ibid.*, 38–39.
29. Coincidentally, Franklin Roosevelt was a member of Wilson's administration when the CPI was first created. Allan M. Winkler, *Politics of Propaganda: The Office of War Information, 1942–1945* (New Haven: Yale University Press, 1978), 5.
30. *Ibid.*, 2–3.
31. Sproule, *Propaganda and Democracy*, 9.
32. Bohn, *Historical and Descriptive Analysis*, 36–38.
33. *Ibid.*, 36–38.
34. *Ibid.*
35. Sproule, *Propaganda and Democracy*, 38.
36. *Ibid.*, 9.
37. *Ibid.*, 19.
38. *Ibid.*, 16.
39. Winkler, *Politics of Propaganda*, 4–5.
40. David Kennedy, *Freedom from Fear*, loc. 6978–81.
41. Bernays, *Propaganda*, 126.
42. *Ibid.*, 64.
43. *Ibid.*, 54.
44. *Ibid.*, 37.
45. Savage, *Teenage*, 227.
46. McBride, *Catastrophe of Success*, 456.
47. Blaine Allan, "*Heritage* and *The Plow That Broke the Plains*," *The Historical Journal of Film, Radio, and Television*, 19, no. 4 (1999): 447.
48. Gilbert Seldes, "Pare Lorentz's *The River*," in *The Documentary Tradition, Second Edition*, ed. Lewis Jacobs (New York: W.W. Norton, 1979), 123–124.

49. Richard Steele, *Propaganda and Open Society: The Roosevelt Administration and the Media, 1933–1941* (Westport, CT: Greenwood Press, 1985), 147.
50. Allan, "*Heritage* and *The Plow That Broke the Plains*," 449.
51. McBride, *Catastrophe of Success*, 481.
52. Kennedy, *Freedom from Fear*, loc. 4603–4607.
53. Steele, *Propaganda and Open Society*, 147.
54. *Ibid.*, 148.
55. Michael C.C. Adams, *Best War Ever* (Baltimore: The Johns Hopkins University Press, 1994), 11.
56. Robert T. Elson, "De Rochenmot's *The March of Time*," in *The Documentary Tradition, Second Edition*, ed. by Lewis Jacobs (New York, W.W. Norton, 1979), 104.
57. Bohn, *Historical and Descriptive Analysis*, 26.
58. Elson, "De Rochement's March of Time," 108.
59. McBride, *Catastrophe of Success*, 481.
60. Elson, "De Rochement's March of Time," 108.
61. *Ibid.*, 110.
62. Steele, *Propaganda and Open Society*, 150.
63. Elson, "De Rochemont's *The March of Time*" in *The Documentary Tradition*, 111.
64. Steele, *Propaganda and Open Society*, 150.
65. *Ibid.*, 150–151.
66. *Ibid.*, 148–149.
67. William K. Everson, "The Triumph of the Will." In *The Documentary Tradition, Second Edition*, edited by Lewis Jacobs (New York: W.W. Norton, 1979), 138.
68. *Ibid.*, 138–139; Peter C. Rollins, "Frank Capra's *Why We Fight* Film Series and Our American Dream," *Journal of American Culture* 19, no. 4 (Winter 1996): 82.
69. Capra, *The Name Above the Title*, 328.
70. *Ibid.*
71. McBride, *Catastrophe of Success*, 466.
72. Siegfried Kracauer, *From Caligari to Hitler: A Psychological Study of the German Film* (New York: Noonday, 1960), 303.
73. Thomas Doherty, *Projections of War: Hollywood, American Culture, and World War II* (New York: Columbia University Press, 1993), 23.
74. *Ibid.*, 23–24.
75. Kracauer, *From Caligari to Hitler*, 280.
76. *Ibid.*, 293.
77. *Ibid.*, 304.
78. *Ibid.*, 307.
79. Bohn, *Historical and Descriptive Analysis*, 95–96.
80. MacCann, "World War II: Armed Forces Documentary," 216.
81. McBride, *Catastrophe of Success*, 456.

Chapter 4

1. McBride, *Catastrophe of Success*, 89.
2. Capra, *The Name Above the Title*, 334.
3. *Ibid.*, 347.
4. *Ibid.*, 334.
5. McBride, *Catastrophe of Success*, 474.
6. Capra, *The Name Above the Title*, 342.
7. McBride, *Catastrophe of Success*, 275.
8. Capra, *The Name Above the Title*, 341.
9. McBride, *Catastrophe of Success*, 472, 454.
10. *Ibid.*, 453.
11. Winkler, *Politics of Propaganda*, 7.
12. Capra, *The Name Above the Title*, 339.

13. McBride, *Catastrophe of Success*, 156.
14. Bohn, *Historical and Descriptive Analysis*, 105.
15. Capra, *The Name Above the Title*, 339–340.
16. McBride, *Catastrophe of Success*, 458.
17. Capra, *The Name Above the Title*, 338.
18. McBride, *Catastrophe of Success*, 472.
19. This changed later, as it proved difficult to find appropriate shots. Instead, basic storylines were constructed so the unit did not have to find specific matching shots. Bohn, *Historical and Descriptive Analysis*, 105.
20. *Ibid.*, 107
21. McBride, *Catastrophe of Success*, 472.
22. *Ibid.*, 473.
23. Bohn, *Historical and Descriptive Analysis*, 102–103. The SCPC in Astoria, which produced film bulletins, historical informational films like *The Battle of San Pietro* and the *Why We Fight* series, employed 287 officers, 610 enlisted men, and 1,361 civilians, housed in 14 buildings. *Ibid.*, 53.
24. Poague, *Frank Capra Interviews*, 58.
25. Bohn, *Historical and Descriptive Analysis*, 103.
26. McBride, *Catastrophe of Success*, 460–461, 464; Capra, *The Name Above the Title*, 335.
27. Barnouw, *Documentary*, 160.
28. Frank Capra actually met Walt Disney for the first time in 1929. Recognizing the young man's talent, Capra advised Harry Cohn to pick up Mickey Mouse, exclusively for Columbia. The deal fell through and Disney ended up distributing through RKO. Capra, *The Name Above the Title*, 104–105.
29. McBride, *Catastrophe of Success*, 474.
30. *Ibid.*, 475.
31. *Ibid.*, 489–490.
32. Capra claimed most of his knowledge of small towns came from his short time as a salesman after World War I. Maland, *Frank Capra*, 24.
33. Adams, *Best War Ever*, 12–13.
34. Poague, *Frank Capra Interviews*, 168.
35. *Time*, August 8, 1938, 37.
36. Kennedy, *Freedom from Fear*, loc. 12697–701.
37. Adams, *Best War Ever*, 86.
38. Kennedy, *Freedom from Fear*, loc.12676–81.
39. This measure passed the House of Representatives by one vote (203 yes, 201 no). Bohn, *Historical and Descriptive Analysis*, 86.
40. *Ibid.*, 93, 89.
41. *Ibid.*, 46–48.
42. *Ibid.*, 108.
43. Doherty, *Projections of War*, 74.
44. *Ibid.*, 27.
45. McBride, *Catastrophe of Success*, 467, 481.
46. *Ibid.*, 467–468.
47. Capra, *The Name Above the Title*, 341; McBride, *Catastrophe of Success*, 481.
48. McBride, *Catastrophe of Success*, 482.
49. *Ibid.*, 480.
50. *Ibid.*
51. Doherty, *Projections of War*, 89.
52. *Ibid.*, 234.
53. *Shooting War*, DVD Directed by Richard Schickel (Burbank, CA: DreamWorks Video, 2004).
54. *Ibid.*
55. Adams, *Best War Ever*, 475.

56. *Shooting War*, DVD.
57. Doherty, *Projections of War*, 250–251.
58. *Shooting War*, DVD.
59. Bohn, *Historical and Descriptive Analysis*, 200.
60. Poague, *Frank Capra Interviews*, 121.
61. McBride, *Catastrophe of Success*, 471.
62. Bohn, *Historical and Descriptive Analysis*, 100.
63. *Ibid.*
64. Capra, *The Name Above the Title*, 330–331.
65. Winkler, *Politics of Propaganda*, 12–13.
66. Peter C. Rollins, "World War II: Documentaries," in *The Columbia Companion to American History on Film: How the Movies Have Portrayed the American Past*, ed. Peter C. Rollins (New York: Columbia University Press, 2003), 118.
67. Capra, *The Name Above the Title*, 345.
68. *Ibid.*, 341.
69. *Ibid.*, 346.
70. McBride, *Catastrophe of Success*, 476.
71. *Ibid.*, 476–477.
72. Bohn, *Historical and Descriptive Analysis*, 109–110.
73. McBride, *Catastrophe of Success*, 462.
74. Bohn, *Historical and Descriptive Analysis*, 121.
75. McBride, *Catastrophe of Success*, 486–487.
76. Capra, *The Name Above the Title*, 352.
77. McBride, *Catastrophe of Success*, 483–484.
78. Frederic Krome, "*Tunisian Victory* and Anglo American Film Propaganda in World War II," *Historian* 58, no. 3 (Spring 1996): 4.
79. *Ibid.*, 5.
80. *Ibid.*
81. McBride, *Catastrophe of Success*, 482.
82. *Ibid.*
83. Bohn, *Historical and Descriptive Analysis*, 107–108.
84. Kathleen German, "Frank Capra's *Why We Fight* Series and the American Audience," *Western Journal of Speech Communication* 54, no.2 (Spring 1990): 245.
85. German, "Frank Capra's *Why We Fight* Series and the American Audience," 246.
86. Schickel, *The Men Who Made the Movies*, 83.
87. Capra, *The Name Above the Title*, 362.
88. *Ibid.*
89. Barnouw, *Documentary*, 162.
90. McBride, *Catastrophe of Success*, 492.
91. *Ibid.*, 491.
92. *Ibid.*, 471; Capra, *Name Above the Title*, 336.
93. Patton, who notoriously admired the Nazis, called the film "bullshit." McBride, *Catastrophe of Success*, 496.
94. *Ibid.*
95. Bohn, *Historical and Descriptive Analysis*, 59.
96. Capra, *The Name Above the Title*, 365.
97. Kracauer, *From Caligari to Hitler*, 277.
98. Bohn, *Historical and Descriptive Analysis*, 59.
99. McBride, *Catastrophe of Success*, 498.
100. *Ibid.*, 499.
101. *Ibid.*, 500.

Chapter 5

1. Bohn, *Historical and Descriptive Analysis*, 122–128.

2. Adams, *Best War Ever*, 88.
3. Bohn, *Historical and Descriptive Analysis*, 131.
4. George Bailey, "Why We (Should Not) Fight: Colonel Frank Capra," in Poague, 127.
5. Barnouw, *Documentary*, 161.
6. Doherty, *Projections of War*, 74.
7. Bohn, *Historical and Descriptive Analysis*, 197.
8. *Ibid.*, 201.
9. The only real exception to this rule is from *Tunisian Victory*, where Allied soldiers are shown in close-up profile prior to invading Africa. The use of the profile in this case, however, seems to emphasize intense concentration, rather than to separate them emotionally from the audience.
10. Joseph McBride, *Searching for John Ford* (New York: St. Martin's, 2001), 51.
11. These same shots were also used effectively in John Huston's *The Battle of San Pietro*.
12. Bernays, *Propaganda*, 123.
13. Doherty, *Projections of War*, 75.
14. Andre Bazin, "On *Why We Fight:* History, Documentation, and the Newsreel (1946)," *Film and History* 31, no. 1 (May 2001), 61.
15. *Ibid.*
16. Bohn, *Historical and Descriptive Analysis*, 223.
17. *Ibid.*, 178–179.
18. Kracauer, *From Caligari to Hitler*, 283.
19. According to Thomas Bohn, the intention of German camera operators when shooting their soldiers was to portray the German soldier as superhuman, strong, and above emotion. As Capra used the shots in a different context, they were seen in the *Why We Fight* films as automatons, devoid of feeling. Bohn, *Historical and Descriptive Analysis*, 196.
20. Bohn, *Historical and Descriptive Analysis*, 144.
21. Adams, *Best War Ever*, 48.
22. Alan Axelrod, *The Real History of World War II* (New York: Sterling Publishing, 2008), 82.
23. Kennedy, *Freedom from Fear*, loc. 7936–41.
24. According to David Kennedy, despite Roosevelt's insistence that the Atlantic and Pacific Oceans could not protect us from invasion, they were actually an extremely powerful deterrent for both powers. *Ibid.*, loc. 13293–95.
25. *Ibid.*, loc. 14389–91.
26. Adams, *Best War Ever*, 61.
27. Kennedy, *Freedom from Fear*, 7090–95.
28. Adams, *Best War Ever*, 39.
29. Bohn, *Historical and Descriptive Analysis*, 153.
30. Karacauer, *From Caligari to Hitler*, 284.
31. Kennedy, *Freedom from Fear*, loc. 7583–86.
32. Barnouw, *Documentary*, 159.
33. Bohn, *Historical and Descriptive Analysis*, 170.
34. *Ibid.*, 135.
35. *Ibid.*, 146–147.
36. Bailey, 125.
37. Bernays, *Propaganda*, 73–74.
38. Axelrod, *The Real History of World War II*, 93.
39. MacCann, "WWII: Armed Forces Documentary," 217–218.
40. Bohn, *Historical and Descriptive Analysis*, 33, 48.
41. *Ibid.*, 33.
42. Barnouw, *Documentary*, 162.
43. Bohn, *Historical and Descriptive Analysis*, 108.
44. According to Capra, the State Department reported that these showings brought in more than $2.5 million, six times the cost of production. Capra, *The Name Above the Title*, 336.

45. Bohn, *Historical and Descriptive Analysis*, 112–113.
46. *Ibid.*, 112–113, 115.
47. Barnouw, *Documentary*, 158.
48. McBride, *Catastrophe of Success*, 482.
49. Bohn, *Historical and Descriptive Analysis*, 112–113, 115.
50. Winkler, *Politics of Propaganda*, 157.
51. Adams, *Best War Ever*, 88–89.
52. *Ibid.*
53. *Ibid.*, 4.
54. *Ibid.*, 138.
55. McBride, *Catastrophe of Success*, 90.
56. Adams, *Best War Ever*, 54; Kennedy, *Freedom from Fear*, loc.13249–50.
57. Kennedy, *Freedom from Fear*, loc. 14907.
58. *Ibid.*, loc. 14910
59. Adams, *Best War Ever*, 75.
60. *Ibid.*, 150.
61. *Ibid.*, 90.

Chapter 6

1. Capra, *The Name Above the Title*, 337.
2. *Ibid.*, 375.
3. John C. Tibbetts and James M. Welsh, eds. *The Encyclopedia of Filmmakers, Volume 1* (New York: Facts on File, 2002), 91.
4. Poague, *Frank Capra Interviews*, 122.
5. *Ibid.*
6. Childs, 96.
7. Maland, *Frank Capra*, 132.
8. Poague, *Frank Capra Interviews*, 122.
9. Gehring, *Populism and the Capra Legacy*, 23.
10. Capra, *The Name Above the Title*, 371.
11. Roger Ebert, *The Great Movies* (New York: Broadway Books, 2002), 230.
12. Poague, *Frank Capra Interviews*, 29 from "Emotional Appeal Capra's Film Goal" by Edwin Shallert, from the *Los Angeles Times* (3/3/1946): 1, 3.
13. Poague, *Another Frank Capra*, 216.
14. Girgus, *Hollywood Renaissance*, 94, 100.
15. Maland, *Frank Capra*, 141–142.
16. Poague, *Another Frank Capra*, 190.
17. Robin Wood, "Ideology, Genre, Auteur," in *Film Theory and Criticism, 5th edition*, eds. Leo Brady and Marshall Cohen (New York: Oxford University Press, 1999), 674.
18. Girgus, *Hollywood Renaissance*, 93.
19. Ebert, *The Great Movies*, 229.
20. McBride, *Catastrophe of Success*, 530.
21. Nichols, ed. *The New York Times Guide to the Best 1000 Films Ever Made*, 496.
22. Ebert, *The Great Movies*, 230.
23. Capra, *The Name Above the Title*, 386.
24. Ebert, *The Great Movies*, 229.
25. Capra, *The Name Above the Title*, 397.
26. Drew, 182.
27. Maland, *Frank Capra*, 163.
28. *Ibid.*, 166.
29. *Ibid.*
30. Capra, *The Name Above the Title*, 443.
31. Poague, *Frank Capra Interviews*, 21 from Daugherty, Frank, "He Has the Common Touch," *Christian Science Monitor*, November 8, 1938.

32. Capra, *The Name Above the Title*, 446.
33. *Ibid.*, 447.
34. *Ibid.*, 451.
35. Maland, *Frank Capra*, 168.
36. Crowther, "Capra's 'A Hole in the Head': Sinatra Is Starred in Story by Schulman," *New York Times*, July 16, 1959.
37. Gertner, *Motion Picture Almanac of 1983*, 40a.
38. Capra, *The Name Above the Title*, 486.
39. *Ibid.*, 475.
40. *Ibid.*, 493.
41. *Ibid.*
42. *Ibid.*
43. Gene Siskel, "Candidly Kubrick," in *Stanley Kubrick Interviews*, ed. Gene D. Phillips (Jackson: University Press of Mississippi, 2001), 187.
44. Capra, *The Name Above the Title*, 494.

Chapter 7

1. Gabler, *An Empire of Their Own*, 165.
2. Poague, *Another Frank Capra*, 231.
3. Nat Hentoff, "Flight of Fancy," in *Clint Eastwood Interviews*, ed. Robert Kapsis and Kathie Coblentz (Jackson: University Press of Mississippi, 1999), 157.
4. Michel Ciment and Hubert Niogret, "A Destabilized America," in *Oliver Stone Interviews*, ed. Charles Silet (Jackson: University Press of Mississippi, 2001), 106.

Bibliography

Adams, Michael C.C. *Best War Ever*. Baltimore: The Johns Hopkins University Press, 1994.
Allen, Blaine. "*Heritage* and *The Plow That Broke the Plains*." *The Historical Journal of Film, Radio, and Television*, 19, no. 4 (1999): 439–472.
American Madness, DVD. Directed by Frank Capra. Los Angeles: Sony Pictures Home Entertainment, 2006.
Arsenic and Old Lace, DVD. Directed by Frank Capra. Los Angeles: Image Entertainment, 2001.
Axlerod, Alan. *The Real History of World War II*. New York: Sterling, 2008.
Barnouw, Erik. *Documentary: A History of the Non-Fiction Film*. New York: Oxford University Press, 1993.
Bazin, Andre. "On *Why We Fight*: History, Documentation, and the Newsreel (1946)." *Film & History* 31, no. 1 (May 2001): 60–62. Accessed online in EBSCO (January 11, 2010).
Bernays, Edward. *Propaganda*. 1928. New York: Ig, 2005.
Bitter Tea of General Yen, VHS. Directed by Frank Capra. Los Angeles: Sony Pictures Home Entertainment, 1997.
Block, Alex, and Lucy Autrey Wilson, eds. *George Lucas's Blockbusting*. New York: HarperCollins, 2010.
Bohn, Thomas. *An Historical and Descriptive Analysis of the Why We Fight Films*. New York: Arno Press, 1977.
Broadway Bill, DVD. Directed by Frank Capra, Los Angeles: Paramount Collection, 2004.
Cover Story, *Time*, August 8, 1938.
Capra, Frank. *The Name Above the Title*. New York: Macmillan, 1971.
Carney, Ray. *American Vision: The Films of Frank Capra*. Hanover, NH: Wesleyan University Press, 1996.
Crowther, Bosley. "Capra's 'A Hole in the Head': Sinatra Is Starred in Story by Schulman," *New York Times*, July 16, 1959.
Dave, DVD. Directed by Ivan Reitman. Los Angeles: Warner Home Video, 1998.
Doherty, Thomas. *Projections of War: Hollywood, American Culture, and World War II*. New York: Columbia University Press, 1993.
Ebert, Roger. *The Great Movies*. New York: Broadway, 2002.
Elson, Robert T. "De Rochenmot's *The March of Time*." In *The Documentary Tradition, 2nd edition*, edited by Lewis Jacobs. New York: W.W. Norton, 1979.
Everson, William K. "The Triumph of the Will." In *The Documentary Tradition, Second Edition*, edited by Lewis Jacobs. New York: W.W. Norton, 1979.
Gabler, Neal. *An Empire of Their Own: How the Jews Invented Hollywood*. New York: Anchor Books, Doubleday, 1989.
Gardner, Gerald. *The Censorship Papers: Movie Censorship Letters from the Hayes Office, 1934–1968*. New York: Dodd, Mead, 1987.
Gehring, Wes D. *Populism and the Capra Legacy*. Westport, CT: Greenwood, 1995.
German, Kathleen M. "Frank Capra's *Why We Fight* Series and the American Audience." *Western Journal of Speech Communication* 54, no. 2 (Spring 1990): 237–248. Accessed online in EBSCO (January 11, 2010).
Gerster, Patrick. "The Ideological Project of *Mr. Deeds Goes to Town*." *Film Criticism* 5, no. 2 (Winter 1981): 35–48. http://ezproxy.rollins.edu:2048/login?url=http://search.ebsco

host.com/login.aspx?direct=true&db=aph&AN=31316448&site=ehost-live&scope=site (accessed online in EBSCO, January 13, 2010).
Gertner, Richard, ed. *Motion Picture Almanac 1983.* New York: Quigley, 1983.
Girgus, Sam B. *Hollywood Renaissance: The Cinema of Democracy in the Era of Ford, Capra, and Kazan.* New York: Cambridge University Press, 1998.
Hargrave, Harry. "Interview with Frank Capra." *Literature Film Quarterly* 9, no. 3 (1981): 189–200 (accessed January 11, 2010).
Just For You / Here Comes the Groom, DVD. Directed by Frank Capra and Elliot Nugent. Los Angeles: Paramount Collection, 2004.
Hemo the Magnificent / Unchained Goddess, DVD. Produced and Directed by Frank Capra. Los Angeles: Image Entertainment, 2003.
Hero, DVD. Directed by Stephen Frears. Los Angeles: Sony Pictures, 1999.
A Hole in the Head, DVD. Directed by Frank Capra. Los Angeles: MGM Home Entertainment, 2001.
The Hudsucker Proxy, DVD. Directed by Joel Coen. Los Angeles: Warner Home Video, 1999.
Huston, John. *An Open Book.* New York: Alfred A. Knopf, 1980.
It Happened One Night, DVD. Directed by Frank Capra. Los Angeles: Sony Pictures Home Entertainment, 2006.
It's a Wonderful Life, Blu-Ray. Directed by Frank Capra. Los Angeles: Paramount Pictures, 2009.
Kapsis, Robert E., and Kathie Coblentz, eds. *Clint Eastwood Interviews.* Jackson: University Press of Mississippi, 1999.
Kennedy, David. *Freedom from Fear: The American People in Depression and War.* New York: Oxford University Press, 1999. Kindle Edition.
Know Your Enemy: Japan, DVD. Directed by Frank Capra. Kaiserslautern, Germany: Aberle-Media, 2005.
Kracauer, Siegfried. *From Caligari to Hitler: A Psychological Study of the German Film.* New York: Noonday Press, 1960.
Krome, Frederic. "*Tunisian Victory* and Anglo-American Film Propaganda in World War II." *Historian* 58, no.3 (Spring 1996): 517–530. http://ezproxy.rollins.edu:2048/login?url=http://search.ebscohost.com/login.aspx?direct=true&db=aph&AN=9607261518&site=-ehost-live&scope=site (accessed February 9, 2010).
Kuntz, Maria Elena de las Carreras. "The Catholic Vision in Hollywood: Ford, Capra, Borzage, and Hitchcock." *Film History* 14 (2002): 121–135. Accessed in EBSCO (January 11, 2010).
Lost Horizon, DVD. Directed by Frank Capra. Los Angeles: Sony Pictures Home Entertainment, 1999.
MacCann, Richard. "World War II: Armed Forces Documentary." In *The Documentary Tradition*, 2nd edition, edited by Lewis Jacobs. New York: W.W. Norton, 1979.
The Majestic, DVD. Directed by Frank Darabont. Los Angeles: Warner Home Video, 2002.
Maland, Charles. *Frank Capra.* New York: Twayne, 1995.
Meet John Doe, DVD. Directed by Frank Capra. Tulsa, OK: VCI Entertainment, 2010.
McBride, Joseph. *Frank Capra: The Catastrophe of Success.* New York: Simon & Schuster, 1992.
———. *Searching for John Ford.* New York: St. Martin's, 2001.
Mr. Deeds Goes to Town, DVD. Directed by Frank Capra. Los Angeles: Sony Pictures Home Entertainment, 2006.
Mr. Smith Goes to Washington, DVD. Directed by Frank Capra, Los Angeles: Sony Pictures Home Entertainment, 2006.
Nichols, Peter, ed. *The New York Times Guide to the Best 1,000 Movies Ever Made.* New York: St. Martin's, 2004.
O'Leary, John, and Rick Worland. "Against the Organization Man." In *The Sitcom Reader*, edited by Mary M. Dalton and Laura R. Linder, 73–86. Albany: State University of New York Press, 2005.
Phelps, Glenn A. "Frank Capra and the Political Hero: A New Reading of *Meet John Doe*." *Film Criticism* 5, no. 2 (Winter 1981): 49–57. http://ezproxy.rollins.edu:2048/login?url=http://search.ebscohost.com/login.aspx?direct=true&db=aph&AN=31316449&site=ehost-live&scope=site (accessed in EBSCO, January 12, 2010).

Phillips, Gene D., ed. *Stanley Kubrick: Interviews*. Jackson: University Press of Mississippi, 2001.
Poague, Leland. *Another Frank Capra*. New York: Cambridge University Press, 1994.
_____ (editor). *Frank Capra Interviews*. Jackson: University Press of Mississippi, 2004.
Pocketful of Miracles, DVD. Directed by Frank Capra. Los Angeles: MGM Home Entertainment, 2001.
Riding High, DVD. Directed by Frank Capra. Los Angeles: Paramount Pictures, 2004.
Rogin, Michael, and Kathleen Moran. "Mr. Capra Goes to Washington." *Representations* no. 84 (Autumn 2003): 213–248. Accessed online in JSTOR (January 12, 2010).
Rollins, Peter C. "Frank Capra's *Why We Fight* Film Series and our American Dream." *Journal of American Culture* 19, no.4 (Winter 1996): 81–86. Accessed online in Academic Search Premier (January 11, 2010).
_____. "World War II: Documentaries." In *The Columbia Companion to American History on Film: How the Movies Have Portrayed the American Past*, edited by Peter C. Rollins, 116–124. New York: Columbia University Press, 2003.
Savage, Jon. *Teenage: The Creation of Youth Culture*. New York: Viking Penguin, 2007.
Schatz, Thomas. *The Genius of the System: Hollywood Filmmaking in the Studio Era*. New York: Pantheon, 1988.
Scherle, Victor, and William Turner Levy. *The Complete Films of Frank Capra*. New York: Citadel, 1992.
Schickel, Richard. *The Men Who Made the Movies*. Chicago: Ivan R. Dee, 1975.
Seldes, Gilbert. "Pare Lorentz's *The River*." In *The Documentary Tradition, 2nd edition*, edited by Lewis Jacobs, 123–125. New York: W.W. Norton, 1979.
Sennett, Ted. *Laughing in the Dark: Movie Comedy from Groucho to Woody*. New York: St. Martin's, 1992.
Sherman, Eric. *Directing the Film: Film Directors on their Art*. Los Angeles: Acrobat, 1976.
Shooting War, DVD. Directed by Richard Schickel. Burbank, CA: DreamWorks Video, 2004.
Silet, Charles L., ed. *Oliver Stone Interviews*. Jackson: University Press of Mississippi, 2001.
Smoodin, Eric. *Regarding Frank Capra: Audience, Celebrity, and American Film Studies, 1930–1960*. Durham: Duke University Press, 2004.
Sproule, J. Michael. *Propaganda and Democracy: The American Experience of Media and Mass Persuasion*. New York: Cambridge University Press, 1997.
State of the Union, DVD. Directed by Frank Capra. Los Angeles: Universal Pictures, 2006.
Steele, Richard W. *Propaganda and Open Society: The Roosevelt Administration and the Media, 1933–1941*. Westport, CT: Greenwood, 1985.
Sterling, Bryan. *The Best of Will Rogers: A Collection of Rogers' Wit and Wisdom, Astonishingly Relevant for Today's World*. New York: M. Evans, 2000.
Tibbetts, John C., and James M. Welsh, eds. *The Encyclopedia of Filmmaking, Vol. 1*. New York: Facts on File, 2002.
Tunisian Victory. YouTube website, http://www.youtube.com/watch?v=gSqMTjONkbI (accessed February 9, 2010).
Winkler, Allan M. *The Politics of Propaganda: The Office of War Information, 1942–1945*. New Haven: Yale University Press, 1978.
Winston, Brian. "Documentary: I Think We Are in Trouble" in *New Challenges for Documentary*, edited by Alan Rosenthal. Los Angeles: University of California Press, 1988.
Wood, Robin. "Ideology, Genre, Auteur." In *Film Theory and Criticism, 5th Edition*, edited by Leo Brady and Marshall Cohen. New York: Oxford University Press, 1999.
WWII: War in Europe, Vol. 1: Here Is Germany, DVD. Renton, WA: Topics Entertainment, 2008.
WWII: War in Europe, Vol. 2: Know Your Ally: Britain, DVD. Renton, WA: Topics Entertainment, 2008.
WWII: War in Europe, Vol. 2: Two Down and One to Go! DVD. Renton, WA: Topics Entertainment, 2008.
WWII: Why We Fight, Vol. 1: Prelude to War. DVD. Renton, WA: Topics Entertainment, 2008.
WWII: Why We Fight, Vol. 1: The Nazis Strike, DVD. Renton, WA: Topics Entertainment, 2008.
WWII: Why We Fight, Vol. 2: Divide and Conquer, DVD. Renton, WA: Topics Entertainment, 2008.

WWII: Why We Fight, Vol. 3: *The Battle of Britain*, DVD. Renton, WA: Topics Entertainment, 2008.
WWII: Why We Fight, Vol. 4: *The Battle of* Russia, DVD. Renton, WA: Topics Entertainment, 2008.
WWII: Why We Fight, Vol. 5: *The Battle of* China, DVD. Renton, WA: Topics Entertainment, 2008.
WWII: Why We Fight, Vol. 6: *War Comes to* America, DVD. Renton, WA: Topics Entertainment, 2008.
You Can't Take It with You, DVD. Directed by Frank Capra. Los Angeles: Sony Pictures Home Entertainment, 2006.
Your Job in Germany. YouTube website, http://www.youtube.com/watch?v=1v5QCGqDYGo (accessed February 9, 2010).

Index

Numbers in **_bold italics_** indicate pages with photographs.

Academy Awards (Oscar) 1, 11, 17, 20, 21, 22, 23, 25, 27, 28, 30, 32, 34, 37, 39–40, 41, 53, 61, 67, 112, 129, 135, 191, 195, 203, 207, 210
Academy of Motion Picture Arts and Sciences (AMPAS) 15, 17, 20, 25, 41, 129
Adair, Jean 46
Adams, Michael 168–169, 171
Air Force 125
Albert, Eddie 197
Alexander, John 46
Alexander Nevsky 156
All Quiet on the Western Front 125
Allied powers 84, 105, 129, 130, 131, 138–139, 142, 143, 145–147, 148, 152, 153, 154, 155–156, 158, 159, 160–162, 163, 164, 165–166, 169, 170, 174, 189, 227
Altman, Robert 53, 207
America (film) 125
America *see* United States
America Calling 103
The American Film Institute 5, 40, 62, 191
American Madness 15, 18, 20, 30, 32, 59, 65, 66, 74, 75, 79, 83, 191, 205; dialogue, 86; "love thy neighbor" 77, 78; mob behavior 95; pacing 71; plot summary 19–20; similarities to *Bitter Tea of General Yen* 30, 59–60, 69; similarities to *Broadway Bill* 29; similarities to *Lady for a Day* 23–24, 26; similarities to *Meet John Doe* 63; similarities to *State of the Union* 193
America's Answer 107
Anderson, Maxwell 38
The Andy Griffith Show 89
animation: in Bell Science Films 197; in *It's a Wonderful Life* 182; in *Why We Fight* 122, 125, **_140_**, 148, **_149_**, **_150_**, 159
Army-Navy Screen Magazine 132
Army Pictorial Service *see* United States Army Pictorial Service
Arnold, Edward 36, 39, 42, 66, 88
Arsenic and Old Lace 1, **_2_**, 9, 15, 35, 38, 45–49, **_50_**, 51, 59, 60, 93, 101, 121, 182, 189; and conformity 167, 187; difference from play 48–49; and freedom 97; and individualism 49, 188; metaphor for America 49–51; and Mortimer Brewster character 84, 97, 99, 188; plot summary 45–48; production of 45–46; similarity to *It Happened One Night* 46; use of light and shadow 69–70
Arthur, Jean 31, 36, 38, **_60_**
Association of Documentary Film Producers 110
Asther, Nils 21
Astoria, New York 120, 226
Auteur Theory 53–55
Avatar 219
Axis powers 75, 84, 95, 103, 105, 128, 129, 130, 138, 142, 144–145, 147–148, 153, 154–156, 157, 159, 164–165, 166, 170

Balaban, Barney 191
Ball Film Laboratory 14
banned films 22, 115
Baptism of Fire 115–116, 153
Barnouw, Eric 133–134, 139, 162, 168
Barrymore, Lionel 36, 176, 190
Battle for Midway 3, 125, 171
The Battle of Britain 130–131, **_140_**, 142, 143, **_144_**, 146, 147, 149, 152, 153, 156, 164, 166, 168, 169
The Battle of China 132–133, 145, 146, 151, 155, 169
The Battle of Russia 131, 143, 144, 152, 154, 155, 156, 158, 166, 168
The Battle of San Pietro 170–171, 226, 227
Baxter, Frank 197–198
Baxter, Warner 28–29, 194
Bazin, Andre 150–151
Beatitudes 78–79
Beery, Wallace 25
Bell System Science Films 196–198
Bellamy, Ralph 18
bells 67, 145, 178
Bernays, Edward 9, 11, 13, 75, 108, 146, 166
The Best Years of Our Lives 175, 191
Big 208–209, 210

237

Billy Jack Goes to Washington 209
Bitter Tea of General Yen 8–9, 15, 17, 19, 21–23, 60, 61, 87; difference from *Lady for a Day* 23; and fascism 22, 96, 98; and freedom 96–98; plot summary 21–22; similarity to *American Madness*, 30, 59–60, 69; similarity to *It Happened One Night* 28; similarity to *Lost Horizon* 35, 95
block booking 51, 103
Bluem, William 112
Bogdanovich, Peter 53–54
Bohn, Thomas 4, 130, 141, 142, 151, 152, 165, 168, 226, 228
bombing of London 104, 122, 170, 174, 189
Breen, Joseph 38
Brennan, Walter 42
Briskin, Sam 121, 175, 204
British Army Film Unit 122, 131–132
Broadway 16, 45–46, 199
Broadway Bill 15, 27, 46, 59, 65, 91, 97, 98; and capitalists 30, 96, 98; childlike behavior 83; close ups 62, 63–64; common faces 68–69; Dan Brooks character 84, 87, 96, 97; ending 61–62; individualism 167; mobs 18, 95; pace 30, 71; plot summary 28–30; and *Riding High* 32, 64, 194–195; similarity to *American Madness* 29; similarity to *It Happened One Night* 29
Bronco Billy 210
Buchman, Sidney 38–39, 56, 103, 176
Byington, Spring 83
Byrnes, Sen. John 103

Cal Tech *see* Throop Polytechnic Institute
Campaign in Poland (Feldzug in Polen) 115, 125
Capra, Frank, Jr. 209
Capra, John 37
Cardwell, LTC Barry 4
Carlson, Richard 197
Carmichael, Hoagy 195
Carney, Ray 3, 8, 11, 24, 62, 64, 70–71, 72, 81, 83, 86, 87, 88
Carrey, Jim 216
Casablanca 48, 191
Catholicism 76–78, 203
Chamberlain, Neville 145, 160
children, depiction of 65, 85, 96, 142, 143, 152, 154–156, *157*, *158*, 161, 162, 164
China 133, 145, 146, 162; *see also* Allied powers
The Christian Science Monitor 36
Christianity 41, 74, 76–79 89, 145, 149, 160–162; in *Bitter Tea of General Yen 21*; *see also* Beatitudes; churches; "love thy neighbor"
churches, depiction of 17–18, 76–77, 81, 133, 141, 152, *161*, 162, 178, 203
Churchill, Winston 142, 145, 147, 158–159, 166, 170
Citizen Kane 18, 191

Clark, Gen. Mark 145
Close Encounters of the Third Kind 208
close ups 62–64, 66, 67–68, 72, 126, 142–144, 195, 227; in profile 63–64, 142–143; in *It's a Wonderful Life* 178, 183; in *State of the Union* 193
Coen, Ethan 211–212
Coen, Joel 211–212
Cohn, David 138
Cohn, Harry 5, 14–15, 22, 23, 25, 33, 35–36, 37, 51–52, 57, 96, 99, 103, 119, 120, 128, 199, 204, 226
Colbert, Claudette *12*, 25–27, 210
Colman, Robert 33
Columbia Pictures 5, 8, 14–15, 16, 17, 19, 25, 35, 51–52, 57, 99, 199, 208, 226; Capra's lawsuit against 35–36; and *Lost Horizon* 33–34; and *Mr. Smith Goes to Washington* 103; *see also* Cohn, Harry
Committee on Public Information (CPI) 106–109, 221, 225
communion 78, 203
communism 74, 103, 121–122, 130, 131, 193, 195, 196, 207, 216
conformity 9, 167, 202; in *Arsenic and Old Lace* 51, 99, 167, 187; in *A Hole in the Head* 201; in *It's a Wonderful Life* 187–189; in *Mr. Deeds Goes to Town* 30, 32; in war documentaries 141, 144, 152
Connolly, Myles 16, 192, 196
Connolly, Walter 21, 25, 28, 194
Conservatives *see* Republicans
conversions 28, 30, 75, 83–84, 98–99, 124; in *Meet John Doe* 43–44; in *You Can't Take It With You* 37
Cooper, Gary 5, 31, 38, 42, 43, 66, *70*, 124, 163, 201, 205
Coppola, Francis Ford 207, 208
Crawford, Joan 25
Creel, George 106–109, 221
Crocodile Dundee 209
Crosby, Bing 32, 194–196, 201, 202, 205
Crouse, Russel 192
Crowther, Bosley 190, 200–201
Curtiz, Michael 120

D-Day 126
Darabont, Frank 216–218
Dave 214–215
Davis, Bette 203
Davis, Geena 212
Dead Poets Society 208, 211
December 7th 3
"The Declaration of Independence" 82
De Gaulle, Charles 140, 145, 163
Democrats 34, 56, 74, 94
The Dick Cavett Show 34, 53
Dirigible 16, 59
Disney, Walt 32, 122, 226
Divide and Conquer 8, 130, 140, 143, 145, 147,

148, *149*, 152, 153, 155, 156, 157, **158**, 163, 164
Doherty, Thomas 141
Dressler, Marie 25
Drums Along the Mohawk 125
Dumbrille, Douglas 29, 31, 194
Dunn, Kevin 214
Dunne, Phillip 56
Durning, Charles 211

Eastwood, Clint 210
Ebert, Roger 190–191
Ecce Homo 110
Eddy, Bob 70
editing 4–5, 6, 13, 14, 34, 51, 61, 65, 70–73, 82, 110, 113, 115, 120–121, 124, 127, 132; in *Broadway Bill* 30; in *It's a Wonderful Life* 178, 181; in *Pocketful of Miracles* 202; in war documentaries 143, 150–152, 164; in *You Can't Take It with You* 37–38
834th Photographic Detachment 6, 8, 118–122, 127, 132
Eisenhower, Gen. Dwight D. 126, 142, 145, 147, 165–166
Eisenstein, Sergei 72, 156
England *see* Great Britain
Epstein, Julius 48, 121–122
Epstein, Philip 48, 121–122
Ethiopia 22, 129, 145, 165
Eyemo camera 126

"faceless" man episode 27–28, 31
Falk, Peter 203
The Family Man 209
Fascism 21–22, 30, 41, 43, 59, 74–74, 79, 88, 95, 96–100, 112, 128, 138–139, 208, 210, 218–219; in *It's a Wonderful Life* 177, 186, 188–190
Field of Dreams 208
Fight for Life 110
The Fisher King 210
Flaherty, Robert 111, 112, 122
Flight 16, 117
Foch, Marechal Ferdinand 156–158
Forbidden 16, 17, 18–19, 20
Ford, Glenn 203–204, 205
Ford, John 3, 7, 11, 54, 59, 60, 71, 103, 104, 112, 120, 122, 125, 143, 171, 219
Foreman, Leo 81
Foster, Lewis R. 38
France 106, 115, 130, 140, 143, 145, 147, 148, ***149***, 152, 156, 157, 161, 168; *see also* Allied Powers
Frank Capra Productions 15, 41, 44, 45
Frank Capra: The Catastrophe of Success 1–4, 104
Frears, Stephen 212–214
Friedman, Arthur 13, 27, 34, 53
Friendly Persuasion 191, 207
Fulta Fisher's Boarding House 13, 14, 67, 105

Gable, Clark *12*, 25–27, 210
Gabler, Neal 15, 208
Garcia, Andy 212
Gardner, Gerald 103
Garrison, Jim 210
Geisel, Theodore 121, 122, 134–135, 136
"The Gentleman from Montana" 38
German, Kathleen 133
Germany 34, 42, 95, 104, 110, 130, 131, 134–135, 140, 142–143, 145, 146, 147, 153–154, ***155***, 156, *157*, 159–160, 161, 162, 164, 170, 174–175, 189; and the CPI 107; war films of 113–116, 117, 124–125; *see also* Axis Powers; Hitler, Adolf; Nazis
Girgus, Sam 39, 40, 181, 187
Glatzer, Richard 84
Gleason, James 42, 48
Goebbels, Joseph 44, 135
Goldwyn, Samuel 38, 175
Gone with the Wind 39, 112
The Good Earth 125
Goodrich, Frances 176
Gordon, Gavin 19, 21
Grant, Cary 1, **2**, 45–46
Grant's tomb 80–82, 147
The Grapes of Wrath 89
Graves, Ralph 16–17
Gray, Colleen 194
Great Britain 22, 23, 33, 88–89, 112, 115, 122, 130–131, 131–132, 136, 138, 140, 142, 143, 145, 146, 147, 149, 152, 153, 156, 158, 160, 161, 162, 163, 164, 168, 169, 170, 202; *see also* Allied powers; bombing of London; Churchill, Winston
Great Depression 6–7, 17, 32, 37, 68–69, 74, 77, 81, 82, 89, 92, 143, 177, 189
The Great War *see* World War I
"The Greatest Gift" 176–177
Griffith, David Wark 125, 221
Griffith, Richard 121
Grodin, Charles 214

Hackett, Albert 176
Hakkō ichiu 136
Hal Roach Studios 94, 126
Harlow, Jean 16
Harry Potter and the Deathly Hallows Part 1 211, 219
Hart, Moss 35–36
Harvey, Joan 101
Hawks, Howard 54, 204
Hawn, Goldie 210
Hays, Will 38
Heisler, Stuart 133–134
Hemo the Magnificent 196–198
Henry, Patrick 158
Hepburn, Katharine 192–194
Here Comes the Groom 191, 195–196
Here Is Germany 127, 134, 135, 142, 143, 148, 153, **155**, 164, 170

240　　　　　　　　　　Index

Hero 211, 212–214, 218
Hersey, John 168
Hilton, James 32–33
Hirohito 136, 147, 165
Hitchcock, Alfred 54, 59, 60, 71, 180, 192, 204, 207
Hitler, Adolf 27, 30, 34, 42, 44, 96, 125, 130, 141–142, 145, 148, 149, 159, 160, 162, 163–164, 165, 166, 177, 202, 219
Hitler Lives? 135
Hoffman, Dustin 211, 212
Holden, Laurie 216
A Hole in the Head 191, 198–202, 203, 205, 207
Hollywood Citizen News 102–103
Holt, Jack 16
Horgan, Paul 119, 121, 122
Hornbeck, William 119, 120, 121
Horton, Edward Everett 48, 203
House of Un-American Activities Committee 103, 122, 196, 205, 216, 218, 219
Housesitter 210
The Hudsucker Proxy 211–212, 218
Hughes, Howard 102
Hughes, Langston 133
Hull, Josephine 46
Huston, John 104, 112, **118**, 122, 131–132, 170–171, 204
Huston, Walter 19, 121

I'm an American 104
imagination, in Capra's heroes 75, 80–81, 83–84, 86, 154, 181, 201, 216
imperialism 33, 50, 65, 136, 169
improvisation 24–25, 26, 57, 83–84, 85–86, 87, 90, 153–154, 178, 194, 196, 197, 203, 215
Information and Educational Division of the War Department 168
It Happened One Night 3, 6, 7, 14, 15, 16, 25–28, 32, 40, 54, 56, 57, 61, 62, 69, 72, 73, 87, 120, 142, 155, 191, 205, 219; effect on Capra 27–28, 30, 61, 101, 190; and Ellen Andrews character 62, 79, 84, 85, 87, 93, 96–97, 142, 210; and Peter Warne character 40, 57, 84, 87, 90, 92, 93, 155, 210; plot summary 25–26; similarity to *Arsenic and Old Lace* 46; similarity to *Broadway Bill* 29, 32, 98; similarity to *Bronco Billy* 210; similarity to *You Can't Take It with You* 37, 66, 98; success of 27–28
Italy 95, 103, 104, 144, 145, 154, 157, 164, 165; see also Axis powers; Mussolini, Benito
It's a Wonderful Life 2, 3–4, 7, 8, 9, 19, 38, 43, 51, 54, 57–58, 60, 62, 76, 99, 175–191, 199, 203, 205, 207, 209, 211, 216, 217–218; and community 180–181, 187, 190; difference from prewar films 179–182; and George Bailey character 20, 76, 176–177, 181–182, 186–188, 189–190, 193–194, 201, 217–218; and "The Greatest Gift" 177; and Harry Bailey character 186–187; and Mary Bailey character 184–185; and Mr. Potter character 22, 177, 178, 187–188, 190, 201; and Peter Bailey character 177; Pottersville sequence 176, 183–184, 187–188; self-reflexivity of 182–185; similarity to *Arsenic and Old Lace* 49, 60, 187; similarity to Capra's prewar films 177–179; similarity to *Meet John Doe* 43, 178–179; similarity to *Mr. Smith Goes to Washington* 41, 178–179; similarity to *Why We Fight* films 187, 189–190; and World War II 185–187, 189
Ivens, Joris 111, 112, 122, 136

Jaffee, Sam 33
Japan 1, 95, 112, 117, 124, 129, 132–133, 135, 136–137, 141, 142, 144–145, 146, 147, 148–149, 152, 153, 154, 155, 157, 159, 162, 164, 165, 170, 174–175, 189; see also Axis powers; Hirothito
Jefferson, Thomas 69, 72, 80, 81, 82, 93, 94, 156
Jesus Christ 76–78
The Jimmy Durante Story 202
Johnson, Van 192
Joseph and His Brethren 199, 207

Kanin, Garson 199
Karloff, Boris 47, 50
Kaufman, George S. 35–36
Kelland, Clarence 30
Kelly, Gene 35
Kendall, Elizabeth 208
Kennedy, John F. 169
Kennedy, Joseph 103
Kesselring, Joseph 45, 49, 51
The King's Speech 210
Kingsley, Ben 214
Kline, Kevin 214–215
Knight, Eric 121, 125
Know Your Ally: Britain 127, 130, 132, 141, 142, 156, 158, 160, 162, 163, 169
Know Your Ally: Russia 130
Know Your Enemy: Japan 127, 132, 136, 137, 141, 142, 144–145, 147, 148, 152, 159, 162, 164, 170
Know Your Enemy: Russia 130
Kracauer, Siegfried 114, 115, 116, 153–154
Kubrick, Stanley 204–205
Kuntz, Maria elena de las Carreras 78

Ladies of Leisure 16, 17, 26, 87
Lady for a Day 15, 21, 23–25, 27, 59, 61, 62, 65, 67, 68, 69, 84, 87, 97, 98, 180; and Apple Annie character 62, 97, 180; and Dave the Dude character 84, 90; and *Pocketful of Miracles* 202–203; similarity to *American Madness* 23, 24, 26; similarity to *It Happened One Night* 26
The Land 110

Index 241

Landau, Martin 216
Lane, Priscilla 1, *2*, 46
Langdon, Harry 14, 51, 61, 77, 83
Lange, Jessica 211
Langella, Frank 214–215
Lansbury, Angela 192–194
League of Nations 145, 147
A League of Their Own 211
Left-wing *see* Democrats
Leftists *see* Democrats
Leigh, Jennifer Jason 211–212
Liberal *see* Democrats
Liberty Bell 67, 145
Liberty Pictures 175, 191–192
Libia 105
Life magazine 111
lighting 37–38, 69, 183
Lincoln, Abraham 38, 69, 80–82, 93–94, 96, 156, 169; imagery in *Arsenic and Old Lace* 50; imagery in *It's a Wonderful Life* 182, *183*; imagery in *Meet John Doe* 82
Lincoln Memorial 39, 63, 67, 68, 69, 81–82, 87, 156
Lindsay, Howard 192
Little Orphan Annie 92
Litvak, Anatole 113–114, 121, 131, 132
Locke, Sandra 210
Lord of the Rings 208, 219
Lorentz, Pare 109–110, 112
Lorre, Peter 47
Los Angeles, California 1, 6, 14, 90, 93, 132
Los Angeles Times 22, 178
Lost Horizon 15, 28, 32–35, 54, 56, 63, 65, 67, 69–70, 72, 76, 79, 82, 89, 92, 120, 126–127, 142, 145, 167, 223; effect on Columbia Pictures 34; and *Mr. Deeds Goes to Town* 34–35; and Robert Conway character 65, 69, 80, 82, 84, 91, 96, 97, 146, 165; similarity to *Bitter Tea for General Yen* 22, 95; similarity to *It's a Wonderful Life* 180; similarity to *Lady for a Day* 98; similarity to *Why We Fight* series 33
"love thy neighbor" 77–78, 96, 160–162, 165, 178
Loy, Myrna 28, 194
Lubitsch, Ernst 54, 134

MacArthur, Gen. Douglas 136, 158
MacLeish, Archibald 128
"Madame La Gimp" 23
Magic Town 57
The Majestic 216–218
Maland, Charles 4, 5–6, 16, 17, 18, 26, 34, 37, 45, 46, 54, 61, 71, 74, 79, 86–87, 182, 194, 195
Mann, Anthony 180
The March of Time 111–113, 116
Marshall, Gen. George 6, 11, 105, 109, 116, 118–119, 125, 129, 135, 158, 168, 221
Martin, Dean 202
Martin, Steve 210
mass media 18, 90, 95, 107, 108, 109, 111, 148
Massey, Raymond 47, 49, *50*
massism 32, 95, 128, 189, 202
Mauldin, Bill 168
Mayer, Louis B. 25
McBride, Joseph 1–3, 4, 8, 11, 27, 56, 96, 104, 105, 168
McCarthy, Frank 109
McGovern, George 40
Meet John Doe 3, 15, 17, 18, 26, 41–45, 54, 56, 59, 62, 63, 64–65, 67, 68, 69, 72–73, 74, 75, 76, 78, 79, 82, 87, 88, 95, 97, 98–99, 101, 139–140, 148, 156, 160, 164, 167, 171, 182, 193, 211; and Ann Mitchell character 142, 143, 165; and D.B. Norton character 22, 66, 88, 91, 96, 145, 148, 163–164, 165; ending of 43–44, 63, 98–99, 139–140, 188, 189–190; and John Willoughby character 45, 57, 63, 78, 79, 82, 83, 84, 86, 90, 91, 92, 94, 96, 97, 98, 146, 153, 154, 165, 180, 181, 189, 208, 213, 214; and montages 60, 72–73, 151; plot summary 42–43; similarity to *It's a Wonderful Life* 178–179, 184
Mellet, Lowell 127–128, 129
Menjou, Adolphe 18, 192
Mercer, Johnny 195
Metro Goldwyn Mayer (MGM) 25, 125
Meyer, Russ 126
The Miracle Woman 16, 17–18, 28
mise-en-abîme 82
Mr. Deeds 209
Mr. Deeds Goes to Town 3, 4, 6, 11, 14–15, 16, 17, 27, 28, 30–32, 38, 41, 43, 45, 51, 54, 56, 58, 59, 62–63, 66, 67, 68, 69, *70*, 71, 72, 73, 75, 77, 79, 81, 82, 86, 87, 89, 91, 92–93, 94, 95, 97–98, 143, 147, 160, 167, 179, 188, 203, 205, 209, 210, 211–213, 219, 223; character of Babe Bennett 86, 98, 215; character of John Cedar 22, 66, 84, 88, 89, 91, 98, 145, 147, 160, 163–164, 166; character of Longfellow Deeds 20, 40, 57, 67, 73, 78, 79, 80–81, 82, 83, 84, 85, 86, 87, 89–90, 91, 93–94, 96, 97–98, 138, 146–147, 153, 154, 157–158, 160, 165, 180, 181, 182, 200–201, 208, 214–215; and *Lost Horizon* 33, 34, 35; plot summary 31; similarity to *The Hudsucker Proxy* 211–212; similarity to *It Happened One Night* 26; similarity to *Ladies of Leisure* 17; similarity to *State of the Union* 193
Mr. Smith Goes to Washington 3, 4, 11, 15, 17, 26, 28, 32, 38–41, 43, 44, 51, 54, 57–58, 59, 60, 62, 63, 65, 66, 67, 68, 69, 71, 72, 73, 78, 80, 81, 82, 83, 85, 88, 95, 98, 99, 120, 139–140, 141, 142, 143, 145, 147, 148, 151, 160, 167, 178–179, 188, 191, 192, 205, 209, 210, 211, 215, 223; character of Clarissa Saunders 86, 91, 99, 215; character of James Taylor 66, 88, 91, 96, 98, 145, 147, 148, 166, 179; character of Jefferson Smith 20, 57, 65,

76, 77–78, 79, 80, 82, 83, 84, 85, 86, 87, 90, 91, 92–93, 95, 96, 97, 98, 138, 146–147, 148, 153, 154, 160, 165, 178, 180, 181, 182, 201, 208, 210, 212, 214, 216, 218; character of Joseph Paine 63, **64**, 66, 77–78, 82, 88, 96, 98, 163–164, 166; controversy of 40, 103; and *Meet John Doe* 45; plot summary 38–39; similarity to *State of the Union* 193
Mitchell, Thomas 92, 176
mobs 18, 20, 95–96, 164–165, 179
Modern Times 32
montage sequences 4, 60, 65, 72–73, 110, 148, 151–152, 153, 164, 182, 198
Morale Branch of the U.S. Army Special Services 105, 133
Moses 156
Moss, Carlton 121, 134
Muse, Clarence 28, 194
Museum of Modern Art (MOMA) 113–114
music 37, 72–74, 85, 152–153, 164, 165, 178, 183, 195–196, 210–211
Mussolini, Benito 22, 95–96, 129, 141, 162, 165, 166; *see also* Axis powers; Italy

The Name Above the Title 1, 4, 13, 14, 18, 23, 27, 28, 41, 49–50, 71, 76, 80, 90–91, 92, 94, 101, 105, 114, 117, 121, 128, 131, 136, 162, 172, 175, 182, 191, 196–197, 198–199, 203
narration 5, 109–110, 112, 113, 120, 127, 131, 135, 138, 150–151, 152, 160, 162–164, 170, 197
National Broadcasting Company (NBC) 103
Nazis 34, 125, 130–131, 135, 138, 139, 140, 142, 143, 147–148, 149, 154, 156, 157, 159, 161–162, 164, 166, 169, 227; propaganda films 113–116, 125, 152, 161; *see also* Axis powers; Germany; Hitler, Adolf
The Nazis Strike 8, 130, 143, 145, 147, 148, 149, 152, 155, 159, 163, 164, 166
Neely Anti-Block Booking Bill 103
The Negro Soldier 8, 122, 127, 132, 133–134
New Deal 56, 91, 110–111
The New York Times 27, 31, 34, 40, 110, 190–191, 200
Newman, Paul 211
"Night Bus" **12**, 25
Noyes, Arthur 170
Nugent, Frank 31, 34, 40

O'Brien, Pat 19
Office of Facts and Figures 128
Office of War Information 54, 119, 123–124, 127–128, 129
On to Tokyo 122, 127, 136–137
One Flew Over the Cuckoo's Nest 27
"Opera Hat" 30–31
Orlando, Florida 132
Osborn, Brig. Gen. Frederick 133
"Our Gang" 83
Our Job in Japan 137

Our Mr. Sun 196–198
Oz, Frank 210

pace of Capra's films 16, 20, 26, 30, 61, 71, 75, 151–152, 196, 202
Palm Springs, California 23, 55–56
Paramount Pictures 16, 119–120, 191–192, 195–196
Patton 109
Patton, Gen. George S. 135, 144, 227
Pearl Harbor 1, 159–160
Pershing's Crusaders 107
Peterson, Edgar "Pete" 113–114, 118, 121
Phelps, Glenn 44
physical labor in Capra's films 86, 90–91, 146, 198
Platinum Blonde 16–17, 26, 28
Plow That Broke the Plains 109–111
Poague, Leland 3–4, 8, 11, 24, 32, 35, 37–38, 60–61, 71, 72, 80, 88, 91–92, 179
Pocketful of Miracles 191, 202–205
Poland 115, 130, 139, 145, 148, 149, 152, 155, 163
Popeye 92
populism 93–95
The Power and the Land 110
The Power of the Press 15
Prelude to War 8, 125, 129, 131, 138, 140, 142, 145, 146, 148, 154–155, 156, **157**, 159, 160–161, 162, 164, 165, 166, 167–168, 169
Production Code Administration 38
propaganda 4, 9, 11, 13, 75, 100, 106, 108, 110–111, 112–113, 120, 121, 127, 128, 129, 138, 146, 153–154, 169, 170, 218; and Nazis 113–116, 120, 125, 141; and World War I 106–108
Propaganda (book) 13, 108
Pyle, Ernie 122, 168

Radcliffe, Daniel 211
Radio City Music Hall 22, 27
Rain or Shine 16
Rains, Claude 39, **64**, 66, 88
The Ramparts We Watched 112
Reader's Digest 111
Reinhardt, Gottfried 134
Reitman, Ivan 214–215
Report from the Aleutians 104
Republicans 56, 74, 94, 146
Rhames, Ving 214
Riding High 32, 64, 191, 194–195, 201, 202
Riefenstahl, Leni 113–115, 218
Right-wing *see* Republicans
Riskin, Robert 15, 16, 17, 19, 21, 23, 24, 31, 36, 38, 41–42, 54–58, 71, 80, 86–87, 88, 99, 124, 175, 176
Ritter, Thelma 199–200
The River 109–111
Roach, Hal 14
Robbins, Tim 211–212
Robinson, Edward G. 199–200

Index

Robson, May 23
Rogers, Will 7, 77, 87, 94
Rollins, Peter 4
Roman Holiday 191–192, 207
Roosevelt, Franklin Delano 91, 94, 109–111, 119, 121, 129, 142, 145–146, 147, 159, 161–162, 166, 225
Roosevelt, Theodore 50
Rosenblum, Walter 126
Runyon, Damon 23, 87
Russia 25, 107, 117, 130, 131, 142, 143, 146, 152, 153, 154, 156, 158, 159, 161, 162, 166, 168, 169, 174, 219; *see also* Allied powers; Stalin, Josef

St. Paul 202, 207
Sandford, John 130
Sandler, Adam 209
San Francisco, California 14, 67, 102, 105, 117
Savage, John 91
Schatz, Thomas 7
Scheuer, Philip 22
Schickel, Richard 42, 44, 52
Schlesinger, Arthur, Jr. 5
Schlosberg, Col. Richard T. 105, 117
Schulman, Arnold 198–200
Screen Actors Guild 102–103
Selective Service Act of 1940 123
Selznick, David O. 52, 112
Sennett, Mack 13, 14, 90, 94, 119
Sennett, Ted 75
Sergeant York 125
Shawshank Redemption 208
Shooting War 126
Shrek Forever After 209
Signal Corps *see* United States Army Signal Corps
Signal Corps Photography Center (SCPC) 119–120, 132, 226
Silence of the Lambs 27
silhouettes, use of 69, *70*, 141, 149–150
Sinatra, Frank 199–201, 202, 205
singles, use of 64–66, 143–145, 164, 165–166, 178, 181
Siskel, Gene 205
Slumdog Millionaire 208
Smith Act 103
Smoodin, Eric 8
Sony Pictures *see* Columbia Pictures
Soviet 25
Soviet Union *see* Russia
Special Services *see* United States Army Special Services
Spewak, Sam **118**
Spielberg, Steven 207, 208
Sproule, J. Michael 107
Stalin, Josef 131, 145, 166
Stander, Lionel 31
Stanwyck, Barbara 5, 16, 17, 19, 21, 42
Star Wars 208

State of the Union 18, 171, 182, 191–194, 205, 207, 211
Steele, Richard W. 112–113
Stein, Elliot 44
Stern, Philip Van Doren 175–177
Stevens, George 131–132, 175
Stewart, James 5, 36, 38, 40, **60**, 66, 88, 124, 163, ***173***, 176, 179–180, ***183***, 190, 191, 205
Sticht, Chet 56
Stiers, David Ogden 216
Stillwell, Gen. Joseph 136, 147
The Stillwell Road 127, 136, 142, 144, 146, 147, 164
Stone, Oliver 210
The Strange Case of Cosmic Rays 196–198
The Strong Man 14
Submarine 16
suicide, in Capra's films 17, 22, 39, 43–44, 63, 177, 178, 187, 211
Superman **92**, 208
Swerling, Jo 16, 17, 56

Teenage 91
Thalberg, Irving 25
Throop Polytechnic 13, 102, 117, 170
Time magazine 41, 45, 111, 117, 123, 133
Tiomkin, Dimitri 73, 119, 121
Tootsie 211
Top Hat 219
Tracy, Spencer 192–194
Treaty of Versailles 107
Triumph of the Will 113–115, 125, 141–142
The Truman Show 184
Tunisian Victory 8, 104, 116, 122, 125, 127, 131–132, 138, 140, 142, 143–144, 145, 147, 148, 149–150, 151–152, 153, 154, 155–156, 160–161, 162, 163, 164, 166, 170, 227
Twentieth Century–Fox 105, 119, 129
Two Down and One to Go! 122, 127, 135–136, 145

Unchained Goddess 196–198
Under Four Flags 107
United Artists 204
United States 3, 7, 49–50, 74–75, 81, 103, 112, 130, 134, 158–159, 160, 167–171, 174, 185–187, 189, 196; *see also* Allied powers; Roosevelt, Franklin Delano
United States Army Pictorial Service (APS) 119, 122, 132
United States Army Signal Corps 1, 105, 106–109, 117, 119, 124, 125, 131, 132
United States Army Special Services 100, 105, 119
United States Citizenship 103–104
United States Customs Service 114
United States Film Service 109–111

Van Dyke, W.S. (Woody) 104
Variety 37, 59, 125

Veiller, Anthony **118**, 121, 134, 192
Victory in the West (Sieg im Westen) 115–116, 125, 153
Vietnam 169
Vorkapich, Slavko 72–73, 151

Wake Island 125
Walker, Joe 102
WALL-E 208
War Activities Committee 123
War Comes to America 127, 132, 134, 144, 146, 152, 154, 157, 158, 159, 160, 165
Warner, H.B. 33
Warner, Jack 45–46, 203–204
Warner Brothers 1, 15, 45, 99, 101, 135, 189
Washington, George 69, 80, 81, 82, 96, 156, 169
Washington, D.C. 1, 6, 38, 40, 65, 72, 80–81, 103, 104, 117, 118, 119, 120, 121, 132, 147, 157, 179
Watson, Emma 211
Weaver, Sigourney 214–215
When You're in Love 57
Why We Fight series 2, 3–6, 7, 11, 13, 14, 15, 30, 33, 41, 67, 70–71, 72–73, 75, 78, 92–93, 99, 104–105, 113, 115–116, 120–134, 139, 141, 145, 148, **150**, 151, 152, 155, 157, 160, **161**, 163, 165, 167–171, 183, 184, 187, 189–190, 205; audience 123, 167; Capra's involvement 5–6, 122; distribution 123, 129, 167–168; effects 167–171; footage used 124–127; goals 105–106, 116, 127–129; production 118–122; roots 106–116; *see also The Battle of Britain*; *The Battle of China*; *The Battle of Russia*; *Divide and Conquer*; *The Nazis Strike*; *Prelude to War*; *War Comes to America*

Wiggins, Roy 13
Wilder, Billy 204, 207
William, Warren 23
Wilson, Woodrow 106, 112, 225
Wingate, Maj. Gen. Orde Charles 147
Wings 16
Winkler, Allan 107
Wood, Robin 187
World War I 13, 102, 104, 117, 119, 148, 156; propaganda films during 106–108
World War II 6, 7, 12–13, 54, 98, 100, 112, 117, 119, 129, 139, 150, 152, 167–169, 170, 171, 202; effect on Capra 172–175, 189–190; and *It's a Wonderful Life* 177, 185–187, 189
Wyatt, Jane 33
Wyler, William 104, 112, 175, 190–192, 204, 207
Wyman, Jane 195

You Can't Take It with You 3, 15, 28, 30, 35–38, 41, 53, 54, 56, 61, 62, 63, 64, 66, 67, 68, 72, 73, 74, 80, 83, 86, 91, 97, 98, 143, 153, 167, 180, 188, 203, 210; and Anthony Kirby, Jr., character 67, 73, 79, 84, 85, 86; and Anthony Kirby, Sr., character 30, 37, 63, 66, 74, 79, 84, 86, 91, 97, 145, 153, 166; and Grandpa Vanderhof character 40, 63, 73, 74, 78, 80, 82, 84, 97, 138, 165; plot summary 36–37; similarity to *It Happened One Night* 37, 66, 98
The Younger Generation 15
Your Job in Germany 127, 134–135, 137, 142, 164, 170

Zanuck, Darryl F. 105, 119
Zemeckis, Robert 207

www.ingramcontent.com/pod-product-compliance
Lightning Source LLC
Chambersburg PA
CBHW051218300426
44116CB00006B/625